LET ME
FINISH

LET ME FINISH

Trump, the Kushners, Bannon, New Jersey, and the Power of In-Your-Face Politics

CHRIS CHRISTIE

hachette
BOOKS

NEW YORK   BOSTON

Hachette Books
Hachette Book Group
1290 Avenue of the Americas
New York, NY 10104
hachettebooks.com
twitter.com/hachettebooks

First Edition: January 2019

Hachette Books is a division of Hachette Book Group, Inc.
The Hachette Books name and logo are trademarks of Hachette Book Group, Inc.

The publisher is not responsible for websites (or their content) that are
not owned by the publisher.

The Hachette Speakers Bureau provides a wide range of authors for speaking events.
To find out more, go to www.hachettespeakersbureau.com or call (866) 376-6591.

Print book interior design by Timothy Shaner, NightandDayDesign.biz

Library of Congress Control Number: 2018956938
ISBNs: 978-0-316-42179-9 (hardcover), 978-0-316-42180-5 (ebook),
978-0-316-45412-4 (large print hardcover)

Printed in the United States of America

LSC-C

10 9 8 7 6 5 4 3 2 1

For my mom, Sandy Christie,
whose strength, toughness, generosity,
and unyielding confidence in me added up
to the greatest love anyone could ever ask for.
I have never had a better cheerleader
or role model.

CONTENTS

CONTENTS

LET ME
FINISH

INTRODUCTION

BANNON BLINKS

Steve Bannon was never big on small talk.

But on this particular Thursday morning, two days after Donald Trump shocked nearly everyone by getting himself elected president, Trump's self-impressed "campaign CEO" was even more abrupt than usual.

"Sit down a sec," Steve mumbled in that distinctive rasp of his, summoning me from a transition-team meeting and into his spartan glass office on Trump Tower's fourteenth floor. Steve Bannon is the only person I have ever met who can look pretentious and like an unmade bed at the very same time. He motioned for me to shut the door and sit down.

"We've decided to make a change," he said, getting right to the point.

"Good," I answered. "What are we changing?"

His response came in a single word.

"You."

Me?

"The vice president is going to be the new chairman of the transition," Steve went on, "and you're out. Going forward, you have no position of any kind in the transition, and we do not want you to be in the building anymore."

I wasn't only being fired. I was being eliminated. Vaporized.

I'd been close to the president-elect for the past fourteen years, longer than anyone else in the inner circle who wasn't related by marriage or blood. I'd been the first governor in the nation to endorse him—the first major elected official of any sort. I'd just spent the past nine months campaigning with and for him. Since May, I had been chairman of his transition team, a huge responsibility he had asked me to take on, designing an entire federal government in his image and likeness.

Was this really how it was all going to end?

I could feel my heart pounding as Steve barreled on, laying out my future as he imagined it. I had to call on all my experience as a US Attorney and governor just to hold my anger in. It was crucial to keep my cool. No way was I letting Steve Bannon see how devastating this development felt to me.

"Whose decision is this?" I asked him.

"It doesn't really matter," Steve deflected.

As far as I was concerned, that wasn't remotely good enough. "I want to know whose decision it is," I repeated. "Did the president-elect make this decision?"

"It's really of no consequence, Governor," Steve insisted. "The decision is made. There is no changing it. We expect you to comply."

I'd been dealing with Steve periodically since August, when he left *Breitbart News*, at least officially, and moved into Trump Tower as chief executive of the Trump campaign. We'd worked together on debate prep. He'd gotten involved in some transition stuff. We'd talked strategy quite a few times. Gruff, bright, and never lacking faith in his own brilliance, Steve saw himself not as a political operative or a campaign adviser but as a high-level executive. From everything I had witnessed, he had one overriding goal: ingratiating himself with the Trump family. Everything else was secondary. For months, Steve had been telling the candidate he had a 100-percent chance of victory—then saying something far less optimistic behind his back. But now that the votes had all been counted and the impossible had occurred, Steve seemed certain that, come January 20, 2017, he'd be moving into the West Wing of the White House as the new president's chief of staff.

I stared at Steve across his desk. So this was how he wanted to play it? Like I was an errant child who deserved no explanation as I was bounced out the door? Steve knew and I knew—and certainly Donald knew—that I'd been one of the very few grown-ups on this wild ride of a campaign. The president-elect and I had an excellent relationship. And now I was being banished—no warning and no fingerprints—just when the time came to execute our carefully crafted, thirty-volume transition plan. Was this where my friendship with the soon-to-be-president was going to crash and burn? I was about to find out.

"Okay, that's fine," I told Steve as I stood to leave.

"By the way," I added, "just so you know. Since you won't tell me anything, I'm going to have to assume it was your decision. You are the one conveying it. Now I'm going to go downstairs to that scrum of reporters in the lobby and tell them I was just fired by Steve Bannon. That it was Steve Bannon's decision and Steve Bannon's alone. And that's not all I'll say. You can count on the fact that I'll have a lot to say. Then you can deal with all the incoming and explain everything yourself. Good to see you."

The reporters in the lobby would eat this stuff up. I was certain of that. If there was anything I'd learned from two decades in New Jersey politics and as a federal prosecutor, it's that reporters like nothing more than a life-or-death feud. Two minutes from now, Steve's cell phone was going to explode.

Suddenly, Steve changed his tune. "No, no, no," I heard him say, not quite as unequivocally as before. "Wait a second. You can't walk out and do that."

"Oh yeah, I can," I told him. "I'm no longer associated with this place. I'm not allowed in the building. You made your decision. Now I am making mine."

"Governor," Steve pleaded. "Sit down, and let's talk about it."

"What do we have to talk about?" I asked, glancing at the open door. "I should leave."

I knew this couldn't be Donald's idea. He and I had been there for each other, time and again. He said to me as far back as Labor Day: "Chris, you and I are so smart, and we've known each other for so long, we could do the whole transition together if we just leave the victory party two hours early!" I loved the self-confidence and appreciated the compliment, but, "No," I'd told him, "we need to do this right." Now that the election was over and victory was ours, I was even more grateful that I'd talked him down from his just-wing-it approach. It made no sense for Donald Trump, who had never held public office, to sever his relationship with one of the few people around him who'd actually run an executive branch of government. How did that serve him? Of course it didn't. And now the momentum in Steve Bannon's office seemed to be shifting my way.

"No, no," Steve said. "I want to talk to you about this."

"Well, I want to know who fired me, because I know it wasn't you," I said. "You're just here as the executioner. Who fired me? The president-elect? Because, Steve, if you don't tell me who it is, I am going to say it was you."

That, right there, is where Steve Bannon blinked.

—

In the decade and a half I have known Donald Trump, I've seen in him many of the qualities that have defined America's leaders through the years. He knows who he is and what he believes in. He has a keen understanding of what regular people are feeling. He commands extraordinary loyalty from his supporters and has unique communication skills. He is utterly fearless. Donald doesn't care who he angers or how things used to be. He just doesn't. The harsher the attacks on him, the more energized he gets. This is a man who wakes up every morning with unparalleled self-confidence.

But he also has deficits, significant gaps in his experience and personality that, if left unchecked, will inevitably hobble him. All presidents have these, even the greatest ones, though Donald's are uniquely his. He acts and speaks on impulse. He doesn't always grasp the inner workings of government, which are different from the intricacies of the business world. And he trusts people he shouldn't, including some of the people who are closest to him.

That is why, as he prepared to take the oath of office, Donald so urgently needed the right people around him and a solid structure in place. Many of the problems he would go on to face during his first two years in office were caused at least in part by the absence of that foundation. The infighting and chaos in the White House. The failure to get important parts of his agenda through Congress. The revolving door of deeply flawed individuals—amateurs, grifters, weaklings, convicted and unconvicted felons—who were hustled into jobs they were never suited for, sometimes seemingly without so much as a background check via Google or Wikipedia.

Here are the facts of the Trump transition: The day after Trump was elected, he was handed a detailed road map that would have avoided many of these pitfalls and launched him on a far more promising path, a plan that was fully consistent with his values, his campaign promises, and his publicly stated views. But that plan was thrown in the trash. Literally. All thirty binders were tossed in a Trump Tower dumpster, never to be seen again. Steve Bannon, Rick Dearborn, Jared Kushner and others, for their own selfish reasons, got rid of the guidance that would have made their candidate an immensely more effective president and would have saved him an awful lot of heartache, too. In so doing, they stole from the man they'd just helped elect the launch he so richly deserved.

The situation isn't hopeless. It can still be reversed. But America and its forty-fifth president have been paying the price for these foolish decisions ever since. Instead of a well-oiled administration with an effective one-hundred- and two-hundred-day legislative strategy, the president got the epic failure of the timing and execution of Obamacare repeal. Instead of a border wall and a merit-based immigration policy, he got an ill-conceived Muslim ban that was immediately blocked in court.

Instead of high-quality, vetted appointees for key administration posts, he got the Russian lackey and future federal felon Michael Flynn as national security adviser. He got the greedy and inexperienced Scott Pruitt as administrator of the Environmental Protection Agency. He got the high-flying Tom Price as health and human services secretary. He got the not-ready-for-prime-time Jeff Sessions as attorney general, promptly recusing himself from the Justice Department's Russian-collusion probe. He got a stranger named Rex Tillerson as secretary of state. He almost got the alleged spouse abuser Andrew Puzder as labor secretary. Worse, he did get the alleged wife abuser Rob Porter as White House staff secretary. He almost got the hotheaded Vincent Viola as army secretary. He got the *Apprentice* show loser Omarosa Manigault in whatever Omarosa's job purported to be. (I never could figure that one out.) Too often, these were the kinds of people he got. Too many Rick Dearborns. Too few Kellyanne Conways. A boatload of Sebastian Gorkas. Too few Steven Mnuchins. Out on the campaign trail, Donald had spoken frequently about knowing "all the best people." Far too often, he's found himself saddled with the riffraff.

I know exactly how this happened. I was there for most of it. I did everything I could to make sure my friend Donald reached the White House fully prepared to serve. But a handful of selfish individuals sidetracked our very best efforts. They set loose toxic forces that have made Trump's presidency far less effective than it would otherwise have been. If this tragedy is ever going to be reversed, it is vital that everyone know exactly how it occurred.

——

Once Steve Bannon started unburdening himself that day in his Trump Tower office, he couldn't seem to stop. "The kid's been taking an ax to your head with the boss ever since I got here," he blurted out. "It's been constant. He never stops. Ancient bitterness, I guess."

In Bannon-speak, *the kid* is only one person. Not Donald Jr. Not younger son Eric. Not Ivanka or Tiffany. The kid is Jared Kushner, the husband of Ivanka Trump and the son of the real estate developer Charles Kushner, a man I once sent to prison for

tax evasion, witness tampering, and illegal campaign contributions. The kid is the soft-spoken son-in-law of Donald Trump.

"What I've learned every day since August," Steve continued,
"is if you want to survive around here, you've got to agree with the
kid ninety-five percent of the time. You have to."

And there it was. Steve Bannon, chief executive officer of the
Trump campaign, had just made clear to me that one person and
one person only was responsible for the faceless execution that
Steve was now attempting to carry out. Jared Kushner, still apparently seething over events that had occurred a decade ago, was
exacting a plot of revenge against me, a hit job that made no sense
at all for the man we had just helped elect. And Steve Bannon, hot-
shot, big-balls campaign executive, was quietly acquiescing to it.

What wimps. What cowards. And how disloyal to Donald
Trump.

It says a lot about Steve that he was willing to fire me to stay
on Jared's good side, yet he couldn't bear to be fingered as the one
who'd done the deed. Back where I come from, which is New Jersey, that's what we call a lying snake.

"It's unacceptable to me that I'm no longer on the team and
that I'm being publicly hung out in this way," I said to him. "So we
need to figure something out."

Up till then, the conversation had lasted less than five minutes. What came next took two and a half hours. Steve and I sat
there, face-to-face in that glass-walled office of his, going back
and forth and back and forth over what my future role would be,
while other staffers paraded up and down the hallway, peering in
on us, wondering what on earth was going on in there for so long.
I got it. Here was the presumptive chief of staff and the chairman
of the transition both looking thoroughly agitated. Just from the
traffic and the glances, I could tell that people were freaking out.

They *had* to find out what was being said in there. Just a tidbit, just a little morsel, so the leaking could begin.

"By the way, you're still a serious candidate for attorney general," Steve said after he'd finally given up on my proposed banishment and I'd agreed to stay on as vice chair of the transition team, however meaningless that might be.

I couldn't believe he was saying that. "Wait a second," I said to him. "How can you tell me I'm a serious candidate for attorney general? Weren't you just firing me? This makes no sense at all."

Steve hinted strongly, without quite saying so, that the attorney general idea was coming straight from America's next president. "There aren't a lot of candidates he'll trust for attorney general," Steve said, immediately ruling out former New York City mayor Rudy Giuliani and US senator Jeff Sessions, from Alabama. "Rudy doesn't want it. He will only take secretary of state. Sessions wants it, and I love Sessions. I'm a big supporter of Sessions, but he doesn't belong as attorney general. He's not strong enough. We need somebody really strong as attorney general, and you're the best person for it. I'm going to advocate for you for attorney general. Please tell me you'll be willing to continue to be considered."

It all sounded nuts to me, and I told him so. "You guys are going to fire me publicly, and then you're going to turn around and make me attorney general? Who's going to buy this?"

Steve insisted it was all on the up-and-up, but I couldn't believe anything I was hearing from him. I needed to get out of that office, out of the building, out of the city, and back home to New Jersey. I needed to be around some people who were sane.

Steve Bannon had just shown his true character to me. If he was telling the truth, he was a traitor, avoiding the heat from me by fingering Jared Kushner as my political assassin. If he was lying, he was blaming a member of the president-elect's family for a deed he or someone else was truly behind. Either way, Steve really was a snake. Donald Trump would discover that in the months ahead, as would Jared, the young man Steve was hoping to curry favor with and was, according to Steve, obsessed with destroying me.

———

I've been waiting to tell this story, the whole story, the way it deserves to be told. To take readers to places they've never been before. To share hard-earned lessons and surprising insights. To clear up some lingering misconceptions. To unmask more than a few phonies, connivers, power grabbers, and snakes. To sing the praises of some overlooked heroes.

Others have written books: journalists with axes to grind, ex-staffers with unhappy exits, assorted hangers-on with dollar signs in their eyes. Not one of them, however, has known Trump for as long or as well as I have—or was right there in the room when much of this occurred.

So hold on tight now. That's what this book is for.

I still talk to Donald. We respect each other's skills, though some in his world sought to drive a wedge between us. I'll get to all that. But to understand my unique kinship with the president, you first have to understand where I came from: a cramped apartment on the west side of Newark and the leafy lawns of Livingston, where I soaked up the Jersey version of the suburban American dream. Pushed by strong women who kept telling me, "You can do anything, Christopher, if you work hard enough." And so I did. Learning to lead in high school and college. Catching baseballs and the political bug. Finding my soul mate early and starting a family with her. Running for small offices, then larger ones. From the rough-and-tumble of Jersey politics, learning how to get in peoples' faces, always prepared to challenge them. Aiming higher than I had any right to. Becoming a US Attorney after 9/11 and sending criminals off to prison, and then serving as governor of my beloved state. Twice. Cutting taxes. Fighting unions. Telling the loudmouths, "Sit down and shut up!" Warning my fellow citizens in the path of danger to "get the hell off the beach!" Healing Jersey from Superstorm Sandy, always in the same blue fleece. Being stymied by bridge traffic and losing the benefit of the doubt. Running for president.

And there stood Donald Trump. Fearless Donald. Disruptive Donald. Upending the process. Breaking the rules. Decimating the competition. Doing it his way, whatever *it* was. *Build the wall. Drain the swamp. Collusion? What collusion? Fake news media!*

I got in early, and I spoke up loudly. I worked hard, and I never forgot where I came from. And I'm still ready for more. Let me finish. I'm not finished. I'm not even close.

PART ONE

BECOMING CHRIS

ONE

FAMILY VALUES

In my earliest conscious memory, I am crying my eyes out.

It is two days before my fifth birthday, September 4, 1967. I am in the car, my parents' big, blue Buick, sitting by myself on the broad backseat. My mother is driving through Livingston, New Jersey, past comfortable suburban houses and the township's last remaining farms. She is delivering me to the redbrick Squiretown School for my first day of kindergarten. I desperately do not want to go. I am happy with my life the way it is. I like spending all day with my mother and little brother, Todd, and hanging out with my father when he gets home from work.

All of a sudden, I've got to go—*where*? For *what*? My mom is trying to convince me what a grand adventure lies ahead.

"You're going to make friends," she's saying through my confusion and my tears. "You're going to have fun." And I'm not buying any of it.

Soon my mother is opening the car door, taking my hand, walking me into the building and finding my teacher, whose name is Mrs. Lukemire. Mrs. Lukemire walks me away from my mother and immediately picks up her argument, as if the two women have just spent the morning comparing talking points. "Oh, Chris, you're going to have a great time here," the teacher says. "We're going to have so much fun." By then, my mother has beat feet out of there.

It turned out, of course, that my mother and Mrs. Lukemire were right. I came to love school: the academics, the athletics, the friendships, and all the rest of it. I just hadn't been convinced yet. My whole life, I have never been shy about expressing my feelings, and I saw no reason to start on that day. If something is in my head or in my heart, it will be on my lips in a hurry for everyone to hear, whether I am kicking and screaming in my parents' Buick or standing up to a privileged whiner at a packed town hall illuminated by TV lights. I've always been that way. I can't imagine ever changing. "There will be no deathbed confessions in this family," my mother used to say, and there never were.

———

Though I remember nothing before that first day of kindergarten, I have heard stories and seen photos, and I can recite some pertinent details. I was born Christopher James Christie in Newark, New Jersey, on September 6, 1962, the first child of Wilbur Christie and Sondra Grasso Christie, Bill and Sandy to their friends and relatives. My parents had been married for fifteen months when I came along. We started out in a two-bedroom apartment on Newark's South Orange Avenue and Fourteenth Street, across from West Side High School, my mother's alma mater. My younger brother, Todd, arrived just after my second birthday.

By the mid-1960s, Newark was really on the edge. Crime was rising. Racial tension was growing. White families like ours were moving to the suburbs. My parents were Newarkers. They didn't want to go. But my father was convinced that the schools were better in the suburbs. He found a three-bedroom, one-bath ranch house at 327 West Northfield Road in Livingston, still in Essex County but eighteen miles to the west. It might as well have been a million, as far as my mother was concerned. "You're taking me to the sticks," she griped to my father.

They borrowed $1,000 from each of their mothers and put the other $20,000 on a thirty-year GI mortgage. In June 1966, a year ahead of the Newark riots, the Christie family joined the great American migration to the suburbs. But the story of our family didn't start with my parents, my brother, and me. We were just the latest chapter in a long-running journey begun by my parents' parents and their parents and God-knows-how-many generations before them, all trying to make their way in a large and unpredictable world.

I never met my father's father. Jim Christie was a hard-charging Irish American factory worker from Newark who bounced from plant to plant—there were hundreds in those days—and smoked two packs of unfiltered Lucky Strikes a day. The son of an alcoholic, he dropped out before starting high school to help support his five siblings and his mother. He was a good man who got the short end of the stick and never complained once. He died of esophageal cancer at fifty-four when my father was twenty. My father's mother, Caroline Winter Christie, came from a German family and lived to be ninety-nine. Grandma was a very difficult woman, almost impossible to get close to. Selfish. Ornery. Quick with a cutting insult, especially for people she supposedly loved. After her husband died, she married a wonderful man named John Pfaff, who had recently lost his wife to cancer.

My mother's people, the Grassos and the Scavones, came originally from Sicily. Her mother, Anne Scavone Grasso, was born in

America. But my grandfather, Philip Joseph Grasso, was not—*not quite*. His mother was pregnant when she and her husband prepared to set sail from Sicily. In those days, when you bought your ticket to America, you did not wait to leave. The danger of a birth on the open Atlantic was a risk the Grassos were willing to take. Fear had no place in this family, even back then.

So, my grandfather arrived somewhere at sea. Years later, my mother would tease him about this. "You're not American," she'd say. "You're not Sicilian. You were born in the middle of the ocean." He didn't think that was funny at all. "I'm an American," he'd stammer. "They made me an American when I came to Ellis Island." He was hugely proud of his adopted home.

My mother's sea-born father—we called him Poppy—grew up to do many jobs, settling finally on being a bus driver in Newark. His marriage to my grandmother—Nani to us—was arranged by their parents. The young couple had barely met before their wedding day. They had three children in a hurry. My mother, Sandy, was first. Then came her younger sister, Minette, and their little brother, Philip Joseph Jr. But things got complicated quickly. My grandfather had a girlfriend. Back in those days, the way my grandmother told the story, Sicilian wives were expected to tolerate such arrangements without complaint. But when my grandmother discovered her husband's girlfriend, Nani was not in an understanding mood. She ended the marriage immediately. This took incredible strength of character for a woman like her in the early 1940s. My grandmother was thirty-three years old with no education beyond middle school. Her oldest child, my mother, was ten. Nani was truly on her own.

Nani found a job at the IRS office in Bloomfield, two hours and three bus rides from home. Every morning, my mother prepared lunches for her brother and sister and dropped the younger ones at day care before she headed off to school. There was so little money, my mother got the same doll for Christmas three years in a row, just so she'd have something to unwrap beneath the tree. My grandfather remained a presence in his children's lives, though he never so much as paid an electric bill.

And so, a pattern was set. My mother had a horrible first marriage of her own. Fresh out of West Side High, she wed a man named Alphonse Nesta. Al was seven years older than my mom, the father figure she never had. What she didn't discover until after her wedding day was that Al was an out-of-control alcoholic and a violent one. He beat my mother badly. When Poppy paid a visit one day to the couple's apartment on Arch Street in Bloomfield, he saw the condition his daughter was in. He and one of his brothers went looking for Al. The way the story's been told, it didn't end well for Al. There were some things the women in my family simply would not tolerate.

My mother was profoundly affected by her violent first marriage and her father's sporadic presence in her life, in ways that were both positive and negative. Those experiences made her incredibly tough, but she also found it hard to trust people. My mother realized early on: "I'm in charge of my own destiny." And that is how she lived—and one of the lessons she instilled in me.

——

My father was a bright kid from a tough neighborhood, Newark's Ironbound. He graduated from the historic Ann Street School and skipped a grade before graduating from Hillside High at sixteen. He couldn't afford college and was drafted into the US Army during the Korean conflict, though the closest he got to combat was Fort Carson, Colorado. Once back home, he landed a spot at the Breyers Ice Cream plant in Newark. He liked the job well enough, but a supervisor kept telling him, "You've got the GI Bill. Why aren't you in college?" Eventually, my father listened. After a brief stop at Columbia University—cut short by a steep tuition increase—he enrolled in night classes at the Rutgers campus in Newark for accounting.

My parents, who'd met briefly in high school, were both twenty-five when they were reintroduced by mutual friends, Shelly and Sheila Kahn. By then, my mother was working at the Remington typewriter offices in Newark. Things moved quickly from there. Once they decided to marry, my mother went to the Archdiocese of Newark to get her first marriage annulled, which would have allowed her to marry again in the Roman Catholic Church. But in those days, annulments were handed out only to those who could pay. No one in her family had that kind of money. My mother was crushed, her mother and my father's mother even more so. But love won out. My mother and father tied the knot in a civil ceremony on June 4, 1961. By December, my mother was pregnant with me. The following June, my father earned his college degree, trading the job at the Breyers plant for a suit-and-tie position with the accounting firm Peat Marwick. There's a wonderful picture of my parents on the day my dad graduated from Rutgers. He's wearing his cap and gown. My mother is six months pregnant. She's beginning to show. The two of them have confident smiles on their faces, like they are ready for just about anything.

"It's our first family photo," my father likes to say, and I suppose it is, though it offers only the vaguest hint of me.

———

Once my parents moved from Newark to Livingston, they threw themselves 100 percent into suburban family life. My mother joined the PTA, rising eventually to president. Both my parents volunteered with the Livingston Little League, where my father coached and my mother ran the 50/50 raffles and flipped burgers in the refreshment stand. My mom and dad were totally committed to their children and seemed to love every minute of it. Livingston in the 1970s was a wonderful place to grow up. The friends I made would remain my friends forever. The joy I feel in my life, the unlimited potential for success I have always believed in—all of that sprang from my immigrant ancestors and my Livingston childhood.

———

My mother's mother was a very different kind of person from Grandma Caroline—in the best possible ways. Nani was a central part of our lives. Mine especially. She'd come to our house all the time. If she wasn't with us, I would often spend the weekend at her garden apartment in West Orange. I'd have dinner with her on Friday. On Saturday, she'd supervise my homework, then let me watch one game on TV—college football in the fall, baseball in the spring. After that, we'd walk to the public library and take out books for both of us, before she prepared Saturday dinner. On Sunday morning, we'd walk to the eight a.m. Mass at Saint Joseph's on Benvenue Avenue. My mother was still angry at the church over her blocked annulment, but Nani was devoutly Catholic. She was really the basis for our Catholic upbringing.

After Mass, we might stop at the bakery for a donut, depending on her mood. When we got back to her apartment, we always watched *Meet the Press*. To Nani, politics was right up there with religion, and her devotion was infectious. Watching Lawrence Spivak and his panelists interviewing all those senators and congressmen didn't instantly make me dream of serving in Washington, but it did spark in me a lifelong fascination with politics.

Once you got to know the characters, Nani explained, politics was one of the greatest stories around. She wrote letters to her congressman, the Democrat Joseph Minish, on every issue that was important to her. The many replies she got could barely fit in a large dresser drawer. "You have an obligation to have your voice heard," she often said.

Nani loved taking her grandchildren on great adventures. To Radio City Music Hall for the Christmas show. To the Feast of San Gennaro in Manhattan's Little Italy. She was really the one who kept us in touch with the Sicilian part of our heritage. This little old Italian lady, barely five feet tall, dragging her grandchildren on a bus or a PATH train across the river to New York City. She was fearless. She always made those trips special and made us feel important. Her Christmas gifts were fifty- or seventy-five-dollar savings bonds. "This is for college," she would say. She wanted all of us to get the education she never had. She carefully saved her money for two or three vacations every year, almost always traveling alone.

Nani wasn't scared of anything. One of the most important things she taught me was to never be afraid. "Fear is your enemy, Christopher—not your friend," Nani always told me, and she was living proof. From her divorce in 1942 to living the rest of her life alone and totally independent to setting an example of courage for her grandchildren, she was an amazing woman, though most people could never tell it just by looking at her.

———

For as long as I can remember, my brother, Todd, was my best friend. We shared a bedroom and much more. My mother constantly warned me, "You have to be a role model. Todd will copy whatever you do." And she was right. Todd followed me into sports and shared my curiosity about the world. He was always smart, but he was more of a cutup than I was. People liked me because I seemed to know what was happening. They liked Todd because he made them laugh. From our earliest years in that tiny bedroom, Todd and I were a team. We fought. We laughed. We played. I stood up for him and vice versa. I knew from the beginning that nothing could pull us apart.

My parents also wanted a daughter, and that wasn't happening. So they put their names on the state adoption registry and hoped for the best. Every three months for nearly seven years, a social worker named Sharon came to visit us. With two healthy sons, our family was considered a low priority. But one day in the summer of 1973, while Todd and I were swimming in our back-yard aboveground pool, we heard a scream from the kitchen and went running into the house. Sharon the social worker and my mom were there with smiles on their faces. Leaning on the table was a three-by-five black-and-white photo of a little dark-haired girl in a Raggedy Ann dress.

"This can be your sister if you want," my mother said to Todd and me.

She told us what the social worker had said to her: "You can take the weekend and think about it. Let me know on Monday if you want her or not."

The girl was two years old. Her name was Julia. She was the daughter of a teenage mother and a father who'd left the day she was born. Her mother didn't initially want to give her up, trying hard to make the situation work. This was why the girl hadn't been adopted quickly. She'd been living on and off with her maternal grandmother and a foster mother.

Todd and I, all of eight and ten years old, talked with our parents all weekend. A sister sounded great to us. On Sunday night, my father said: "We need to take a vote, yes or no." Each of us wrote an answer on a small piece of paper and folded it up. When my father unfolded the papers, there were four yes votes.

On Monday after school, the four of us went together to the New Jersey Division of Youth and Family Services. "She'll stay with you for a few weeks," Sharon said. "If everything goes well, you can keep her. If you want to send her back, you can send her back." There was a return policy? That was impossible to imagine. We wanted a sister.

We were all in the waiting room of that drab state office—my mother, my father, Todd, and me—when the door opened and in walked a beautiful little girl, carrying a tiny suitcase and speaking with the cutest southern accent. She'd never left New Jersey. But her foster mother came from the South, and that's how she picked it up.

When we got home, we gave her the guest room. It was now hers. She was part of the family immediately. Only one question lingered about our new little sister, and it came from my father. He wanted to know if we could change her name. She was two and a half years old. Was it too late?

"I think she's still young enough," our social worker said.

It was time to take another vote. When my father unfolded the paper ballots, two votes said *Sharon,* for the nice social worker who'd made all this possible. Two said *Dawn.*

"Looks like we have a tie," my father said. "I guess we'll have to pick the name out of a hat."

Sharon won.

At this point my father stood up glumly and walked to his bedroom. My mother and I remained at the kitchen table. We'd both voted for Sharon.

My mother and I looked at each other. "He obviously really wants Dawn," my mother said. "Do you really care that much?" Democracy had failed him. So had chance.

"I don't care," I told my mother truthfully.

"Then go down the hall, and you tell your father that you and I want to change our votes. We'll name her Dawn."

When I got to my parents' bedroom, my father was taking off his shirt and tie. "You know, Dad," I told him, "Mom and I talked about it. We were the ones that picked Sharon, and you really want Dawn. We're going to change our votes. We'll go with Dawn."

My father looked like he'd just won the lottery. A big smile spread across his face. "I've always wanted a daughter named Dawn," he confided. And now he had one. Our family was complete.

TWO

JERSEY BOY

Politics wasn't a huge topic around the Christie kitchen table. My parents were keenly interested in what was happening in Livingston—but state and national politics? Not so much. My father was a registered Republican. My mother was a Democrat. But neither was a strict party-line voter. On election morning, November 5, 1968, as my father was leaving the house, he mentioned he'd be stopping to vote for Richard Nixon on his way home from work. That was enough to motivate Mom.

"Come on," she said. "Let's go vote."

She took me behind the curtain and into the booth. I watched as she pulled the lever for Hubert Humphrey. "I had to cancel out your father's vote," she explained as we climbed back into the Buick for the short drive home.

Those weekends with *Meet the Press* at Nani's must have already had an effect. I found the experience fascinating. I was in seventh grade when Richard Nixon was driven from office over Watergate. Mom, Dad, and I watched his resignation speech on

TV. As the 1976 presidential election took shape, I was still four years away from being eligible to vote. But I watched every night of the Democratic and Republican conventions as Georgia's governor, Jimmy Carter, sealed the Democratic nomination and the former California governor Ronald Reagan almost snatched the Republican nomination from President Ford. The speeches, the backroom maneuvering, the craziness on the floor—all of it felt so dramatic to me.

After listening to Ford's acceptance speech, I turned to my parents and said: "I'm a Republican." To me, the Democrats seemed to put their faith in government. The Republicans put theirs in people. That might sound overly simplistic now, but that's how it struck me at the time. I was moving toward Dad's party, not Mom's.

That winter, our state assemblyman came to speak at Heritage Junior High. His name was Tom Kean. A Princeton graduate whose father had been a congressman and grandfather a US senator, he lived near us in Livingston. There was already talk he'd be running for governor that year. I was incredibly impressed. He made me feel like political office was truly a noble calling. This was a guy I really wanted to help. Until that day, I had never thought much about making politics my career.

When I got home from school, I told my mom all about the assemblyman's visit. She could see how excited I was. This is where aggressive Sandy Christie showed her true stripes. "Volunteer for his campaign," she said.

I asked how.

"Get in the car," she said. "Let's go to his house."

I was petrified. We crept up the long driveway off Shrewsbury Drive, and my mother kicked me out to knock on his door. Tom

Kean answered, and I told him I wanted to help him campaign for governor. He smiled and walked me toward my mother's car, and then he spoke to her.

"I'm going up to speak in Oradell tonight," Kean said to her. "Why don't you let him come with me and see if he likes it?"

My mother said yes, and so my political career began.

———

Livingston High School is where I came into my own. The way I am today—the traits like outspokenness and intense focus on winning that have come to define my political career—emerged in those years. I was a type-A leader-achiever. President of my high school class all three years. Captain of the baseball team. I led a boycott of the Heritage Diner when the manager tried to impose a ridiculous minimum-purchase rule. I organized the junior and senior proms. That was me. I wanted to be the one who decided things. I liked taking charge. I never encountered much resistance or resentment. Most people seemed to appreciate that someone was stepping up, as long as you were a decent person. I just thought being a leader was cool. And having those opportunities only motivated me to seek more.

I had Nani's voice inside my head: "Don't be scared . . . Don't be a victim . . . Don't be shy . . . You can be anything you want if you are willing to work hard enough, Christopher."

At some time or another, I played basketball, baseball, soccer—you name it. But early in high school, baseball became number one. I wasn't a fast runner. So no one was putting me at shortstop or in the outfield, especially now that we were playing on full-size fields. But I had good hands, a good arm, and, just as crucial, a good brain. Catcher was perfect for me. The pitcher defers to the catcher. The catcher calls the pitches, even if the pitcher occasionally shakes one off. The catcher is the boss on the field. What more could I ask for?

I had a core group of close male friends. Scott Parsons, Bill Giuliano, Steve Slotnick, Stan Yagiello, George Alpert, Fritz Alworth, Phil Ortolani, and some others. Many of these friendships, like the one I had with the future bestselling author Harlan Coben, went all the way back to Little League. We grew up together, experienced winning and losing together, and we have stuck together as loyal friends for forty years. We played on teams together, hung out at each other's houses, and tooled around in Scott's VW bug, cranking up the volume on songs by a singer we liked who'd grown up a couple of towns away and had really hit it big—Bruce Springsteen.

━━━

Although there was lots of marijuana and some cocaine around Livingston in the late 1970s, I never smoked or did drugs in high school. I wasn't a big drinker, either, though I drank beer with my friends sometimes. The drinking age was eighteen then, so it wasn't hard to find, even though we weren't quite old enough to buy it legally for ourselves. Thank God I never lost a friend to a drunk-driving crash or a drug overdose. Unfortunately, I can't say the same about violence. My friend and classmate Joey Kernan was stabbed to death at an end-of-summer party the night before classes began for junior year. He was sixteen years old. Joey and I had played Little League together. Our dads both coached. His parents and my parents were friends.

Some kids from another town were at the party, and people were drinking. A couple of boys got into a dispute over a girl and decided to take it outside. The punches started flying in front of the Livingston police headquarters on South Livingston Avenue, and Joey was getting the better of his opponent. That's when the other kid pulled out a knife and stabbed Joey in the chest.

I was at another party that night when someone rushed in and said: "Joey Kernan got stabbed." No one could believe it. This was Livingston. Stabbings didn't happen in Livingston. Not to people we knew. When I got home, my parents were stricken. It was incredibly jarring for the entire community.

The next morning, the principal asked me, as class president and Joey's friend, to go on the morning announcements and say something. I did my best. But it took a month or so for the school year to feel normal.

—

In those years, there were always lessons to be learned playing sports. I got some of my greatest thrills on the baseball field—and one of my greatest disappointments. I was starting catcher junior year. ("Go, Lancers!") We made it to the Essex County finals and the state semifinals. By senior year people were saying we might go all the way. We'd played together, many of us, since we were nine years old. This was the season we'd been practicing for our whole lives.

Except for one small development. His name was Marty Writt.

Marty and I had been childhood friends. We used to walk together to Squiretown School and Heritage Junior High. In eighth grade, Marty had left for the private Newark Academy, where he'd been a standout catcher on the baseball team. Marty had dreams of playing Major League baseball. Everyone kept telling him he was good enough. Figuring that Major League scouts might notice him more if he was playing on a winning team, Marty decided to transfer to Livingston High just for the second half of senior year.

And where did that leave me? On the bench, that's where.

My friends were in an uproar. "This is bullshit," one fumed. "I can't believe he's transferring," another said. "You should just walk, quit the team." My father was upset, too. Years later, I would hear people say he threatened to sue the school district. I never remember him saying that. But he was upset. So was my mother. All of us were.

I thought about quitting the team. I really did. But only for a minute. In the end, it didn't feel right. My high school girlfriend, Melina Maritato, also urged me not to quit. She believed I might eventually beat Marty out. I told myself I would find a way to make it work. And I did.

I went from starting catcher to designated hitter to bench-warmer over the course of the season. I was elected one of the captains anyway, perhaps the first backup catcher in the history of baseball who was also a captain of the team. I still talked to the pitchers like I always did. I was the loudest guy on the bench, and I just kept leading from there.

Sitting on the bench, watching my lifelong friends win game after game, I was left with a real empty feeling. I had led them to a Babe Ruth League state championship as MVP when we were fifteen years old. Now, as we headed to a possible high school state title, I was sidelined, and that sucked. I'd worked my whole young life toward this goal. That season was going to be my reward. And in a funny way, it really was. We went 28-2. We won the county championship. We won the state championship. My friend Scott Parsons went to the University of Miami on a baseball scholarship. And Marty, my replacement at catcher, was drafted by the Cleveland Indians.

In retrospect, that season on the bench was one of the most important experiences of my life. I was elated to be on the field when we won the state championship, celebrating with my teammates and friends. But I also learned to deal with being disappointed. Seeing the lineup card without my name on it that season would inform my attitude about quitting for decades to come, as challenges I couldn't even imagine in high school would enter my life. I had to keep going, just pushing through. That was hard at seventeen. But it also made me tougher. It became embedded in my DNA. And my friends on that team—Scott, Steve, Bill, Stan, George, Fritz, Troy, Phil, and the rest—stood by me as I stood by them for that magical season. That taught me about perseverance and real friendship. Those lessons proved indispensable.

———

Every year at Livingston, some members of the senior class would climb up on the roof and paint the number of the graduation year. The class of 1977, the class of 1978, the class of 1979—they'd all done it. But when our turn came, we found ourselves facing an energetic new principal named Al Berlin. Mr. Berlin was eager to set a new tone. He had been vice principal at Freehold High School, where, he liked to joke, he'd called a young Bruce Springsteen into the office one day and declared: "If you don't put down that goddamned guitar and start studying, you're not going to amount to anything."

But the new principal wasn't joking when he called me in one Friday morning and said, "Chris, we're done with painting the roof. It's vandalism, pure and simple. Someone could get hurt. There can't be any painting of the roof this year. I'm asking you to take a leadership position. Get the word out as president of the senior class."

I told Mr. Berlin I understood what he was asking. Then I left the office and called my friends together. "Okay, guys," I said. "The principal called me in and told me the roof is not to be painted this year. We paint tonight."

I told my parents what I was planning to do. They seemed to understand. My father even went out and bought the white paint. That night, my friends and I shimmied up to the roof—not the safest thing, I grant you. We painted a big *80* up there.

Monday morning, Mr. Berlin called me to the principal's office again. "Did you see the roof?" he asked. "There's an 'eighty' up there."

"It's kind of a tradition in the school," I said.

"Really?"

"Yeah."

Mr. Berlin's response? He had the roof painted black. Our white *80*? Vanished. Now I had a decision to make.

I waited two weeks. Then, once again, we climbed up to the roof and painted our *80*, even bolder than before. And this time, we brazenly signed our first names.

Monday morning, I was in Mr. Berlin's office again.

"The names up there sound very familiar," he said to me. "Including Chris."

"There are a lot of Chrises here," I reminded him.

He stared at me, and I stared at him. "Let me ask you something, Chris," he said, saying my name extra clearly. "If I paint over it again and I don't keep armed guards there twenty-four hours a day, what's your guess as to what will happen?"

"I'm pretty sure it will get painted again," I said.

"Do you *know* that?" he asked me.

"I don't know it," I said. "Just my instinct."

At that point, I noticed that Mr. Berlin had a small smile on his face.

"Okay," he said. "We understand each other."

I left his office, and he never touched the roof again.

Winning that stare down with Mr. Berlin gave me an enormous feeling of accomplishment. I realized that if you had a clear goal and you kept your cool under pressure, there was no end to the things that you could achieve. The roof was clearly important to Mr. Berlin, but it was more important to my classmates and me. We were not going to be the first class that failed to paint its class number. Some battles, you just have to win.

THREE

LEARNING CURVE

I had a rough transition out of the house.

I dreamed of going to Boston College or Georgetown. But the University of Delaware was less expensive than either of those private Jesuit universities and offered more financial aid. Delaware was the practical choice. Thirteen thousand students, two and a half hours from home, far enough but not too far. For the first time in my life, I'd be moving out of New Jersey, a full twelve miles over the state line to the historic Delaware city of Newark, a name that certainly had a familiar ring. And I wouldn't exactly be going alone. Thirteen of my Livingston classmates also said yes to Delaware.

In August 1980, just as I was packing to leave, my mother was diagnosed with breast cancer. She was forty-eight years old. For the first time in my life, I felt genuine terror. The doctors said it was advanced enough that she needed a mastectomy and probably radiation after that.

Her surgery was scheduled for the day before I was supposed to leave for Delaware. Even from a hospital bed, my mother wouldn't hear of my delaying anything. My father and my aunt Minette, my mother's younger sister, drove me to campus. That first month as a college student wasn't fun at all. Worried about my mother, I felt lethargic and depressed, feelings I wasn't used to. My mother wasn't recovering well from the surgery. I couldn't focus on my studies, and I didn't feel like going out. But when I told my father I was thinking of coming home for the rest of the semester, he was adamant. "No, no," he said. "You wouldn't be helping your mother. She'd feel like she took you out of college."

On the last Friday in September, I didn't say anything. I just got on a bus in front of Rhodes Pharmacy on East Main Street and rode to the Port Authority Bus Terminal in New York, where I caught the DeCamp 77 bus to Livingston. As I came walking up Northfield Road from the Route 10 circle with a duffel bag of dirty laundry, my mother was sitting alone on the porch. She spotted me before I saw her. By the time I hit the driveway, she was out of her chair, smiling and crying at the same time. I hadn't seen her express joy like that since my first Little League home run.

"What are you doing here?" she asked me. "Why didn't you tell me you were coming?"

I could have turned around and gone back to campus right then. I saw that she was okay. I felt like my job was done. I stayed the weekend and bussed back to campus with a clear conscience and a bag full of clean clothes, finally ready for college life.

———

Once I gave it a chance, the University of Delaware was a perfect fit for me. I was challenged and inspired by some brilliant teachers. My political science professor Jim Soles, an older Southern gentleman, made politics seem fascinating and became my academic adviser. My civil liberties professor, a young Boston liberal named Jim Magee, made constitutional law come alive. I began to ponder a career in law.

Meanwhile, just as I had in high school, I found my way quickly into student government. I was elected president of my dorm. Then I chaired the lobbying committee of the Delaware Undergraduate Student Congress, pushing our issues at the state capital in Dover. In that role, I testified for a bill that would install a student representative on the university's board of trustees. We actually got a yes vote in the senate committee before the university came back full guns blazing and got the bill killed on the senate floor. "I gotta give you credit," John Brook, the university's government-relations guy, said to me afterward. "You're the only kid that ever got that bill that far. You made me a little nervous."

It was around that time that I got to know a fun-loving business student named Mary Pat Foster. The ninth of ten children from an Irish American family in the Philadelphia suburb of Paoli, she was a year behind me. We met the first day she arrived on campus. I was helping a freshman friend from Livingston move into Smyth Hall. Mary Pat and I literally bumped into each other. She seemed energetic and smart. And she was definitely pretty, with long, brown hair. We had a short conversation, but that was it. As the year went on, we'd see each other on campus from time to time. Like me, she was involved in student government.

In the spring of junior year, I decided to run for student body president. At Delaware, that meant pulling together a slate of candidates. For our Campus Action Party, I recruited one of my best friends from high school, Lynn Jalosky, to run as my vice president. Lynn was smart and popular, and she knew me as well as anybody. She could tell me the hard truths when I needed to hear them. She was a perfect number two. I asked Mary Pat to run as secretary. I always liked Mary Pat. She, too, was very smart. She gave us a presence in the College of Business and Economics and was a prodigious worker. I was sure she'd be a tireless campaigner. Lee Uniacke, the student I was running against, was the sitting vice president. He just might have been the most popular guy on campus, a wonderful kid who seemed to be everybody's best friend. He also happened to be a dwarf. He certainly never let that interfere with anything. Lee and his slate were formidable opponents, but we went dorm to dorm and just out-campaigned them, capturing all six positions and 62 percent of the vote.

It was clear to me that I was more conservative than most of my classmates and almost all of my professors. On our campus in the early 1980s, here was the conventional wisdom: Nuclear power was a dire threat to the environment. Ronald Reagan was a warmonger, ready to blow up the world. Things would be better if we elected as president someone like Walter Mondale or Mario Cuomo. Those weren't my views, and I was always up for a lively political debate. But I wasn't an ideologue. I was never active with the College Republicans. *Student* government was my thing, and the issues I pushed there were day-to-day concerns. Faculty evaluations. Activity fees. We fought federal financial-aid cuts and got the university to hold its first commencement ceremony for winter graduates. I also learned the importance of being quoted in the student paper, *The Review*, and having my issues highlighted there. I started a real friendship with Tobias Naegele, the liberal New Yorker who was the paper's editor, though some people considered us an unlikely pair.

Looking back at that time, I can see the seeds of my adult political career. I tried to be practical, well informed, and open-minded, whatever the topic was. I didn't use politics to settle personal scores. I tried to unify the student body behind issues that affected all of us and to combat apathy.

I loved being student body president. But my greatest personal achievement up till then happened the Saturday night before spring semester of my senior year. I was sitting with a couple of friends in the Deer Park Tavern, a famous bar on campus where Edgar Allan Poe supposedly wrote "The Raven," years after George Washington supposedly slept there.

The band was playing. We were throwing back some drinks. I was watching a young woman on the dance floor. She was facing away from me. But I could see she was an enthusiastic dancer and had short, brown, wavy hair. Only when she turned around did I realize that the dancing girl was Mary Pat, with short hair. She'd been in Paris for winter term, and she'd decided to cut her hair. I don't know if it was the new Euro haircut, but I found myself looking at Mary Pat in a very different way.

She came over to the table. We talked and then we danced. I walked her back to Christiana Towers, the university apartment complex where both of us lived. We chatted some more along the way. As we walked up to her building, I thought to myself, *I'm gonna try and kiss this girl and see what happens.*

She looked surprised. "What's that all about?" she asked.

"I don't know," I answered.

"Okay," she said with a shrug. "See you soon."

Nothing more came of it until we ran into each other the following week, and I said to her, "Why don't we go to a movie Saturday night?" She agreed.

We stayed up really late that night. At dawn we went to Howard Johnson's for breakfast. And that was the real beginning of Chris and Mary Pat. She wasn't just a friend or a fellow officeholder anymore.

As spring semester rolled along, Mary Pat decided she wanted to be my replacement as student body president. I was committed to helping her win.

This set the stage for my most aggressive political maneuver up to that point.

———

Mary Pat was going to have a challenger in her bid for student body president. I persuaded the guy to step aside. "You really don't want to run," I told him, "because, if you do, I'm gonna work as hard as I can to make sure you lose, and that would be humiliating. You should go to Mary Pat and offer to be on her ticket."

He went for it. Mary Pat ran unopposed. And I gave a quote to *The Review*. "This is not an election," I said. "It's a coronation."

For her part, Mary Pat didn't like any of it. She felt like the quote in the paper had diminished her accomplishments. I thought I was being pithy, but she had a point. She especially didn't like it when the paper's editorial cartoonist drew a ballot with "Mary Pat Foster" listed six times. "Choose one," the cartoon said.

She blamed me for that, too.

In September, as Mary Pat began her term as University of Delaware student body president, I was off to a new adventure: Seton Hall University School of Law in Newark, New Jersey. But the distance didn't cool our relationship at all. At Thanksgiving, I decided that I would ask her to marry me. I told Nani before I told anyone else. "I just want to know if you think I'm nuts," I said to her.

"No, absolutely not," Nani gushed. "She's fabulous, and she's just perfect for you. If you love her, you should marry her." And then Nani said, "Wait here."

She went into her bedroom and came out with a tiny box. Inside was a diamond ring. "This is the engagement ring your grandfather gave to me. I want Mary Pat to have it." After all the bitterness of her marriage to Poppy, who knew that Nani would still have the ring? "You'll want a different setting," she went on. "This isn't the style anymore. My granddaughters are going to be upset. But I'm going to tell them, it's not about them. It's about Mary Pat."

I told my mother and father on Christmas Eve. My father pointed out how young we were, twenty-two and twenty-one. But I told my parents I was certain, and that was good enough for them. I popped the question to Mary Pat at her house after Christmas dinner. We sneaked away to her room where I presented her gifts one by one. The last one was Nani's ring. She agreed immediately.

We then broke the news to her folks in a quiet corner of their bedroom. When I asked her father's permission, the first thing he said to me was: "Well, Chris, we really like you, but how do you intend to support my daughter?" Jack Foster was a Wharton business graduate. He thought in practical terms.

"We'll work it out," I stammered.

"That's not a plan," her father cautioned me.

But I hung tough. "We have confidence in each other," I said. "We'll be able to work it out."

He turned to his daughter and asked, "Do you love him?"

She answered, "I do."

Her father melted at that. "Okay," he said. "You have my permission."

When we stepped back into the dining room, seventy Foster relatives already seemed to know. They broke into applause before anyone said a word. By then, Mary Pat was halfway through her senior year. I had finished my first semester of law school. I'd met the woman I was going to marry, and soon we set a wedding date—

March 8, 1986, spring break the following year. My mother was almost five years cancer-free. Mary Pat and I were visiting back and forth on weekends. She was applying for finance jobs. I felt like my life had a clear path. I was heading toward a law career. If the opportunity arose, I told myself, maybe at some point I'd get into politics.

———

Eight days before our wedding, Mary Pat was fired from her first grown-up job. She'd graduated in June 1985 and gone to work as a municipal-bond analyst at Printon, Kane & Company, a New Jersey brokerage firm. And now, on the last day of February— invitations mailed, a dress waiting, flowers ready, and a huge crowd of Christies and Fosters expected in Paoli for the big day— her supervisor came to her and said, "We love you. But we're cutting back in your area, and you're the junior person."

"I'm getting married in a week," Mary Pat protested.

"Sorry," the supervisor said.

Not only were we about to get married, we had just signed a lease on a $600 studio apartment above a liquor store on Ashwood Avenue in Summit, New Jersey. What were we going to do? I had a job as a part-time law clerk, but my entire monthly salary was less than $1,000. Mary Pat's yearly salary of $25,000 was gone.

Then, I had a thought. Louis Krutoy, one of the senior partners at Printon, Kane & Company, was a lifelong friend of my parents. He was even coming to the wedding.

"I'm going to see Lou," I told Mary Pat.

"You can't do that," she warned.

"I'm doing it," I said and drove to Lou's house in Livingston.

"Lou," I said after he waved me inside. "You're coming to the wedding, and she got canned?"

"It's complicated," Lou protested. "I'm sorry."

"It's not complicated," I countered. "You can't do this. You've got to help us figure out a solution."

Honestly, I don't know why I believed this would work. But Lou thought for a minute and then he said: "I have an idea. Have Mary Pat call me in the morning."

Lou set up an interview for her with a woman named Angela Puccia at Donaldson, Lufkin & Jenrette, the New York investment bank with a thriving junk-bond practice. "Angie is a great girl," he said. "She's an old friend of mine." On Monday morning, Mary Pat had an interview at 140 Broadway in Lower Manhattan. On Tuesday, she went down to Pennsylvania for last-minute wedding details. On Thursday, she called me and said, "I got the job!" She'd be a DLJ desk assistant for $20,000 a year with endless possibilities for upward mobility.

It had been a crazy week. But now with smiles all around, Lou and his wife were among the guests when we tied the knot at Mary Pat's local parish, Saint Norbert's, and celebrated with a reception at the Portledge Manor Mansion. After a weeklong honeymoon in Jamaica, a gift from my parents, I returned to law school. Mary Pat began her exciting new career on Wall Street. And we discovered the joys of married life, which at first glance appeared to be vastly overrated.

———

Marriage was a difficult adjustment for both of us. Until then, Mary Pat and I had essentially been weekend partners. Now we were a full-time unit. Our lives were far from glamourous. I was in law school and working three or four nights a week at a small law firm. She was getting up at six in the morning and taking the train into New York. The apartment was bare-bones and cramped. A half wall separated the living and sleeping areas. The kitchenette had a hot plate, a minifridge, and no freezer or oven. Our only luxury appliance was a small TV. After rent and my law school expenses, money was still extremely tight, even with Mary Pat's salary. The first time her parents came to visit, even our wedding china wasn't enough to put their minds at ease. Years later, after a few cocktails, my father-in-law would tell me what my mother-in-law had said on the drive home to Paoli: "Can you believe the dump he put our daughter in?"

There was another issue, too. Until we got married, Mary Pat didn't fully grasp how mammoth a baseball fan I was. She knew I played in high school. She knew I followed the New York Mets. But 1986 was going to be an epic year. All Mets fans could feel it.

Opening Night was Tuesday, April 8, one whole month after the wedding. The Mets were facing the Pittsburgh Pirates at Three Rivers Stadium. Dwight Gooden, the young phenom, was starting for New York. Of course I had the TV on. And right at the national anthem's impossible-to-reach high notes, Mary Pat announced, "Dinner's ready."

I grabbed my plate and utensils off the Ikea white ceramic tabletop with blue-and-red sawhorse legs and carried my dinner to the couch.

"Where are you going?" Mary Pat asked sharply.

"Dwight Gooden is starting for the Mets," I said. "It's Opening Night."

She shot me a contemptuous look. "We don't eat dinner in front of the TV."

"Tonight, we should eat dinner in front of the TV," I answered, "because it's Opening Night for the Mets, and I want to—"

"Chris," she cut me off. She was serious. "I'm not going to eat dinner in front of the TV."

"Well," I countered, "I'm not gonna miss the first pitch of the season, so I'm going to go in there and eat."

Nineteen eighty-six turned out to be the amazing year Mets fans expected. The team won night after night. I watched night after night. The team won 108 games and the World Series. As the summer progressed, Mary Pat seemed to grow more accepting. She actually went to a World Series game with me. But there's no denying it. My obsession with the Mets put an enormous strain on our first year of marriage.

My part-time job was with a lawyer named Myron Kronisch. He was a taskmaster and a real stickler for legal-writing style. One of his rules was that no sentence could have more than seven words. I could plead for exceptions, and sometimes he granted them. It all seemed a little rigid. But I had to admit that my boss's rigor did sharpen my writing. I second-sat him in a medical malpractice trial. We had the plaintiff. The doctor was represented by the attorney Russ Hewit. Gregarious, physically large, incredibly friendly, Hewit was everything Kronisch wasn't. Our opponent kept whispering to me during the breaks, "What's it like to work for Myron Kronisch? Does he ever tell a joke?" When the trial was over, Hewit slipped his business card into my palm and said, "If you ever want to come work for the good guys, give me a call." I called him in the fall of third year.

I went in for some friendly catch-up with Hewit and an "instant feedback interview" with his partner, John Dughi, who barely looked up from signing a tall stack of papers until he asked "What characteristic do you think is most important in a successful trial lawyer?" and I answered, "The discipline to focus on only one thing at a time."

Then a smile slid across the partner's face. He stopped signing and lay down his pen. "Okay, Mr. Christie," he said, "you have my attention." He summoned Hewit. They offered me a job and told me I could start the following September as a young trial lawyer at Dughi & Hewit.

That summer, Mary Pat found us a roomier apartment, the second floor of a two-family house in Westfield. I can still hear the excitement in her voice when she found it. I was away at a deposition, so I couldn't come to the walk-through. But she wanted the apartment and was afraid if we waited we'd lose it. I said yes sight unseen. Two years later, we bought a handyman special at 515 Elm Street in Cranford. My parents, her parents, some of our siblings—just about everyone!—told us not to buy. We didn't listen. Big mistake. Our careers were going fine, but our lives were still in turmoil. That house really was the nightmare on Elm Street, and it became a painful symbol of our fixer-upper marriage.

The issues went a lot deeper than home repair.

Mary Pat and I weren't getting along. Twice we separated. I moved out and went back to live with my parents. After we reunited, Mary Pat moved out for six months. We went for marriage counseling. We went for more. We even made a conscious decision not to have children. We weren't at all sure the marriage would last. We weren't enjoying each other's company anymore.

Looking back, I can see we were both immature. We were two people who had never learned to compromise. We kept ramming heads with each other. It was a thousand big and little things. Mary Pat was resentful that she had to leave Pennsylvania and move to New Jersey. I was resentful that we didn't spend as much time with my parents as they wanted since we lived so close. I was trying to manage my parents' expectations about our independence, and I didn't think I was getting credit for that. I refused to change some long-standing habits even if they were inconsiderate to my new wife. Even though a reservoir of love was always there, we weren't liking each other all that much.

One day, I was sitting in my office when my secretary said, "Jack Foster is on the phone."

Oh, no, I thought. *This can't be good.* But I didn't want to dodge my father-in-law.

"Hey, Dad," I said. "How are you?"

"Good," he said. "How are you?"

"Good days and bad days," I replied.

"Listen," he continued. "I was sitting here today thinking about you. I just want to tell you I love you, and I'm praying for you every day."

With all that had happened between his daughter and me, he could have been angry and bitter. Instead, he called to tell me he loved me and was praying for me. That's how great a person Jack Foster was every day.

"I really appreciate that."

"Okay," he answered. "Time for us to get to work."

"Yep," I agreed.

"Good," he said. "Get back to work. Work hard. I'll talk to you soon."

Jack Foster was all heart.

The three years that Mary Pat and I lived in that house on Elm Street was the darkest period of our married lives. But we kept working at it. We weren't quitters, neither of us. We came to recognize we had something special that was really worth saving, and we both learned to compromise. That whole experience forced each of us to grow up.

Just before Mary Pat moved back in, my brother, Todd, asked me: "How do you know it's the right thing to do?"

"I don't," I told him. "But I know getting divorced is the wrong thing to do." That wasn't based on religion or money or fear. It was based on our mutual refusal to give up.

We sold the house on Elm Street—at a $30,000 loss—in March 1992. We built a beautiful new house in Mendham, the town where we have lived ever since. I was working at the law firm. Mary Pat was rising on Wall Street as a highly successful junk-bond saleswoman. We were socking money away. She was pregnant by December. Our first son, Andrew, was born the following August. What an extraordinary time that was, becoming a father. I would stare at him in his crib and dream big dreams for him.

Mary Pat and I felt like we'd gotten through a rough patch and had put all that stuff behind us. We were happy with each other. It was a wonderful time for us.

It was at that point I began to feel a familiar itch: politics.

FOUR

HURRY UP

liked my clients. I loved standing up in court. Russ Hewit was a generous mentor, and the money was nice. But by the summer of 1992, I was getting antsy.

I'd been hooked on politics ever since *Meet the Press* with Nani, the Ford and Carter conventions, and volunteering on Tom Kean's first governor's race. I had never *stopped* being interested in politics. I called Bob Grady, an old friend from Livingston who was working at the White House as deputy director of the Office of Management and Budget for George H. W. Bush.

"I want to get more involved in politics," I told Bob. Not as a candidate necessarily. Working behind the scenes. "Is there some way I can get involved in the president's reelection campaign against Bill Clinton?" Bob arranged a breakfast for me at the Westfield Diner with Bill Palatucci. A hard-charging young Republican operative, just four years older than I was, Bill was twenty-seven when he ran Tom Kean's 1985 reelection as governor of New Jersey. Now, at thirty-four, he was state director of the Bush-Quayle campaign.

"If you really want to get something out of this," Bill told me over the omelets and oatmeal, "you should take a leave of absence from your law firm and work with me full time."

That was music to my ears. I didn't even care that the position came with a salary of zero.

I had never met anyone quite like Bill, at once utterly familiar and completely unique. The youngest child of an Italian American father who owned a bar in Wanaque, New Jersey, and a German American mother, he was a Rutgers graduate and Jersey guy through and through. He also had a reputation of being more than a little tough and direct.

Bill had almost no filter. If you asked a stupid question, he'd tell you it was stupid. If you did something wrong, he'd call you out. But he was incredibly loyal to you if he thought you were smart and worked hard. He would always give you the next opportunity: "Okay, you screwed this up. Here's how you're going to avoid that mistake next time."

With the blessings of Mary Pat and Russ Hewit, I joined Bill's campaign team at the start of August and spent the next three months running around New Jersey for President Bush. I shared an office with a pair of smart, hardworking women, Mary Warner and Susan Doctorian, who became friends for life.

We worked from a drab suite of offices off exit 138 of the Garden State Parkway. I didn't have a title. My job was to do whatever Bill told me to do. Every day I got another crash course in the nuts and bolts of electoral politics. New Jersey was considered a swing state that year. Between August and November, President Bush visited eight times. I was expected to manage everything that happened while he or one of his surrogates was on the ground, which meant interacting with the White House staff, the Republican

National Committee, and the national reelection campaign—and at least that many conflicting agendas. To succeed, I discovered, I had to accomplish three things: Put on events that the president loved. Make sure the Jersey people got a lot of face time with the candidate. And avoid getting rolled by the White House, the party, or the reelection campaign.

Clinton won the presidency, of course. At 8:05 on election night, I was sitting with Bill Palatucci and Governor Kean when New Jersey was called for Clinton.

I was disappointed. But at this point in my life, I knew how to find the silver lining. I had learned a tremendous amount about politics. I had gotten to know Bill, who would remain an integral part of my life and my career. And when I returned to work at the law firm, he agreed to join us, bringing his lobbying practice to what would eventually be known as Dughi, Hewit & Palatucci.

———

My first real stab at Jersey politics started in my own front yard. Literally. In 1993, the Morris County Board of Chosen Freeholders, the elected body that runs the county government, decided to widen Tempe Wick Road near our house in Mendham. Lots of children lived in the neighborhood. The road was fine. Almost all the neighbors were opposed. A group of us brought our concerns to the freeholders, who rolled their eyes and were incredibly dismissive. So, as election time neared the following year, I decided to run for the board. I recruited two others to run with me, a politically active homebuilder and Livingston native named David Scapicchio, and Jack O'Keeffe, a highly principled engineer and former freeholder with a great Irish smile. Together, we challenged three incumbents, Frank Druetzler, Cecilia Laureys, and

Ed Tamm, who called themselves the DLT Team for the first letters of their last names. They thought that was cute, I suppose. The Republican primary was scheduled for June.

Bill ran a very aggressive campaign for us, and I agreed to fund it. We portrayed the three incumbents as poor stewards of the county's finances and ethically challenged political hacks. We said DLT actually stood for "Delivers Less than Promised." We went all out, buying time on local cable TV, which got super ratings because the Knicks and the Rangers went to NBA and Stanley Cup Finals that year. We zeroed in on the DLT team for holding secret meetings in violation of the state's sunshine law. I called Mike Murphy, the county prosecutor, and asked him: "Is it fair to say you're investigating them for violation of the sunshine act?"

"Yes," he said.

Bill produced a TV commercial in which I spoke straight to camera, ticking off the incumbents' alleged misdeeds and ending with: "And now, they're under investigation by the Morris County prosecutor."

The DLT team went berserk and sued me for defamation, a case that would drag on for years.

On primary day, O'Keeffe and I beat Laureys and Tamm, though Druetzler hung on against Scapicchio. I got more votes than anyone, and the hard feelings lingered. When I showed up for the first board meeting, the remaining incumbents didn't exactly lay out a welcome mat. Me? I just got busy being the good-government reformer I'd promised to be. I introduced a resolution reducing freeholder pay by 25 percent and another eliminating freeholder health insurance. "We're only part-time employees," I pointed out. When both of those measures went nowhere, I cut my own $25,000 pay by 25 percent and refused to take the county health benefits. I made sure the savings was shifted to the Daytop

Village drug-treatment program. Though the voters seemed to appreciate the gestures, the insiders thought I was trying to make them look bad. Everything I did was worthwhile, though I can't deny that I did enjoy watching some of my colleagues squirm.

——

It had been a blast winning that race and starting my term as a freeholder reformer. I decided: Why leave well enough alone? Two months into my term, I announced my candidacy for state assembly. Our district was losing both its assemblymen, two long-entrenched veterans. Rodney Frelinghuysen was headed to Congress. Art Albohn had decided to retire. To me, the State House in Trenton sounded like a much bigger stage than the county building in Morristown. My mother was dead set against my running again so soon. "This is a stupid idea," she said, never one to sugarcoat anything. But Bill was pressing me. "These seats don't come up often," he pointed out.

The race got ugly fast. One of my opponents, Tony Bucco, sent out a mailer that featured a cartoon of a baby in a diaper. "What do this baby and Chris Christie have in common?" the copy asked. "Neither one of them knows what he wants to be when he grows up."

I was a young man in a hurry, my opponents said, a too-cocky thirty-two-year-old who didn't want to pay his dues. Apparently the voters agreed.

Other than getting clobbered, what I most remember from election night was my mother, smoking furiously in the hotel room, lighting one cigarette with another, then taking Bill out into the hallway, just the two of them. Later, I asked her what she'd said to my campaign manager and friend. She was perfectly happy to share.

"I told him, 'Bill, you're like a member of the family, and we love you. That's why I'm going to tell you this. You get one of these. The next time you give my son such horrible advice, you'll be out of here.'"

Yep. That was my mom.

I don't think she really could have banished Bill Palatucci, but she certainly thought she could. Now it was my turn to learn another painful lesson. *Patience. Don't be in such a hurry. Your time will come.* I just kept learning, one stumble at a time.

And the stumbles kept coming.

They came at me hard in the June 1997 Republican freeholder primary. I lost my reelection. As I was waiting by the stage to give my concession speech on election night, Chuck Dawson, who managed the campaign against me, grabbed my arm.

"You hear that sound?" he asked me.

All I heard was a bunch of glasses clinking and people milling around.

"That's your fuckin' career going down the toilet," Dawson said.

I didn't enjoy being talked to like that. But I was too young and driven—some might even say cocky or delusional—to feel all that defeated. Plus, the voices of my mother and grandmother were still in my head, saying I could do anything if I worked hard enough. I'd figure it out. And even among my fellow freeholders, not everyone thought my career was spinning helplessly down a white porcelain bowl.

My last day in office at the end of December, Frank Druetzler, my strongest adversary, came up to me. "I know you're not going to believe this," he said, "but this is the best thing that ever happened to you. You don't belong here."

"You've made that clear," I said.

"You're missing my point," Frank continued. "I want you to really listen to me, Chris. You don't belong here. You're too good for this place. You're meant for bigger things. I promise you."

Frank and I had really bumped heads. He didn't have anything to gain being nice to me. So he had my attention.

"It didn't work out here," he told me, "but it's not because you lacked skill or talent. I'm betting on you."

——

Our oldest son, Andrew, was four by then. Our first daughter, Sarah, was born in 1996. So she was one. I was loving being a father, and now I could really give parenthood the time and attention it deserved. Mary Pat and I were doing great together. Our marriage had, at last, found a wonderful rhythm, even despite sad times. We lost a baby in 1998. Mary Pat had a miscarriage that we discovered together during an ultrasound in her doctor's office. Though that was terribly sad and cast a shadow over our house for a time, it also pulled us even closer together. Our son Patrick would come along in 2000. As our family was growing, so was I. I returned to Dughi, Hewit & Palatucci and resumed my private practice of law full time. It wasn't just the humbling experience of political defeat that I was learning from. Even more important were the joys and challenges of being a husband and a dad.

But even though I wasn't in a political office, it wasn't long before I found a new way to engage with politics. Right after the 1998 midterm elections, Bill Palatucci was in New Orleans for a meeting of the Republican Governors Association. There he ran into an old friend, Texas governor George W. Bush, who was walking around with his brother, Jeb, the newly elected governor of Florida. Their father was six years out of the White House, but this was a heady time to be young and named Bush.

"I'm having trouble with Governor Whitman in your state," George W. confided to Bill. "I'm thinking about running for president, and I'd like to have her on the team. But she's playing hard to get."

Christie Whitman was the leader of New Jersey's Republican Party. She wanted to take her time on the presidential endorsement. George W. had a very different timetable.

"Do you think you can put together a good group of ten or twelve really prominent New Jersey Republicans and bring them down quietly to visit me in Austin?" he asked Bill.

"I'd be happy to do that for you, Governor," Bill said.

"Great, talk to *him*," Bush said, nodding toward a short, balding man standing a few paces back. "He'll square it away for you." The man introduced himself as Karl Rove.

As soon as Bill returned to the office, he and I got busy, rounding up an A-list of Jersey Republicans. Senate president Don DiFrancesco. Assembly Speaker Jack Collins. Assembly Appropriations chairman Rich Bagger. State senators Bill Gormley and Joe Kyrillos. Bergen County executive Pat Schuber. Governor Tom Kean's finance chairman, Jon Hanson. They all agreed to pay their own expenses and to keep the visit quiet. Bush and Rove didn't want Whitman to interfere with getting important New Jersey Republicans behind Bush for 2000.

We landed in Austin on January 8, 1999. The group was invited to lunch with Bush, his wife, Laura, and Rove at the governor's mansion. They'd been having similar lunches, it became clear, with groups from other states. We went around the table and all the guests from Jersey said: "Governor, if you run, we're with you."

As we were about to leave, Bush cornered Bill and me. "You guys did a great job," he said. "Can you do another one next month?" We took groups to Austin almost every month until Bush officially declared his candidacy on June 12. No one made any public announcements, but those lunches effectively undercut the prospect that Governor Whitman might support another candidate. The entire leadership of her party was already with Bush. And suddenly, Bill and I were known across the state as conduits to the inevitable nominee of the Republican Party, George W. Bush.

——

The Sunday after Thanksgiving, Mary Pat and I decided to take a group of her clients to a Bruce Springsteen concert in Minnesota. The show was amazing, but what happened the next morning was even better. Mary Pat and I boarded an eleven a.m. Northwest flight back to New Jersey. Our tickets put us in the front row. We were just putting our bags in the overhead when I heard a familiar voice say, "I think I'm sitting right back here." It was Bruce.

He was by himself—no wife, Patti Scialfa, no E Street bandmates—just Bruce, a baseball cap, jean jacket, *New York Times,* and *Minneapolis Star-Tribune.*

The plane was delayed at the terminal for thirty minutes. Why not? I shrugged to Mary Pat. She and I walked back to Bruce's row. We introduced ourselves. I told him we had flown in for the show last night and were headed home. He smiled and said, "Me, too." We thanked him for the excellent performance and for the many other great nights we'd had at his concerts. He was incredibly gracious. The three of us chatted briefly about where we all lived before heading back to our seats.

When we landed in Newark, Bruce walked off the plane right behind us. I asked him if I could tell him a little story. He said sure. I told him about a concert I'd been to a few months earlier, August 11, at the Continental Airlines Arena in the New Jersey

Meadowlands. My six-year-old son, Andrew, and I were sitting in the front row with tickets we won in an auction for the Kristen Ann Carr Fund, which raises money to fight sarcoma. I reminded Bruce how he'd thrown a pick early in that evening to my little boy and how, around eleven p.m., he had looked down at us, acknowledged my still completely awake son and gleefully shouted, "He's still going?" before launching into "Land of Hope and Dreams." The concert encores were winding down. There was just one song left to play. Bruce introduced "4th of July, Asbury Park," a song known to many fans simply as "Sandy." Bruce pointed right at Andrew and said: "Here's a lullaby for the little guy."

As I finished this story in the Jetway, Bruce said he remembered that night. "That was your little guy?"

"Yes," I said. With a big grin and chuckle, he called Andrew "crazy" and then told me he was glad the kid had such a good time and that he should come back again. I told Bruce how much that dedication meant to both my son and to me. "He calls Sandy his song," I said proudly.

All this, of course, was twelve years before the name Sandy would take on a whole new meaning in my life and in the lives of everyone in the state that Bruce and I both called home.

I asked Bruce if he could sign an autograph to Andrew and his three-year-old sister, Sarah, who had already been to two shows—one in Philly and one in Jersey. He happily signed to both of them before shaking my hand and asking Mary Pat to make sure the kids got the autographs. His ride was waiting at the gate. He wished us a merry Christmas before walking away.

By then, my unofficial role in the Bush campaign had become an official one. I was asked if I would be counsel to the campaign in New Jersey. Throughout the primaries, the convention, and the general election race against Al Gore, Bill and I were there every step of the way. Victory didn't come easy—a razor-thin margin, competing court decisions, and a thirty-seven-day legal fight. But when the Supreme Court ruled 5–4 that Bush was indeed the next president, we all felt tremendous joy and relief.

I was in Washington for the inauguration in January 2001 when I saw Rove, who was now the new president's chief political adviser. "So," he asked, "are you coming down?" meaning, "Was I coming down to take a job in the new administration?"

"I really don't want to," I told him. "I will tell you what I do want. I want to be US Attorney."

———

To me, United States attorney for the District of New Jersey sounded like a dream job. If the new president appointed me the chief federal prosecutor in the state, I could combine my two greatest interests outside of my family: lawyering and government. I loved being a trial lawyer, making my arguments and getting the best results I could for my clients. But how amazing would it be if I had only one client, and that client was the United States of America? The issues I'd be handling would be so much more important than the financial interests of any private client. Every day, I'd be standing up for America.

Rove didn't react one way or another. But a few weeks later, Bill sent him my résumé with a handwritten note: "This is the guy you should consider for US Attorney in New Jersey."

Rove could get an awful lot done in the new Bush administration. But he couldn't snap his fingers and make someone a US Attorney. There was a process for that. Bill and I did what we could. We approached the process as if it were our next political campaign. We got just about every major Republican politico in the state to write letters to President Bush endorsing Christie for

US Attorney. By the time we were done, we had a stack of written endorsements an inch and a half thick.

In such situations, the most important person to have in your corner is the state's highest-ranking elected official from the president's party. Christie Whitman had already stepped down as governor to run Bush's Environmental Protection Agency. New Jersey's two US senators, Bob Torricelli and Jon Corzine, were both Democrats. That left Don DiFrancesco, the senate president, who also served as acting governor. I had interacted with Donnie D., as he was known in New Jersey political circles, for ten years. He was a quiet person but very effective in managing his caucus in the state senate. That effectiveness made him a force to be reckoned with in the government and the party.

"I'm with you," Don kept telling me.

Everything seemed lined up. But the Friday before Labor Day weekend, I got a call from Chris Bartolomucci, a lawyer in the White House counsel's office and the guy who was overseeing US attorney appointments. "We're hearing rumblings out of New Jersey that the acting governor may be changing his mind," Chris warned me.

"I have no indication of that."

"Well," the White House lawyer continued, "I'm just telling you I'm getting ready to send your packet home with the president for him to consider, but I can't unless the governor is firm."

"Okay," I said. "I'll work on it."

I was devastated. Bill and I had been working on this for nine months. Was my appointment really slipping away now? I really thought I should talk directly with Governor DiFrancesco. That afternoon, the governor had an event on the boardwalk in Wildwood, where he was scheduled to sign an amusement park safety bill.

"I guess I'm going to Wildwood," I told Bill.

"What are you going to do?" he asked.

"I'm going to corner the governor and say, 'What the fuck? This is ridiculous.'"

"Give it your best shot," Bill said.

I was there when the governor arrived, and I made sure he couldn't miss me.

"Hey, Chris," he said. 'What are you doing here?"

"I'm here to see you." The governor's face turned a slight shade of red.

We agreed to talk after the bill signing.

The signing was on a pier. So I positioned myself so he had no escape route. He signed the bill. He gave his remarks. As he walked away from the podium, I stepped forward into his path. "What's the problem?" he asked me.

"The White House is calling and telling me that you're backing off your support of me," I told the acting governor. "As a result, they can't send my packet to the president for approval. That's not true is it?"

"Absolutely not," the governor answered. "Complete bullshit. I don't know who the hell is telling you that, Chris. But I'm totally with you."

I slid my phone out of my pocket and handed it to him. "I have Chris Bartolomucci's number right here," I said. "Hit send and tell him that."

This was the moment of truth. Either the governor of New Jersey was going to do it, or he wasn't. He hit the call button. He put the phone to his ear. I heard him say: "Mr. Bartolomucci, this is Governor Don DiFrancesco from New Jersey. I am one hundred percent for Chris Christie for US Attorney. I made it clear in a letter I sent to all of you. Nothing has changed. And I want you to convey, please, to my friend, the president of the United States, that I am for Chris Christie."

I couldn't hear what Bartolomucci was saying. I could hear only Don's side of the back-and-forth. "Yes, Chris. Absolutely . . . You have a nice weekend yourself." But I knew I'd gotten what I came for.

The governor ended the call, handed the phone back to me, and said: "Anything else?"

"Nope."

"I can start my weekend now?"

"Yes, you can, Governor. Thank you."

We shook hands and I walked back to my car. As soon as I was inside, I called Chris Bartolomucci at the White House.

Before I even said hello, he started in on me. "How the hell did you get that done?" he asked. I told him the story, and he said to me, "You are going to be one hell-on-wheels US Attorney. I'm sending your packet tonight with the president to Camp David."

PART TWO

CORRUPTION FIGHTER

FIVE

LAW MAN

I got the call from the White House on September 10, 2001, saying George W. Bush was nominating me for US Attorney. For completely unrelated reasons, that turned out to be a tragic and historic week.

When terrorists struck the World Trade Center and the Pentagon on the morning of September 11, New Jersey lost nearly seven hundred people, more than any other state but New York. Everyone had a story to tell. My wife and my brother were in downtown Manhattan at the time of the attacks. Mary Pat was two blocks from the towers at the offices of the Seaport Group, and Todd was at his post on the floor of the New York Stock Exchange. I didn't hear from either of them until after two thirty p.m. Mary Pat and I had three children by then, ages eight, five, and one. Visions went through my mind during those interminable six hours about what life might be like for all of us without Mary Pat.

When she finally got a call through to me that afternoon from a bar near Gramercy Park where she and her stunned colleagues had taken refuge, my heart started to beat fully again. When I

heard her voice, I started to cry. The feeling of relief was inde-
scribable. I wanted to go and get her as quickly as I could. How
could I make that happen? I determined her best option home was
a boat—a ferry from Manhattan that gave its passengers a harrow-
ing view of the smoldering wreckage of the Twin Towers.

It would be several more hours until we were reunited. I
finally drove to the Jersey Shore to pick her up at the Atlantic
Highlands terminal. She approached me soaking wet. Local firefighters had hosed down the passengers from Lower Manhattan
to remove contaminants from their clothes. It was all surreal. But
I was a very lucky man. I was also soon to have responsibilities I
could hardly have fathomed days earlier. One of those planes had
taken off from Newark International Airport, soon to be in my
jurisdiction as the US Attorney.

The FBI was so slammed that fall, there weren't enough agents
to complete my background check. Some New Jersey Democrats
also objected that I was too much of a Republican partisan. The
Star-Ledger editorial page was drenched in skepticism. "Christie
is a smart attorney by all accounts and a man of some charm," the
piece allowed. "No one challenges his integrity." Then, came the
but, a big one. "But he is not yet qualified for the job of US Attorney. . . . He is 38 years old, can claim no distinguished academic
or legal accomplishment and works primarily as a lobbyist and
mediator. . . . Christie's history as a partisan rainmaker not only
fails to qualify him, it could undermine trust in the office."

To help allay these concerns, I promised Bob Torricelli and
Jon Corzine, New Jersey's Democratic US senators, that I would
appoint a Democrat as my first assistant US attorney, balancing
any partisan hue. With their support, I was unanimously confirmed by the Senate five days before Christmas.

In law enforcement circles, I was still a complete unknown. When I pulled up to the underground garage on Orchard Street in Newark for my first day of work, January 17, 2002, the guard refused to let me in. Even my driver's license didn't persuade him that I was the new federal prosecutor for the district of New Jersey.

"So, your name is Christopher J. Christie," he said, staring down at the license then glaring up at me. "So what?"

It took three phone calls before Michael Chagares, a guy I'd sat next to in law school who'd become an assistant US attorney and would one day be a judge on the Third Court of Appeals, came down to the guard shack to vouch for me.

"Okay, Mr. Chagares, if you say so," the guard relented and finally lifted the gate.

My old friend Joel Pisano, who'd become a district judge, agreed to swear me in. When I was summoned into my first meeting with the senior staff, they figured they'd have no trouble rolling the new guy into signing a major public-corruption indictment without even reading it. You should have seen their faces when I said, "No way."

I'd be leading a staff I hadn't hired. Thankfully, I had the perfect role model. Eighteen months earlier, my friend Mike Brey had left the University of Delaware to become the head basketball coach at Notre Dame. He too had to lead a team he hadn't recruited. "I knew the players saw me as a young coach from a midlevel school, and I'm coming to the University of Notre Dame," Mike said when I called for advice. "What could they possibly learn from me?"

At his first team meeting, Mike recalled, he stood beside a blank poster board on an easel. 'I know I didn't recruit any of you," he told his skeptical players. "I know you all came here to play for Matt Doherty or John McLeod. Now you've got me, and I know there's a lot I can learn from all of you."

The players stared back at him.

"But there's one thing that I've done that you and this school haven't done in a very long time," Mike went on. That's when he flipped the poster board, revealing the brackets from the previous season's NCAA tournament. "I've been here two out of the last three years. You guys haven't been here in a decade."

They got the point.

I tried to come up with my version of that, studying the strengths and weaknesses of the office I'd just walked into. One of the weaknesses, I had learned, was that the line prosecutors had a terrible time getting decisions from the boss. *Are we bringing the case or not?* A yes or no could take months.

"There's one thing you'll never have to worry about with me," I told my new team in our first all-hands meeting, doing my best Mike Brey. "I know how to decide. Once I have the information, I will never, ever hesitate to decide. And when we make a decision, we will stand behind it. I will always have your back."

I meant it.

A prosecutor's office is almost militaristic in the way the people follow orders of a leader they respect. Over the next seven years, as our mutual respect solidified, no one would ever call me "Chris" or even "Mr. Christie." I was always just "Boss." We were a focused, unified army, fighting for a common cause.

Once I had a chance to read that first indictment, I was more than happy to sign. It was an extortion and bribery case against Martin Barnes, the mayor of Paterson, the state's fourth-largest city. The evidence showed that Barnes had pressed city contractors to cover the cost of his pleasure trips with "female companions," among other misdeeds. It was a fortuitous first prosecution for me.

Since the mayor was a Republican, the case helped quiet any lingering concern that I was a political hack who would look the other way when my fellow Republicans engaged in wrongdoing.

Arriving in the office so soon after 9/11, I knew that terrorism would be a top priority. I established a terrorism unit with eight assistant US attorneys and brought two of the highest-profile terror prosecutions in the nation: We convicted Hemant Lakhani, an Indian-born British man who had tried to sell shoulder-launched missiles to shoot down American passenger jets, and the so-called Fort Dix Six, a cell of Muslim jihadists who plotted to attack soldiers at a New Jersey military base. But I quickly discovered that my tenure as US Attorney would be defined by our public-corruption prosecutions, 130 convictions of elected and appointed officials without a single acquittal. With Marty Barnes, we were just clearing our throats.

———

As I settled into the job, I made appointments to visit with each of the judges at the main US courthouse in Newark and at the satellite courts in Trenton and Camden. I hardly knew any of them, other than Pisano. Maryanne Trump Barry had been a popular assistant United States attorney in New Jersey with a fast-rising career when Ronald Reagan appointed her to the district court in 1983. Sixteen years later, Bill Clinton elevated her to the Third Circuit Court of Appeals. Judge Barry also happened to be the sister of the real estate developer and New York tabloid fixture Donald Trump. I'm not sure how much weight that carried around the federal judiciary, but it was certainly a piece of trivia known by all the lawyers and courthouse staff.

How would I describe Judge Barry when I visited her chambers in the Newark federal courthouse? In the 1950s, she would be called a dame. Tough, edgy but also very classy, someone who might say, "Don't mess with me, honey. I've seen some world." No one ran roughshod over Judge Barry, but she was also practical and treated everyone with respect.

We had a lively conversation that morning. She said we had some mediocre lawyers on staff who had to go if we were ever going to inject some real energy into the office. How right she was! She had other smart suggestions about how the US attorney's office could be improved. She obviously still loved the place. It was where she'd met her husband, the attorney John Barry, who had died of cancer two years earlier at age sixty. Despite her obvious exuberance, the judge still seemed heartbroken about his death.

"Chris," she asked when I stood to leave, "would you be willing to do a favor for me?"

"I'm happy to try."

"Would you be willing to have dinner with my little brother?"

That's exactly how she put it: "my little brother."

"Donald?" I asked.

"Yeah," she said, "my little brother, Donald."

"Well, Judge," I told her. "Donald can feel free to call my office and set something up."

"No," she said, shaking her head. "He doesn't know you. I told him I was having a meeting with you. He was concerned that calling you directly would be inappropriate."

I shot her a quizzical look: *Donald Trump? Inappropriate? Seriously?*

"He asked if I would set it up."

"Judge," I said. "I'll have dinner with your brother. You just tell him to have someone call Nancy Manteiga, my assistant. I'll tell her to be expecting a call from his office. We'll do it assistant to assistant. He and I don't even have to speak."

"Great," Judge Barry said.

So, one night in May 2002, I met Donald Trump for dinner at Jean-Georges, the grand nouvelle cuisine restaurant in the Trump International Hotel and Tower at Columbus Circle. Just the two of us. Donald strode in like he was the landlord, which he was. He gave me a warm handshake. We sat at a large, round table, perfectly positioned beneath the L'Observatoire lighting sculpture at the center of the bright white dining room, where we could be seen by everyone. He ordered for me.

Seared scallops and cauliflower with caper-raisin sauce as my appetizer—I'm allergic to scallops—and roasted lamb loin for my entrée. I've always hated lamb.

I didn't complain, though I had to wonder: *Who does he think I am, ordering for me like that? One of his chicks?* Donald had divorced his second wife, Marla Maples, two years earlier. According to the *New York Post's* Page Six column, his new "gal pal," as the *Post* put it, was the Slovenian model Melania Knauss. I was just grateful the Jean-Georges portions weren't too large.

I could detect no agenda on Donald's part, other than getting to know the new US Attorney in New Jersey, a state where he owned a golf club in Bedminster and casinos in Atlantic City. He didn't ask for any favors. As US Attorney, I didn't have regulatory authority over gambling casinos. The state handled that. He just seemed to want to sit and chat and get to know me. For my part, there wasn't anything I wanted from him, but I figured it didn't hurt to know Donald Trump.

He told a lot of stories, and I told some, too. We talked about people we knew in common. We talked about how the city was doing after 9/11 and what he thought of George W. Bush, which wasn't much. Donald was opinionated. He was bombastic. He was entertaining. He talked about his business with infectious enthusiasm and considerable detail. I came away with the impression that public Donald and the private Donald were pretty much one and the same.

We walked out of the restaurant together into a beautiful New York City night. There was a couple waiting outside the hotel. Tourists. "Mr. Trump," the woman said as we got closer. "My husband and I are huge fans. He's the biggest fan of yours. Is there any way he can have a picture with you?"

Donald rolled his eyes. "I'm running," he said. "I've got another appointment."

"Please, Mr. Trump," the woman pressed. "We've been waiting out here for an hour because we were told you were inside the restaurant. Would you please take a picture with him?"

Donald glanced at me, then at the husband. "Okay," he said. "Come over here."

The man stepped forward. Donald put his arm around the man's back. The woman had one of those black-and-yellow Kodak disposable cameras that were popular in 2002. She aimed and pushed the button, and the shutter did not click.

She pushed again. Still no click. And again. Nothing. Probably she'd forgotten to turn the little knob to advance the film.

"I'm sorry, Mr. Trump," she said. "I don't know why it's not working."

I could tell that Donald was growing impatient. I had a sense this wasn't going to end well. Then, I watched in amazement as Donald deftly extracted himself from the situation in a way that I now recognize was classic, trademark Trump.

He looked at the woman and said matter-of-factly to her: "Sweetheart, let's do this the next time we get together."

Then, without so much as a breath, he turned and was gone. He pivoted into the back of his waiting black limo and closed the door.

I was still standing there. The couple had no idea who I was and no interest in me. But I stood there for another moment shaking my head.

"Did he really just leave?" the woman asked me.

"He did," I said.

"We're never going to get together again, are we?" she asked.

"I think that's the point," I said.

They wandered off into the crisp Manhattan evening. I walked back to the parking garage to get my car. I was still shaking my head as I drove back home to New Jersey.

Sweetheart, let's do this next time we get together.

If that didn't perfectly encapsulate the real Donald Trump, I don't know what would.

———

I loved being United States attorney. I still call it the best job I ever had. If you did it right—and we tried to do it right—you got to be Batman every day. Taking criminals off the street. Punishing people who've violated the public trust. Protecting honest citizens from being victimized. What's not to like?

Given New Jersey's abundant corruption, finding worthy cases wasn't all that hard. We got busy, and the convictions started piling up: Hudson County executive Bob Janiszewski for bribery. New Jersey Senate president John Lynch Jr. for tax evasion and mail fraud. State Senator Wayne Bryant for bribery, wire fraud, and mail fraud. Over the course of seven years, we would charge nearly 10 percent of our state legislature. These were major players in New Jersey politics. Soon, they were known by their Bureau of Prisons IDs.

Middletown mayor Raymond O'Grady, who once told an undercover agent—on tape!—that he could "smell a cop a mile

away," for bid rigging and accepting bribes from FBI agents at
Chili's. Ocean Township mayor Terrance Weldon for extorting
cash from real estate developers itching to have their projects
approved. Five members of the Pleasantville school board for taking bribes to influence insurance contracts. Deputy US Marshal
Dominick Russo for turning the asset forfeiture account into his
personal piggy bank. If they were guilty and we could prove it
beyond a reasonable doubt, we headed into court.

We targeted business criminals and street thugs, too. Interstate gun dealers. Bloods, Crips, and Latin Kings. A brothel owner
who kept Mexican teenagers in slavery as prostitutes. The chairman and chief operating officer of the fraud-ridden Cendant
Corporation. Doctors taking kickbacks from the artificial-hip-
and-knee industry. The pharma giant Bristol-Myers Squibb for
defrauding shareholders.

I couldn't possibly do this alone. I had a first-rate team of
professionals to advise me. Ralph Marra was a longtime public-
corruption prosecutor who had been in the office for seventeen
years when I joined. He was introduced to me by Walter Timpone.
A former public-corruption chief, I initially considered Walter
for first assistant US attorney. I immediately liked Ralph. He
was smart, tough, and clever. He'd led the prosecution of former
Newark mayor Ken Gibson. He had respect inside and outside the
office. Charlie McKenna was one of a kind. Born into a working-
class Queens family, he went to work as a janitor in the New York
City public school system, using that job to put himself through
Fordham University magna cum laude and the night division of
Saint John's University School of Law, summa cum laude. Charlie
was an entertainment lawyer at first and also played drums in a
band. He joined the US attorney's office in 1991 to prosecute street

crimes, bringing a bold, profane, and commonsense approach to his cases. He gave our team a street-smart, practical edge.

Paula Dow was a seven-year veteran of the US attorney's office for the Southern District of New York, hired by Rudy Giuliani. She came to the New Jersey office to prosecute public-corruption cases. An African American woman in an office that was nearly devoid of minorities when I arrived, she was my first counsel. In 2003, on my recommendation to Governor Jim McGreevey, she left my office to be Essex County prosecutor. Paula was replaced by Michele Brown, who had previously worked in the white-shoe firm of Latham & Watkins. A savvy Jersey girl and a perfect foil to Charlie McKenna, she prosecuted white-collar crimes—paper cases, the assistants called them—and delivered shrewd, no-nonsense legal advice to me.

That team, with the former Camden County prosecutor Lee Solomon running our South Jersey offices, established the office's high standards and restored public trust in various governments of New Jersey. Most of them would stay with me for much of the next sixteen years.

I made certain that the public-corruption unit got some of the best talent we had. Louie Allen, the FBI agent in charge of the Newark field office, assembled an entire additional squad of FBI public-corruption agents for us. But it was the unit's leader, a brilliant assistant US attorney named Jim Nobile, who became its heart and soul. Dogged, quirky, inspiring, Jim grew up in New Jersey, a long-suffering Mets and Jets fan. I've met few people as paranoid as Jim. Jim didn't trust direct deposit. He refused to use E-ZPass or carry an ATM card. And he was so demanding in the way he grilled his trial assistants that they had their own special term for a case-review meeting with Jim: "getting the Jimmy sweats."

"Jim," I asked him one day after I'd gotten some pushback from the Justice Department payroll office about his insistence on paper checks, "what's the story here? No direct deposit, no E-ZPass, no ATM card?"

"I don't want *the man* to know what I'm up to," he confided.

I absorbed his answer for a moment, then I said, "Jim, you *are* the man. You're the head of political corruption for the federal government in the state of New Jersey. *You're* the person people are worried about, not the other way around."

———

Mary Pat was turning forty on September 15, 2003. I still remembered what she'd said four months earlier when I got home from my dinner with Donald: "Oh, my God, Jean-Georges! I want to go to that place. I can't believe you went without me."

I called and asked Donald if he could get us a reservation. He said he'd be happy to, only to call me back a week before the birthday with a piece of bad news: "They're closed for a private event that night." He insisted on getting us a table at the legendary (but now shuttered) Le Cirque instead.

I felt his large presence from the moment we walked in.

"Mr. and Mrs. Christie," the maître d' at Le Cirque welcomed us, "we're so happy you're here tonight." Before we'd even reached our table, I was summoned to the phone. "Chris, I'm so embarrassed about the Jean-Georges thing. But it's going to be a very special evening. You tell Mary Pat happy birthday."

It was like that all evening. Course after fabulous course. Everything impeccably served, right down to the absurdly elaborate Le Cirque Stove, a signature dessert that Donald ordered for Mary Pat. It was a milk chocolate stove with sponge cake inside and three little fruit sauce pans on top. A woman at the next table had tried to order one and was told that the dessert was unavailable. "Who are you?" she leaned over and whispered to Mary Pat.

Finally, the maître d' asked if there would be anything else. "Just the check, please," I said.

"There's no check tonight," he said. "The check has been taken care of by Mr. Trump."

Everything until then had been lovely. But *that* I couldn't do.

"No, no," I said firmly. "I can't accept that from Mr. Trump. You need to bring me a check."

The maître d' looked pained. "You don't understand, Mr. Christie," he said. "Mr. Trump has asked me to charge him for the dinner."

"You don't understand," I countered. "I'm the United States attorney. I'm the chief federal law enforcement officer in New Jersey. I cannot accept a gift from him like this. I need to have the check."

"You'll have to straighten that out with Mr. Trump," the man said. "I'm not getting in the middle of it."

"Then, please bring the menu back," I said.

He returned with the menu. I wrote down the prices of everything we'd ordered. The next day in the office, I added it all up, threw in a nice tip, and wrote a note on my US Attorney stationery:

Dear Donald,

Thank you so much for setting up the dinner. We had a wonderful time. Thanks for the phone call. I really appreciate your checking in. However, your picking up the check was unacceptable. So enclosed, please find my check. You say you want to be my friend. If you do, you'll cash this check.

Thank you,

Chris Christie.

I mailed the check.

He didn't cash it.

I checked my bank statement for the next two months. The check still hadn't cleared. Then I called Donald's incredible executive assistant, Rhona Graff, and told her I needed to speak to Donald.

"I'm not happy right now," I said when he picked up. "You haven't cashed my check."

"Of course, I haven't cashed it," he said. "I framed it."

"You framed it?"

"I framed it," he said. "You're the first person in public life who's ever sent a check to *me*. So, I framed it."

"Listen," I said. "This isn't funny. Take a Xerox of it, and frame the Xerox, if you want. You need to cash the check. I'm not kidding, Donald."

He let out a long, pained sigh. "Is it very important to you?" he asked.

"It's very important to me," I answered.

"Incredible," he said. "You're the most honest public servant I've ever met in my life. You sent a check to *me*. All right. I'll cash the check."

And finally, the check cleared through my account. On the back was an endorsement, in a sweeping script that would become unmistakable: a big, fat *Donald J. Trump* signature.

SIX

SUMMER CHAOS

I really thought my mom was indestructible.

She'd beaten breast cancer a quarter-century earlier. She had barreled through the treatments and gotten right back on her feet. She survived a brain aneurysm in 1999—a feat hardly anyone accomplishes—coming through with no damage at all. She was always a smoker, and that didn't help. But whatever life threw at her, my mother approached it with the same can't-stop-me attitude. In her own unique way, she'd been a wonderful wife to my father and an intensely dedicated mother to my brother, sister, and me. If you'd asked any of our children, they'd tell you she was the world's most-loving grandmother.

But early in 2004, my mother was having dizzy spells and went to see her doctor. Before she and my father returned for the follow-up, the doctor called my office. "I'm going to give your parents some news," he said to me. "You need to be there. They're not going to take this well."

The news was that my mother had three large brain tumors. It was Valentine's Day.

I loved both my parents dearly but in different ways. Over the years, I had come to see—and be grateful for the fact—that I had my father's keen mind. But I also had my mother's heart and soul. Temperamentally, my brother, Todd, was far closer to my father. By comparison, I was definitely my mother's son. Her in-your-face view of life, her refusal to back down from anything, her insistence on always speaking her mind—I'd inherited all of that.

My mother took the doctor's news fatalistically. My father looked like he'd been hit by a truck. Todd, Dawn, and I hardly knew what to say or do, other than to drop by my parents' house constantly to tell my mother how much we loved her. In April, I was at the US attorneys national conference in San Diego when Todd called.

"Mom's back in the hospital," he said. "It's really bad. The doctors are saying she could die at any time. If you want to see her again, you probably need to come home."

I jumped on the Thursday-night red-eye and landed at Newark on Friday morning. I got into my car at the airport and drove straight to Saint Barnabas Medical Center in Livingston. My mother was sleeping when I walked into her room. I sat beside her bed for a while, not wanting to wake her. When she stirred, she didn't even say hello to me.

"What day is it?" she demanded.

"It's Friday," I said.

"What time is it?"

"It's nine thirty in the morning."

"Go to work," she said to me in the same impatient tone I had heard from her thousands of times before.

"Hey, Mom," I told her, "I just flew back from San Diego to see you. I'm taking the day off to spend it with you."

She wasn't having it at all. I immediately felt like I was back in second grade, and I was complaining about a tummyache so I could stay home from school. "Christopher," my mother snapped. "It is a work day. You don't need to sit here. Go to work."

I started laughing out loud. "What?" I asked her. "You're afraid you're not getting your money's worth today as a taxpayer? Don't worry about it. I'll make up the time. I want to be here with you."

My mother reached over and grabbed my hand. "Go to work," she said. "It's where you belong. There's nothing left unsaid between us."

Right then is when tears welled up in my eyes.

"All right," I said. "I'll go to work, Mom."

"Good boy."

I gave her a kiss on her forehead. I forced a smile and left the room. I drove to my office in Newark and got back to work. It was the last time I would ever speak with my mother.

About three hours later, my brother called and told me she had slipped into a coma. She survived the weekend and died on Monday, May 3, two weeks shy of the three months her doctor had predicted.

Ever since then, whenever people have asked me to explain what I'm made of or who I am and why I act the way I do, I tell them how extraordinary my mother was. To look at her child on her deathbed and say, "There's nothing left unsaid between us"— and to really believe that. No untold stories. No buried secrets. What an extraordinary way to go out.

———

People across the country were noticing that something was happening at the US attorney's office in New Jersey. The *Washington Post* and *Los Angeles Times* published major profiles, highlighting our corruption prosecutions. Suddenly, I was being asked to deliver ethics-in-government speeches—in and out of the state. We were getting job applications from top graduates of the nation's most prestigious law schools. And why not? We were no longer an invisible backwater between the glamourous Southern District of New York and the Eastern District of Pennsylvania. We were a place where interesting stuff was happening and talented prosecutors could make their careers.

Not everyone was charmed by our equal-opportunity approach. This was not how New Jersey usually worked. Jim Treffinger was the Essex County executive, most famous for refusing to issue a filming permit for *The Sopranos* because he didn't like the way the HBO series depicted Italian Americans. Treffinger was also the leading Republican candidate to take on Democrat Bob Torricelli for the US Senate in 2002. That's until, early in my tenure as US Attorney, he was indicted for extortion, fraud, conspiracy, and obstructing a federal investigation. During that prosecution, Bill Palatucci got a call from a Republican county chairman who complained I was being too tough on our fellow Republicans. "What the hell is Chris doing?" the county chairman roared at Bill. "I thought he was *our* guy."

"You don't know Chris," Bill told him. "He's not *our* guy. He's the United States Attorney." Most people in the state, Republicans and Democrats, seemed to appreciate that. They just never believed it was possible.

When Treffinger saw the pile of evidence our people had assembled against him, he did what many of our other targets did. He pleaded guilty before the case ever got to trial. He admitted that he had solicited an illegal $15,000 campaign contribution in exchange for a county contract and had placed two campaign workers on the Essex County payroll.

Just another day in a changing New Jersey. And he was worried how *The Sopranos* made us look?

———

Two thousand and four was one crazy summer in New Jersey politics, and the trouble was inching closer to Governor Jim McGreevey. We got a conviction and a two-year prison sentence for one of the state's top Democratic Party fund-raisers, David D'Amiano, a close McGreevey ally. D'Amiano tried to shake down a Piscataway farm owner, Mark Halper, who was in a development dispute, demanding a $20,000 donation to the Democratic state committee and a $20,000 cash bribe to "State Official 1," as the governor was described in the indictment. There was even a secret code word, which Halper suggested without our permission: "Machiavelli." When Halper got some quality time with the governor, right after "Hello," McGreevey said to him: "I understand you're a big fan of *The Prince* by Machiavelli," which could be interpreted that the governor was in on the deal. But D'Amiano refused to flip on McGreevey, and that statement alone was not enough for us to charge the governor, who later blasted me in the media for overstepping my bounds. "No one has ever questioned my honesty," he steamed.

Guess the Machiavelli line was one big coincidence.

That same summer, an entirely different extortion allegation enveloped McGreevey—only this time the governor insisted he was the victim. On the morning of August 12, we got a call from McGreevey's lawyer, Marc Elias, asking us to investigate a blackmail attempt by the governor's secret gay lover, Golan Cipel, a former naval officer in the Israel Defense Forces who was until recently the governor's homeland security adviser.

Within hours, McGreevey, with his wife, Dina at his side, announced he was "a gay American" and would resign from office effective November 15. By the time the day was over, Cipel was threatening to file a sexual-harassment lawsuit, claiming he'd been fired for deflecting the governor's persistent sexual advances.

How quickly careers can come crashing down.

———

I ended that stunning day in the conference room of the US attorney's office in Newark, with several of my senior staffers. First assistant Ralph Marra was there. So were executive assistant Charlie McKenna, counsel Michele Brown and political-corruption chief Jim Nobile.

As we were taking it all in, my assistant, Nancy Manteiga, buzzed.

"A call for you," she said to me. "It's Donald Trump."

"Put him through," I answered, reflexively placing the call on speaker.

It didn't surprise me that Donald might have thoughts about Jim McGreevey's shocking news. But did we ever get an earful! "Can you believe what's going on?" he roared out of the speaker-phone as my staffers shot silent looks at one another. "I'd always heard the guy was gay, but I didn't know he was going to resign over it."

Donald liked being in the know. He also liked people knowing he was in the know. We went back and forth about the implications of the governor's sudden move. I explained that by delaying the resignation until November, McGreevey ensured there would be no special election to replace him. Since New Jersey had no lieutenant governor, the state senate president, Richard Codey, would serve as acting governor for more than a year. But Trump kept coming back to McGreevey's personal life. "You know, Chris, he's different than me and you, right? We may have all kinds of problems ourselves, but not this one. Me and you, just chicks—right, buddy? Just chicks."

The senior staffers all stared at me, wondering how I was going to field that one. I answered as vaguely as I could. "Yeah, that would be right, Donald," I said.

Donald, I was coming to realize, was a collector of people and of relationships. He didn't always know whether or not the relationship would help him. But he chose people he thought were interesting and might be of some value someday. I believe that's how he saw me. I was in the middle of some interesting professional adventures, and I probably had more to come. I felt pretty much the same about him.

Along the way, our guy dinners often turned into couples' affairs. Donald would bring Melania. I would bring Mary Pat. Mary Pat and I both found Melania smart, worldly, very intuitive, and immensely likeable. A two-hour dinner with Donald could be overwhelming. Mary Pat put it best: "He's exhausting." But if he was talking too much, Melania would sometimes reach over and lay her hand on his forearm. That was the signal: *Let others get in a word.* She seemed to have a calming influence on him. Given all that, it was only natural that Donald and Melania would invite us to their wedding. And it was only natural that we would go.

———

It was a grand, Trump-level event, of course, January 22, 2005. The wedding was at the Episcopal church of Bethesda-by-the-Sea in Palm Beach, Florida. It was followed by a lavish reception in the ballroom at Donald's Mar-a-Lago estate. Billy Joel serenaded the couple and their guests with "Just the Way You Are." The guest list was high profile if eclectic. Rudy Giuliani, Simon Cowell, Katie Couric, Matt Lauer, Heidi Klum, Sean Combs, Shaquille O'Neal, Fred Wilpon, and Barbara Walters. And, of course, Bill and Hillary Clinton, whose presence at the wedding would eventually become a mark of Donald's admirable bipartisanship or conflicted history, depending on your point of view.

This was my first time around the former president and his wife. I was fascinated by the contrast between them. Bill, who was five years out of office by then, made his way around the cocktail reception like he was running for office all over again. Saying hello to everyone. Posing for pictures. Making warm and funny comments. He couldn't have been friendlier to Mary Pat and me, even though barely anyone there knew who we were.

Hillary, on the other hand, stood beside a pillar and allowed the guests to line up in front of her. She shook hands and moved each person swiftly along. While her husband was working the room like an old precinct captain, she held court like a queen.

At some point during the reception Donald pulled me aside and asked in that direct Trump way of his, "So, are you going to leave the US attorney's office and run for governor?"

"No," I said straight-out. I had been in the position for three years at this point. I told him I still liked being the federal prosecutor and we had important cases still to bring. I had already made that point in the media, but I guess Donald thought maybe I was just being coy.

"I've been hearing things," he said. "People want you to run. Are you really not?"

"I'm really not," I said.

He shrugged and said, "Okay," before wandering off to greet other guests.

———

The cases just kept on coming. Corrupt New Jersey mayors became a virtual subspecialty of ours. Orange mayor Mims Hackett and Passaic mayor Sammy Rivera for attempted extortion. Keyport mayor John Merla and West Long Branch mayor Paul Zambrano for extortion. Hazlet mayor Paul Coughlin for extortion, conspiracy, and accepting a bribe. But to me, one of our most personally satisfying was the successful prosecution of Newark mayor Sharpe James, though he wasn't arrested until he was out of office. Sharpe James had been the mayor of New Jersey's largest city since 1986. He'd been investigated numerous times, though nothing ever stuck. People swore Sharpe was untouchable. He seemed to have an explanation for everything.

Our single most memorable run-in came soon after he left office in the summer of 2006. The city's new mayor, Cory Booker, called to tell me that his people had discovered something interesting in City Hall: a pile of credit card statements that indicated that the former mayor had a Newark Police Department credit card that hardly anybody knew about. And he'd made a number of questionable charges.

The new mayor wanted us to subpoena the records so that he could legally turn them over to us. I went down the hall to Jim Nobile's office. He called the FBI and asked for an agent to serve the subpoena on Newark City Hall, which was a block down Broad Street from our office. It seemed like a simple request, but the FBI supervisor said he couldn't spare an agent on that August afternoon. "Everyone's on vacation," he explained.

Jim and I both shook our heads. The fifth-largest FBI field office in the nation? Not a single agent? I sent Jim Nobile down the block. The chief of special prosecutions served the subpoena himself and came back to the office with a box of records.

We interviewed officials at the police department. We kept hearing about a woman we already knew a little about. Tamika Riley was her name. She was Sharpe James's girlfriend.

"I'm sure you know the PC Richard stuff," a police officer who'd been part of Mayor James's personal-security detail said to one of our investigators. "The air conditioner . . ."

"No. I don't think so."

"Yeah," the officer said. "The mayor made me go and buy a window air conditioner one day. He told me to bring it to this woman's apartment, Tamika Riley. It's actually a funny story because when I got there that day, I didn't know where to put the air conditioner. So I called the mayor. I said 'Mayor, where do you want me to install the air conditioner?' He goes, 'In the bedroom, you fool. That's where I need to stay cool.'"

Those credit card records that Cory Booker called about turned out to be Sharpe James's undoing.

It wasn't the window unit that ultimately did him in, though his obvious affection for Tamika Riley played an undeniable role. The evidence showed that Newark's five-term mayor had rigged the sale of nine city lots to his mistress, who quickly resold the properties for hundreds of thousands of dollars in profit.

After a five-week trial, a federal jury convicted Sharpe James on five counts of fraud. Judge William Martini sentenced him to twenty-seven months in prison, most of which he served at a federal prison camp in Petersburg, Virginia. While there, the ex-mayor wrote a 389-page book called *Political Prisoner*. You can't make this stuff up.

A lot of people followed the story of Sharpe James's prosecution and conviction. His was a big name. But Sharpe James wasn't the case that would follow me forever.

Charles Kushner was.

SEVEN

FAMILY FEUD

It wasn't the kind of meeting I would normally take.

In spring of 2004, two years into my tenure as United States attorney, I got a call from a lawyer I knew. Edward Dauber represented Esther and Bill Schulder, the sister and brother-in-law of a New Jersey real estate developer, Charles Kushner, who also happened to be the single largest Democratic Party campaign donor in the state. The lawyer wanted to bring his clients in to speak with me.

"Talk to Scott Resnik," I said. "He and his people are handling the case."

For more than a year, Resnik, who was part of Jim Nobile's public-corruption team, had been investigating the wealthy real estate developer for possible violations of federal tax and election laws. Those allegations bubbled out of a bitter family-business feud. I had never met Charles Kushner or any of his relatives, but I knew there was anger on all sides. From what I could gather, Charles's brother, Murray, and sister, Esther, were accusing him of running the family business like his own private domain, squeezing the others out of the decision making and what they considered their fair share of the profits. For his part, Charles claimed his siblings were greedy ingrates who ought to be more appreciative of the huge success he had made of the firm. All the usual family-business finger-pointing, in other words—just with bigger dollars attached. Murray and Esther had already sued Charles, though nothing criminal had been proved—not yet.

"Mr. US Attorney," the Schulders' lawyer said to me on the phone that morning, "you're gonna want to take this meeting. Trust me." I said okay and asked Resnik, Nobile, first assistant US attorney Ralph Marra, and my counsel, Michele Brown, to join us.

When the Schulders and their attorney arrived, Esther looked like a woman who felt seriously aggrieved. Bill looked like a beaten dog. After brief pleasantries, the lawyer removed a fat manila envelope from his briefcase and placed it on the conference table.

"It's a videotape," he said.

"A videotape?" I repeated.

"We believe that Esther and Bill are being blackmailed and retaliated against. This videotape is the proof."

"Okay," I answered, not quite sure what the lawyer was getting at. "What's on the video?"

"It's a video of Bill having sex with a woman at a motel in Somerville, New Jersey."

Of all the sordid cases my office had been involved with over the past few years, this was a new one. Not what I was expecting. But, really, what did it have to do with us? Esther calmly stated that she knew that her brother Charlie was behind it.

Ralph, Jimmy, Michele, and Scott all exchanged incredulous glances. Esther's husband was caught with a woman in a New Jersey motel room and somehow it was his wife's rich brother's fault? I'd heard a lot of stories in my time, but I'd never heard this one before.

"Wait a second, Esther," I said. "I know you don't get along with Charles. But what gives you the idea that your brother is responsible for this videotape, whatever may be on it or not?"

Esther didn't hesitate. "Charlie plays on people's weaknesses," she said. "Billy has a weakness." She patted her husband's shoulder and nodded at the envelope. "Charlie played on it."

"Well," I said, "someone had better explain all this to me."

Bill took it from there.

Almost every morning before work, Bill said, he stopped at the Time to Eat Diner, just south of the Bridgewater Commons mall. One morning, he was having his usual breakfast when an attractive, young blond woman said hello.

"She said she was from out of town and was here for a job interview," Bill told us. "She said she had car trouble, that her vehicle had been towed. She asked if I could possibly give her a ride to her hotel."

Bill said sure and drove the woman to the Red Bull Inn on Route 22, about ten minutes away.

Time to Eat? Red Bull? You can't make these names up!

When Bill and the woman arrived at the motel, he said, she asked if he'd like to come up to her room. No, he answered. He had to get going. "Well," he recalled her saying, "I'm going to need a ride to the car dealership tomorrow morning. I don't know anybody out here. If you're around, do you think you could give me a ride to pick up my car?"

Bill said he gave a noncommittal answer: "I'm not sure if I'll be here or not." But they did exchange phone numbers. "If you really need a ride," he told her as she got out of the car, "you can give me a call."

The next morning, the woman called. Bill drove back to the Red Bull Inn. This time, he said yes when she invited him to her room, where the two of them had sex.

What Bill discovered only later—and his wife certainly didn't know at the time—was that his morning encounter with the blond woman from the diner, whoever she was, was being videotaped by a tiny camera hidden inside an alarm clock that was sitting next to the bed.

The first Esther or Bill learned about any of that was months later when a manila envelope arrived in the mail. Inside the envelope was an X-rated video, starring Bill. "It came just as we were getting ready for my son Jacob's engagement party," Esther explained to us. She said the envelope also included several glossy photos of her husband and this woman in poses that could certainly be described as compromising.

"The envelope had no return address," Esther added. "But I knew right away who it came from. Charlie was sending a message to make me miserable and humiliate my husband and me."

It was an incredible story. But as Esther and Bill laid it out there, I couldn't help thinking like a prosecutor who would one day need to present this evidence to a grand jury or a judge. Suspicion was one thing. Where was the proof? "All right," I said to the couple and their lawyer. "You believe Charles is behind this. But how do we know? It could be anybody."

My senior staffers seemed to share my hesitance. "It could be an old girlfriend of Bill's," Jim Nobile said.

"It could be anyone," Scott Resnik said.

"I know it's Charlie," Esther insisted. Of my three senior staffers in the room, only Ralph Marra seemed to think that Esther might well be right. Then a thought occurred to me.

I said to Bill, "You mentioned that you exchanged cell phone numbers with this woman."

He nodded.

"Do you still have her number?"

Bill stared down at the conference table. He thought for a second. "Yeah, I have it," he said.

"We're going to need that number from you now," I said.

———

The children of Holocaust survivors, Charles, Murray, and Esther grew up in Elizabeth, New Jersey. Their construction-worker father started his own contracting company and did very well, becoming one of the state's largest landlords. By the mid-1960s, he owned nearly four thousand apartments. But it wasn't until Charles took over that the family-owned Kushner Companies really hit the big time, transforming it into a billion-dollar real estate empire with office buildings, condominiums, and apartment complexes in half a dozen states. Along the way, Charles deftly positioned himself as a major power broker in the state, contributing millions of dollars to Democratic politicians as well as to synagogues, hospitals, schools, and other charitable causes. He was free with his advice to ambitious officeholders. He had access to everyone.

Bill Clinton turned up several times at Kushner headquarters in Florham Park. Israeli prime minister Benjamin Netanyahu came around, too. But no politician had benefited more from

Charles Kushner's support than Jim McGreevey, whose election to governor of New Jersey in 2001 was greased with barrels of Kushner cash. One month after taking office, McGreevey nominated Kushner to be chairman of the Port Authority of New York and New Jersey, a hugely powerful post overseeing a significant part of the region's infrastructure, including the Newark, John F. Kennedy, and LaGuardia airports.

The chairmanship was eventually scuttled by opponents in Trenton. By then, Charles was already grooming his eldest son, Jared, now in his early twenties, as only a wealthy father can.

The allegations against Charles Kushner were an important matter, one of many, involving a major player in the politics of New Jersey who had behaved in a manner that might be criminal. But that's all it was. As United States attorney, I was interested in only two things: Were federal laws broken? And could our prosecutors prove it beyond a reasonable doubt? I knew this would take some sorting out.

Ralph Marra, who'd spent fifteen years prosecuting public-corruption cases as he rose through the ranks, grabbed his favorite FBI agent, Tom Marakovits, and they dug in. They subpoenaed the records for the cell phone Bill had called. The number belonged to a woman named Susanna, a high-priced, European-born call girl on Manhattan's Upper East Side. The videotape was date- and time-stamped. So Ralph and Tom retrieved her phone records for that period. Immediately after the tape ended, Susanna had called a number that was registered to a private detective, Tommy O'Toole of Utica, New York. That seemed strange. Utica is way upstate. Why would a Manhattan prostitute in a New Jersey motel room call a private detective 250 miles away?

Our guys subpoenaed the private eye's cell records to see who he called immediately after hearing from Susanna. He called his brother, Captain Jimmy O'Toole of the East Orange Police Department in New Jersey. And who did Captain O'Toole call immediately after hearing from his private eye brother?

He called Charles Kushner.

Game. Set. Match.

That was the connective tissue we needed, tying the conspirators together in a provable criminal act. Those phone records linked the Red Bull motel room to the politically wired real estate mogul whose brother-in-law costarred in a movie he had no idea he'd been cast in.

That was more than enough to get search warrants. At the private eye's office in Utica, FBI agents seized a copy of the explicit Bill-and-Susanna video. At the East Orange Police Department, O'Toole immediately squealed on everyone, saying he'd agreed to help Charles Kushner, an old friend, ensnare his brother-in-law. He admitted he'd introduced Charles to his private eye brother, who'd planted himself in an adjoining Red Bull motel room. Jimmy O'Toole said he had gone to Kushner's office in Florham Park a few days after the tape was made and held a private screening for Kushner and Kushner's wife's brother, Richard Stadtmauer, who also worked at the Kushner Companies. He said he felt nauseated at the men's raucous guffaws as they watched the raw video. It was Charles Kushner, the police captain added, who'd first suggested the hidden-camera-and-hooker routine and had ultimately recruited Susanna.

Meanwhile, FBI agent Art Durrant was ringing the bell at Susanna's Manhattan apartment. Ringing and ringing and ringing some more, announcing into the intercom that he was from the FBI. No one answered. He kept ringing. He had a search warrant. But it was a really nice building, and Art didn't want to bust down the door. So he kept ringing—by his count, sixty times.

Finally, Susanna opened and allowed the agent in.

He began to question her about the Time to Eat Diner and the Red Bull Inn. He asked about a story of a towed vehicle and a mild-mannered middle-aged man named Bill. She remembered all of it and didn't hold back. Then Art showed her a picture of Charles Kushner.

"Do you know this person?" he asked.

"Oh, yeah," Susanna said without hesitation, "that's the guy who hired me to do this."

———

Jimmy O'Toole, the East Orange police captain, was an especially cooperative witness, even agreeing to wear a wire for a meeting with his old friend Charles Kushner. Kushner's lawyer, the New Jersey criminal-defense attorney Michael Critchley, actually patted Jimmy down—but not very well, apparently. He missed the hidden microphone. An interesting role for a criminal-defense attorney to play. Based on that and other sleazy conduct he was involved in, we had Critchley recused from the case. In the taped conversation, the politically connected developer tacitly acknowledged his role in orchestrating the X-rated revenge.

With all the evidence we'd amassed, we had more than enough to arrest Charles Kushner. This was our call, in consultation with the FBI. It wasn't an especially close one. At six a.m. on July 13, Ralph Marra called Alfred DeCotiis, a well-regarded New Jersey defense lawyer who'd been leading Kushner's legal team since Critchley had compromised himself with his questionable conduct. At noon, the real estate developer and New Jersey power broker surrendered at the FBI office on McCarter Highway in Newark.

He was fingerprinted, photographed, and asked the question that's been put to countless criminal defendants before him:

"Do you have any interest in cooperating?"

"I do not," he answered unequivocally.

At the downtown federal courthouse, Kushner pleaded not guilty to charges of witness tampering, obstruction of justice, and violating the Mann Act, a 1910 federal law prohibiting promoting prostitution across state lines. He was released on $5 million bail.

There was quite a media scrum outside the court that day and in the weeks that followed. The Jersey papers, the New York tabloids, the major wire services, local and network TV—all of them found the story irresistible. "NJ Scandal: Sex, Money & Politics," CBS News trumpeted. "Sex Gal Now Helping Feds—Hooker Turns on Kushner," blared the *New York Post*. "Senator to Return Contributions from Donor Facing Charges," announced the *New York Times*.

Behind the scenes, Kushner's legal team was beefing up. The famed New York City attorney Benjamin Brafman joined Al DeCotiis and his partner Jeffrey Smith. Brafman's initial position was "There's nothing here. Let's go to trial. We're not pleading guilty to anything." Brafman displayed similar bravado in front of the media. "Once the facts are fully disclosed in a courtroom," he said of his client, "he will be completely exonerated."

No such luck.

Brafman's tone changed quickly as the defense attorneys absorbed the evidence. We started discussing a potential plea bargain within a few days. The negotiation was the usual one: Precisely which counts would Kushner plead guilty to? Which would we drop? And, especially, how much prison time could he expect to receive? The defense team was proposing twelve to eighteen months, a level 13 under the federal sentencing guidelines. We were pushing for eighteen to twenty-four months, a level 15. The tax charges, election violations, plus the humiliating personal attack—this was definitely not a case that could end with a slap on the wrist.

We went back and forth on the numbers. Kushner seemed eager to avoid a trial, where all the sordid details would be thrown into the open and, if the jury convicted, he might receive considerably more prison time.

After a month of negotiations, we were close, but we weren't quite there. I went to speak to a civic group at the Loews Glenpointe Hotel in Teaneck. Waiting in the parking lot afterward was Al DeCotiis, whose law office was in the same complex. He said he'd heard that I was in the neighborhood, and he had a proposal to make.

"How 'bout this?" Al asked. "Charlie is willing to donate $3 million to set up a new shelter for homeless people in Newark or wherever you want in New Jersey. If he does that, can you lower his guideline to a level 13?"

Al's a good lawyer, but I didn't like the sound of that. "Your guy thinks his money can buy anything," I said. "Not from me, it can't. As a prosecutor, it's not my responsibility to worry about homeless shelters. He can go talk to his friend, the governor. I have no interest in discussing this anymore."

Al grabbed my arm and said, "C'mon, Chris. It will help a lot of people."

"Al, I can't care. It's not my job. No."

Al got the message. I assume he passed it back to his client. We never budged off the 15, the level carrying a possible sentence of eighteen to twenty-four months.

———

On August 18, Charles Kushner was set to appear before US District Judge Jose Linares to admit his criminal wrongdoing and plead guilty in federal court. Kushner had finally agreed to the deal.

But at six o'clock that morning, Mary Pat and I were dead asleep at home in Mendham when I heard the doorbell ring.

"What the hell is that?" I asked Mary Pat.

"Sounds like the doorbell," she said.

I threw on gym shorts and shuffled downstairs. When I peeked out the window, Al DeCotiis and his partner, Jeff Smith, were standing there. I rubbed my eyes and opened the door.

"Al," I groaned. "You've gotta be fuckin' kidding me! It's six a.m. What are you doing here?"

"Chris, I'm so sorry," he said. "I have to come in."

"You're— No, you're not coming in. Call me at the office when I get there."

"Chris, we've been up all night," Al said. "Charles Kushner is withdrawing his plea."

What? I could hardly believe it. *After all our efforts, hours before his court date, Kushner's decided not to plead?*

"Okay," I told the lawyers. "Come in."

The three of us—Al, Jeff, and I—went into my kitchen and sat down. Al got me up to speed. When I'd gone to sleep the night before, we had an agreement that Charles would plead to witness retaliation, violating federal election law, and conspiracy to commit tax fraud. But after a heart-to-heart between Charles and his wife, Seryl, the deal was now off.

"We were there all night talking to them," Al said. "He will not plead guilty to the conspiracy count under any circumstances. He'll go ahead with a trial." Admitting to the conspiracy, his wife believed, could implicate her brother Richard in Charles's criminality. That was unacceptable to her. According to Al, she told her husband she would divorce him if he did that.

Al was still recounting the all-nighter with Mr. and Mrs. Kushner when my ten-year-old son, Andrew, came downstairs for breakfast before school. He'd met Al before and, for some reason, didn't think there was anything unusual about two grown men sitting at the kitchen table with his father not long after dawn, talking about criminal counts and prison terms.

"Mr. DeCotiis, you want some Cheerios?" Andrew asked.

Al looked at me like he wanted some.

"Why not, Al?" I said to him. "You're already here."

So Andrew got a bowl and a spoon for himself and another one for Al, then pulled the cereal from the cabinet and the milk from the fridge. I got Ralph Marra, Michele Brown, and Jim Nobile on the phone. In the end, we jiggled the counts slightly, settling on eighteen substantive ones, and managed to get this runaway train back on track in time for our date with the judge.

———

Three hours after Andrew's Cheerios with Al, Charles Kushner walked into Judge Linares's courtroom. It was the first time I had ever personally laid eyes on him. I'd overseen his prosecution. I'd pulled it back from the edge a couple of times. But I had never actually seen the man in person. I was struck by how small and quiet and beaten he seemed. He certainly didn't look like the demanding and volatile real estate baron I'd been reading and hearing about for years. He may have had family members in the courtroom with him—his wife or his children or other relatives. He probably did. But I had no reason to notice them. I was transfixed on one thing.

Charles Kushner stood before Judge Linares and pleaded guilty to eighteen counts of filing false tax returns, retaliating

against witnesses, and making illegal campaign contributions—
no conspiracy—answering each with a flat "yes." We had previously agreed to drop the alleged Mann Act violation.

In the courtroom, Kushner offered no explanation for his
behavior. He slipped in and out of the building without speaking
to the media.

Brafman did the talking for him, saying his client "wanted
to accept responsibility by acknowledging that he did something
wrong" and would be stepping down as chairman of the Kushner
Companies.

What a fall Charles Kushner had taken. From the highest
heights of the state's business and political worlds to convicted
criminal. The only question left was exactly how much prison
time the state's newest federal felon would receive.

——

Charles Kushner's sentencing was held on March 4, 2005. The
lawyers got one final chance to pitch Judge Linares on exactly
how much time would be fair. Eighteen months? Twenty-four?
Something different? The sentencing hearing lasted nearly two
and a half hours. The defense lawyers emphasized that their client had never been in legal trouble before. They noted he'd run a
successful business and given millions to charity. The prosecutors detailed the wealthy businessman's long-running plot to vio-
late the law, obstruct justice, and harm his relatives. There was a
spirited debate over whether he had accepted responsibility for his
crimes.

He sat at the defense table, dressed in a navy blue suit with a
white shirt and polka-dot tie, taking all of this in. Then he rose
and spoke briefly to the court. He told the judge that he didn't

believe he was quite the saint that his lawyers made him out to be or quite as evil as the charges implied.

"The actions which bring me before you today were disgraceful and reprehensible," he said.

When Judge Linares finally spoke, he said he had tried to weigh the "horrific" nature of the defendant's conduct against his many philanthropic deeds. "It is difficult for me to reconcile the generous man with the revengeful, hateful man," the judge allowed.

But in the end, Judge Linares didn't sound swayed by the philanthropy or the defense lawyers' praise. "I must take into consideration the vengeful nature in which this was done," the judge said. "In light of all the relevant circumstances, I find that you be imprisoned for twenty-four months."

The judge gave him the max.

And that, I assumed, was the last I would ever hear about the convicted felon Charles Kushner and his deeply tortured family.

Little did I know.

PART THREE

TOUGH GUV

EIGHT

MINORITY PARTY

Taking out a sitting governor is never easy. It is especially difficult in a state like New Jersey when the governor is a Democrat who has already spent $105 million on his first two races and has vowed to keep spending. New Jersey is a very blue state. Dems have a solid voter-registration advantage. Dems have entrenched political machines in Newark, Jersey City, Paterson, Trenton, Camden, and most of the state's other urban areas. The New York and Philadelphia media markets encompass all of northern and southern Jersey. That's no benefit to Republicans. Only a different kind of Republican can win in a state like New Jersey. Someone who's anti-tax. Someone who's seen as a problem solver and a government reformer. It also helps if the Democrats have been screwing up.

Was I that guy? Would 2009 be that year? I was about to find out. The way I looked at it, I was more Jersey than Jon Corzine, less robotic than Jim McGreevey, more conservative than Christie Whitman, less dour than Jim Florio, and at least as politically calculating as Tom Kean.

I thought my chances were pretty good.

Four years earlier, there'd been talk about my running for governor when Jim McGreevey resigned and Richard Codey, the state senate president, was keeping the seat warm as acting governor. Jon Corzine, who'd been a Goldman Sachs executive before getting elected to the US Senate, was hinting that he and his deep pockets might run, scaring away other candidates. My refusal to jump in then irked some New Jersey Republicans. Lew Eisenberg, a former Port Authority chairman who went on to be US ambassador to Italy, delivered an especially ominous warning. "Let me guarantee you something," Lew said to me. "If you don't do it now, you're never going to get anybody's support again." But I couldn't shake the lesson of my botched assembly race in 1995: *Wait until you are ready.* I told Lew I would take my chances with the future. I wanted to keep sending corrupt politicians to prison. I wasn't ready to leave the US attorney's office yet.

I waited until Barack Obama was elected president on November 4, 2008. Then I submitted my resignation, effective December 1. I didn't want to hang around the US attorney's office until the bitter end. At my recommendation, Attorney General Michael Mukasey appointed Ralph Marra, my longtime first assistant, as acting US attorney. Everything was orderly inside the office, but I was an emotional wreck. Stepping down from the chief prosecutor's job was a whole lot more traumatic than I ever imagined it would be. These weren't just my colleagues I was leaving. I was leaving my friends, my security blanket, and my self-identity. We had a massive going-away party, and I was suddenly sitting around the house in Mendham feeling lonely and lost.

I had no job. I missed our cases. I had nowhere to go. To keep all my options open and to avoid any conflicts, I'd decided against signing on with a law firm in New Jersey or New York City. Was it finally time for me to run for governor? With my old friend Bill

Palatucci and my brother, Todd, I spent December trying to game out a possible campaign. Who would run it? How would we raise the money? What issues would we hit? I wasn't doing a very good job of answering any of those questions. I was still feeling too big a letdown from leaving the best job I ever had. Mary Pat had never seen me like this.

"What's wrong with you?" she asked as Christmas neared. "There's another challenge ahead. Go get it like you normally do." Sound advice, but I wasn't ready to act on it. First I had to get through the grief.

We took a family vacation to Jamaica the week between Christmas and New Year's. The first night we got there, while the kids were playing cards in the room, Mary Pat and I took a walk on the beach. "I think I want to do this," I said, "but I really need you to be on board. I want to know what you want."

"I don't care either way," she said. "I can be happy doing it or not. But here's what you have to promise me: If you're not going to run, then you have to do it with no regrets. I have no interest in spending the rest of my life with a man full of regrets."

Mary Pat's answer was perfect. "If that's the case," I said to her, "then I'm running."

Mary Pat and I made a deal right away. If I was fortunate enough to win, we wouldn't move the family to Drumthwacket, the governor's mansion in Princeton. It's a beautiful home, a short drive from the State House in Trenton, where the governor's office is. The land was once owned by William Penn, the Quaker proprietor of the Province of Pennsylvania. But we wanted our children—ages fifteen, twelve, eight, and five—to have lives as normal as possible, remaining in their schools, staying with their friends, and sleeping in their own beds at night. If that meant I'd be commuting an hour and twenty minutes each way, so be it.

We told the kids the next morning at the pool. One by one, we called them out of the water and broke the news. Andrew, Patrick, and Bridget, ages fifteen, eight, and five, were all instantly on board. They all reacted with some version of "That sounds like fun." Sarah, who was about to turn thirteen, was far from enthusiastic. "Okay," she said. "Thanks for ruining my life." Then, she turned around and jumped back in the pool.

"Four out of five isn't bad," Mary Pat said with a shrug.

When we got home after New Year's, I called Palatucci and said, "Let's do it." I made a soft-launch announcement January 8 after picking up Patrick and Bridget at Assumption School in Morristown, telling the media I had just filed papers to run. "I decided I could make a difference," I said with the two littlest ones at my side. "If you're looking for the same old stuff, you've got the wrong person."

Palatucci was already assembling a campaign staff that would stand by my side for years. State Senator Joe Kyrillos was our statewide chairman. Palatucci took over as finance chair with his cochair the real estate investor Jon Hanson. Mike DuHaime, an old friend of mine who'd worked in the Bush White House, was chief strategist. Bill Stepien, a New Jersey political hand with state and national experience and a protégé of DuHaime's, was campaign manager, running day-to-day operations. For communications director, I tried to hire a friend of DuHaime's, twenty-nine-year-old Maria Comella, who'd been Sarah Palin's press secretary. She had such PTSD from the Alaska governor's vice-presidential campaign that at first she didn't seem to want the job. Eventually I would convince her.

Before I could take on Corzine, I had to survive a June 2 Republican primary against Bogota mayor Steve Lonegan. He never caught fire. I won the Republican Party endorsement in all twenty-one counties and stomped past him on Primary Day 55 to 42 percent. Now I would get what Jersey politicos had been waiting for since 2005, a clear shot at Governor Corzine.

I woke up the morning after the primary and was treated to the first of many Corzine attack ads, this one tying me to the then-unpopular George W. Bush. The tagline? "Same policies, same results." I couldn't afford to answer the paid attacks with ads of our own. Broke from the primary, we had to start raising money all over again.

——

By the time I was running for governor, I was long done with the Kushner family. I thought I was, anyway. Charles Kushner's prosecution had been major news when it happened in the busy summer of 2005, but that was ancient history. He'd already done his time—fourteen months at the federal prison camp in Montgomery, Alabama, followed by a short stay at a Newark halfway house. I was long gone from the US attorney's office. All I was thinking about was the governor's race.

But some stories refuse to end.

It was at one of our couples' dinners with Donald and Melania—Donald's usual table at the 21 Club—that he shared some big news with Mary Pat and me. His older daughter, Ivanka, who was twenty-seven, was going to marry her boyfriend, twenty-eight-year-old Jared Kushner, Charles Kushner's older son. The engagement wasn't public yet. But Ivanka had told her father she was in love with Jared, and they'd decided to tie the knot.

"That's wonderful," Mary Pat said to Donald and Melania.

"Congratulations to both of you!" I said.

The only wrinkle, Donald said, was that Jared had informed Ivanka that he couldn't marry a woman who wasn't Jewish.

Ivanka, like the other Trump children, had been raised Presby-terian. Ivanka had told her father she'd decided to convert to the religion of her fiancé and his family, Judaism.

It was a little hard to gauge Donald's reaction to all of this. He was greeting the news, especially Ivanka's religious conversion, with what I would describe as acceptance. *She's a big girl. She's a smart girl. If that's what she wants to do, then that's what she wants to do. I support her. I trust her.*

Said Donald: "You never know what your kids will do next!"

What struck me at our dinner that night was how much Don-ald obviously loved Ivanka and how important she was in his life. He spent a long time talking about her many fine qualities. How smart she was. How thoughtful she was. What a catch she was for this guy Kushner. As the evening wore on, Donald circled back to one point of curiosity. He asked me to tell him the story of my brush with Ivanka's future father-in-law.

"Remind me," he said. "There was some sleazy stuff, right?" As Donald often does, he pushed me for all the key details, includ-ing the steamy ones.

"He really did that?" Donald asked me.

"Yes, he did."

"Oh, that's not good."

Later, Mary Pat and I would receive a call from Donald, ask-ing if we would consider coming to Ivanka's wedding. I knew Donald was reaching out so we'd feel included. There was no way we could attend. We told Donald we appreciated the thought but it just didn't feel like it was right to go. I am confident he was relieved that we didn't make things awkward for him, Ivanka, and his son-in-law-to-be.

—

All summer long in 2009, I kept getting pounded by the Corzine team.

I was soft on guns. I was going to stop women from getting mammograms. I was pals with the "dreaded" Karl Rove. The solid lead I had coming out of the primary shrank as Corzine's ads landed, blow by blow.

The Corzine people dug up my driving record, which wasn't good. They seized on a $46,000 mortgage loan I'd made to my friend and former counsel Michele Brown, whose husband had lost his job. To gather opposition research, Corzine hired a former *Star-Ledger* reporter named Jeff Whelan. Whelan had covered me as US attorney for seven years. He was someone I'd spoken with frequently in confidence. When I called the move sleazy, the ex-reporter promised he wouldn't use anything that I'd told him off the record. *Yeah, right!* He then proceeded to bury the US attorney's office in so many Freedom of Information Act requests, it couldn't possibly keep up.

I was still ahead by Labor Day, but my lead had slipped into single digits. The Republican National Committee, under chairman Michael Steele, agreed to spend some money on my behalf. But the Republican Governors Association was initially reluctant. "New Jersey is like Charlie Brown, Lucy, and the football," the association's chairman, South Carolina governor Mark Sanford, had told me when we'd met for five minutes earlier in the year. "I don't see investing in your race."

It was only when Sanford got swept up in a sticky scandal with a woman from Argentina that the defeatism finally evaporated. "I believe in you, baby," Mississippi governor Haley Barbour called to tell me when he took over as chairman. "We're jumping in with both feet." Operating independently, the governors' association produced hard-hitting TV spots answering Corzine's attacks. It also produced an ad slapping the independent candidate Chris Daggett, who was starting to register in some polls after complaining I'd somehow been unfair to him: "Chris Daggett. Just like Corzine, only worse."

By the time Corzine and I met for our first debate, October 1 at the New Jersey Network studios in Trenton, the hostility between us was at a fever pitch. That's why I was surprised by what happened when I came off the stage that night and began shaking hands in the audience. One man stood and reached out his huge palm to me. "Good job tonight," he said. "I look forward to working with you." It was State Senator Steve Sweeney, head of the ironworkers union in New Jersey, a lifelong Democrat who'd just announced he was running for Senate president.

When I learned later that Sweeney had been playing me in the Corzine debate prep, his congratulatory message that night took on an even deeper meaning.

What was most memorable from the second debate, held on October 16 at William Paterson University in Wayne, was the topic of agreement Corzine and I discovered we had. It may have been the only one. This was just before we went onstage. The governor nodded toward Daggett, who'd just been complaining again about how unfair I was being to him. "He's really becoming a pain in the ass, isn't he?" Corzine said.

——

On election morning, I had no idea who was going to win. Mary Pat and I predicted a loss, which I think reflected our view of New Jersey as a blue state and probably a bit of self-protection. The polls had Corzine and me within a couple of points of each other, though they couldn't agree who was on top. The *Star-Ledger* had endorsed Daggett, not Corzine or me. Election morning, my internal pollster, Adam Geller, said we'd win by four or five points. I thought he was just trying to make the client feel good.

"Adam," I said. "You don't have to sell me. You've already been paid."

Friends, family, staffers, volunteers, Governor Kean, Governor Whitman—they all joined the Christie family in our suite at the Parsippany Hilton to await the election night results. The larger crowd was in a ballroom off the lobby with TVs and an open bar. The Republican National Committee funded a war room for us, outfitted with the latest vote-tallying software. By eight p.m., when the polls closed, nothing official was being said.

At 8:45, I got a call from Mayor John McCormac of Woodbridge, whose job Jim McGreevey had once held. "We've just finished counting," he reported. "You won." Woodbridge is a Democratic town in a Democratic county. I went looking for Mary Pat.

"Let's go in the bedroom," I said.

I closed the door and said to her: "I just got off the phone with John McCormac. We won Woodbridge."

"Oh, good," she said.

"No, no, no. You don't understand. If I won Woodbridge, I'm going to be the governor."

"You're kidding," she said to me.

"I am not kidding. You probably have two hours to wrap your head around this before we have to go downstairs in front of a room of screaming people and a bank of TV cameras, when our lives will change forever."

I went into the bathroom to put on a new tie. Mary Pat was at the sink beside me doing her makeup. At one point, we both looked at each other in the mirror and just burst out laughing.

"I can't believe we did it," she said to me.

"Neither can I," I replied.

———

Word was already beginning to spread. For the first time all night, I saw Bill Palatucci smiling. He walked over to me holding out his BlackBerry. I took it. The email on the screen was from George Norcross, a legendary Democratic leader in South Jersey. It said simply: "It's Governor-Elect Christie for sure."

I didn't know George well, but I knew he'd lived through a lot of close elections in his time, and he had a reputation for being a shrewd vote counter. Eventually, official word came in. My team in the Republican National Committee war room and their complex data projections came to the same conclusion that my informal callers and texters had.

We had this in the bag.

Since he was my brother, Todd was given the honor—or was it the duty?—of slipping discreetly up to the suite and delivering the news to me. He almost did. Unfortunately, he got sidetracked in the hotel bar by exuberant staffers and friends. When DuHaime, Stepien, and Comella couldn't reach him for too long, the three decided to tell me themselves.

"Can we see you alone with Mrs. Christie in the bedroom?" DuHaime asked me.

"Sure. What's up?" I already knew what was up, but I didn't want to take away anybody's thrill.

DuHaime looked at me and turned suddenly serious. "We just all came up here, sir," he said, choosing his words carefully, "to congratulate you, Mr. Governor-Elect."

I looked at Maria, and she had tears in her eyes. Stepien looked exhilarated and exhausted at the same time. It was an incredibly emotional moment with these three people who had given their all to me for the better part of a year.

I hugged all three of them and thanked them for everything they had done. And then I heard a scream come from the living room of the suite. I knew that voice. It was the voice of the last Republican to have been elected statewide in New Jersey, way back in 1997, Governor Christine Todd Whitman. Fox News had just declared me the winner of the New Jersey governor's race.

I got 48.5 percent of the vote to Corzine's 44.8 percent and Daggett's 5.8 percent. Just as my pollster had predicted, we'd won by 4 percent.

Michael Steele had flown up from Virginia when the race seemed to be going our way. I told him how much I appreciated the national party's $3 million in support. Haley Barbour, the governors' association chairman, called, along with executive director Nick Ayers. "God damn!" Haley exclaimed. "We were right! You're the winner, buddy!"

Daggett called to concede. After all his moaning and wasted endorsements, he hadn't even cracked 6 percent. I didn't take his call. Corzine called to concede. I was happy to speak with him. Our conversation was cordial though slightly stiff.

"Good evening, Governor," I said.

"Chris, good evening. I guess congratulations are in order."

"Thank you, Governor. I appreciate that very much."

The crowd was cheering wildly in the ballroom. They'd had plenty to drink. Eleven o'clock was closing in. I was still backstage with Mary Pat and the kids. But before I stepped in front of the TV lights to deliver my victory speech, I had a personal message to relay.

"Everybody get in a huddle here," I said to the five of them.

"I want you all to understand something," I said. "This is important, so listen carefully. We are going to walk out on that stage in two minutes, and our lives are going to change forever.

All of us are going to make some new friends—some real friends. But there are also going to be people who act like they're our new friends, but they only want to be around us because of the job that your dad just won. So, here's what you have to remember for the next four years or the next eight years. The most important people in your life, the people who you can count on no matter what, are the people in this circle right now. This circle. No bigger than that. I want you all to look at me and tell me you know that."

They all looked at me and nodded.

"Okay," I said. "Now we're ready to go."

I woke up the next morning. Actually, that's not true. I never went to sleep. I went down to the hotel gift shop at six a.m. to buy the morning newspapers. When the clerk looked at the papers and then looked at me, she smiled and said, "Well, that doesn't happen every day."

I'd agreed to meet the senior staff for an early breakfast to figure out how I'd spend my first day as governor-elect. We met in the hotel lobby with lots of people staring and photographers taking pictures. This was important, I knew. Everyone would be watching. Whatever we did would set a tone as we moved toward Inauguration Day.

The theme I wanted to hit was inclusiveness. If I was going to accomplish anything as governor, I knew I would need Democratic support. Wasn't that what got me elected in majority-Democratic New Jersey?

"Let's go to my favorite charter school," I said.

Early that afternoon, we pulled up in front of the Robert Treat Academy, a charter school run by Steve Adubato Sr., the Democratic boss of Newark. You couldn't get much more Democratic than that.

Meeting us on the sidewalk, along with a couple hundred cheering students, were Adubato, Newark's Democratic mayor, Cory Booker, and Democratic Essex County executive Joe DiVincenzo. All of this for the incoming Republican governor of New Jersey.

Crazy, huh?

I could not have imagined a more inspiring first stop. We went inside, where the students were blowing whistles and waving signs. All the media were there. After everyone said a few words, Steve reached under the conference table where we were sitting and said to me: "I have a gift for you. This is how much confidence I had that you were going to win."

It was a blue fleece. Stitched on the front were the words CHRIS CHRISTIE, GOVERNOR.

I had no idea how much use I would get out of that fleece, but I had to tease him. "Come on," I said. "Where's the fleece for Corzine? I know you printed up two of them."

A few weeks before I took the oath of office, I called George Norcross for lunch. Years before, George had been the Camden County Democratic chairman. He had stretched his influence across South Jersey, believing that the region was constantly being shortchanged in Trenton. With aggressive organizing and some hard-hitting commercial buys on Philadelphia TV, he managed to pick off several Republican legislators, replacing them with his Democrats. George had a legendary reputation—politically savvy, personally wealthy, and ruthless. By the time he and I met, George had no official position at all, but he was still one of the most powerful men in Trenton. People feared him. He could get anyone on the phone. All you had to say was "George." Everyone in New Jersey politics knew exactly who you were talking about.

I knew some people in my party wouldn't like the idea of my meeting with him. But in my view, I was elected to govern.

If I didn't get some Democratic support, I would be a dead man walking.

We met in Philadelphia. We talked about the recent campaign and the makeup of the upcoming legislature. At the end of the meal, I said to George: "I want to see if we can do business together."

George took a second to absorb that.

"Well, Governor-Elect," he said, "let me ask you a question. What are you more interested in? Making headlines or putting touchdowns in the end zone?"

That was easy. "I'm more interested in putting touchdowns in the end zone."

"Okay," George answered. "Let's see if we can work together then."

We shook hands and walked out.

And so began one of the three relationships that would define the bipartisan success of my governorship over the next eight years: George Norcross, Senate president Steve Sweeney, and Essex County executive Joe DiVincenzo. They would become my partners, all Democrats. I was in no position to go for short yardage. If I wanted touchdowns, I would have to throw some long balls. As long as we could do it in ways that were up front and transparent, I would happily work with Steve, Joe, George, or anyone else who wanted to get this vital work done.

When I came home from lunch with George, Mary Pat asked: "How did it go?"

"You know what?" I said. "I can do business with him. I think I'm going to be good at this."

NINE

YOUTUBE GOVERNOR

Mary Pat can sleep through just about anything—grinding garbage truck gears, bumpy airplane rides, kids kicking a soccer ball down the hall. But she was up with the birds on January 19, 2010. When I rolled over at five thirty, she was already sitting straight up in bed.

This was a day we'd both worked hard for, as had so many others. Finally, it was here. I was being inaugurated as the governor of the state where I was born and raised. We kept reminding ourselves to take a deep breath and remember what this felt like.

Our first stop was Newark's Cathedral Basilica of the Sacred Heart, which rivals any church I've ever seen in Europe. Faith had played such a role in my life, it was important to me to start the day with a Catholic Mass. Archbishop John Myers presided. Two thousand people came. Our oldest son, Andrew, did the reading. I sat in the left front pew with Mary Pat, Andrew, Sarah, Patrick, and Bridget. In the right front pew were Donald and Melania,

Cory Booker and Joe DiVincenzo—the Trumps, and two big Democrats!

The inauguration ceremony at the war memorial in Trenton was another family affair. Patrick and Bridget led the Pledge of Allegiance. Sister Merris Larkin, the principal of their elementary school, did the invocation. Father Joseph Hennen, who ran a drug-treatment program in Mendham, said the benediction. David Samson, who chaired my transition, was the emcee. And the oath of office was administered to me by Stuart Rabner, the chief justice of the New Jersey Supreme Court, who had worked for me in the US attorney's office. I raised my right hand, put my left on the Bible given to me by Nani and held by Mary Pat and our four children, repeated a few words, and became the fifty-fifth governor of New Jersey.

It was all so emotional. Behind us, along with my family, were the men and women who would fill my cabinet and senior staff—twenty-nine of them from the US attorney's office. To me, it felt like a continuation of the same adventure, only now we were running the entire state.

We had a massive party that night—not a stuffy inaugural ball—at the Prudential Center, the hockey arena in Newark. The B-Street Band, a Bruce Springsteen cover group, performed. "You said to me that if we hired this band, we'd go out and sing with them," Mary Pat reminded me as the night got late. "Are we doing this or not?" She grabbed a tambourine and the newly inaugurated lieutenant governor, Kim Guadagno. Together, we all went out onstage and joined the band for "Badlands," "Glory Days," and "Born to Run."

Yes, I knew all the words.

And the next morning, the work began.

———

I knew that the national recession had kicked New Jersey hard, and poor state leadership had made things worse. But until I got into the governor's office, I had no idea just how rotten the state's finances were. We'd been told by Jon Corzine there was a $500–$600 million deficit in the current fiscal year's $29 billion budget. The new state treasurer, Andrew Eristoff, came to me and said, "No, it's $2 billion." And we had five months left to fill the hole.

Immediately, the Democrats said, "Let's raise taxes, retroactive to January 1." During the campaign, I had promised I wouldn't raise taxes. There was no way I was doing that. Instead, I called in Eristoff, Kim Guadagno, my chief of staff, Rich Bagger, my chief counsel, Jeff Chiesa, and budget guru Lou Goetting, and we got busy, combing through the current budget and asking ourselves: Can we cut programs for the elderly? Highway upgrades? Youth sports leagues? Every slice was painful. People relied on those funds. After four hours of brutal slashing, I asked, "All right, are we close to $2 billion?"

The distressing answer I got: "No, we cut about $120 million," or 6 percent of what we needed. We met four hours a day, three days a week, until we reached $2 billion. And then the political uproar began. The largest single cut—about half a billion dollars— was the surplus money being held by the state's hundreds of local school districts. I told their boards, "However big your surplus is, that's how much I'm cutting your state aid. You'll need to tap your surplus to pay your bills."

They howled, of course. They considered those surpluses their piggy banks. I marched into a joint session of the legislature and told the members how badly they and the previous governors had screwed things up. As they rustled uncomfortably in their chairs, I announced I was declaring a state of emergency under New Jersey's Disaster Control Act, which gives the governor enormous powers to make cuts by executive order. It was a very aggressive speech and a very aggressive approach.

"This isn't a dictatorship," objected Steve Sweeney, who was now state senate president. He compared me to Napoleon—or was it Stalin? I forget. "We're not going to accept this," Steve vowed to the State House press corps.

The next morning, when I arrived in the State House parking lot, Steve was also getting out of his car. "Hey," I told him, "I read your statements in the paper about dictatorship and how you guys weren't going to put up with it. You've given me a lot to think about, Steve. So, I'm going upstairs right now. I'm going to retract the executive order and let you guys fix the budget."

Steve put his big arm around my back. "Governor, Governor," he said. "C'mon now. Don't overreact."

To me, that was a perfect window into the difference between what people say in public and what they sometimes mean. It also taught me that, if I was willing to take the heat, I could get big things done. The last thing Steve and his members wanted to do was whack $2 billion in state programs that people liked. If I had the balls to do it, why stand in my way? Despite the outraged rhetoric, the legislators never lifted a finger to stop me. My poll numbers took a hit, but the cuts sailed through.

That first budget fight was just a taste of things to come. The new budget would start July 1. That one, Eristoff informed me, had an $11 billion hole. I had plans for that, too. If New Jersey teachers would pay 1.5 percent of their health benefit and pension costs, we could close a big gap in educational funding. I wasn't talking about cutting anyone's benefits, just having employees pay a small share, just like most private-sector employees do. The New Jersey Education Association, the state teachers' union, went berserk, but many of the local school board members were reluctant to confront them. I wasn't. "I'm voting no on the school budget in my town," I said in early April at an economic-development event in Princeton. "I think everybody else should, too."

Almost every day for the next two and a half weeks, I did a public event urging no votes. Bagger, my chief of staff, had an interesting statistic. In a normal year, he said, eighty percent of New Jersey's school budgets are approved. "Unless we come in lower than eighty," he warned me, "this will be seen as a political defeat for you." Exactly the opposite happened on April 20. Sixty-three percent of the budgets got voted down. I wasn't the only New Jerseyean craving fiscal sanity.

Democrats in the legislature kept coming back with new taxing ideas, including a new levy on millionaires. I kept rejecting them. Not everyone was charmed. On May 17, a journalist expressed concern about my combative approach. "Governor," he asked, "do you think this sort of confrontational tone can increase your odds in getting this through the legislature?"

I had to laugh at that. "Ya know," I said, "you must be the thinnest-skinned guy in America. If you think that's a confrontational tone, you should really see me when I'm pissed."

That drew some smiles of recognition.

"That's not confrontational," I continued. "I love when people say they don't want to have an argument. That's what we were sent here for. They believe in certain things. They believe in bigger government, higher taxes, and more spending. . . . I believe in less government, lower taxes, and in empowering local officials who are elected by their citizens to fix their problems."

I lowered my voice in mock politeness. "That may lead to a disagreement or two," I said. "Now, I could say it really nicely. I could say it in a way that you all might be more comfortable with. Maybe we could go back to the last administration, where I could say it in a way you wouldn't even understand it. But the fact of the matter is, this is who I am. And this is who the people elected."

That exchange, which was posted on the paper's website, exploded on YouTube. I don't think a lot of people had ever heard a governor talk like that, certainly not to a journalist. And a lot of people liked it. Suddenly, my answer was being played by Fox News, Rush Limbaugh, Glenn Beck. Conservative Republicans across the country were paying attention to me. More important, they saw it on YouTube. I became the "YouTube governor" on that day.

After that, Maria Comella, my communications director, made sure her staffers videotaped my public appearances. She started posting the interesting stuff on YouTube. I had a message to deliver. Why not let people hear it?

———

Senate president Steve Sweeney and assembly Speaker Sheila Oliver made a promise to me: If I wouldn't raise taxes for the fiscal year beginning July 1, 2010, they would shut down the government.

"Go ahead," I said.

Jon Corzine had closed the government in 2006 and had famously moved a cot into the governor's office. "I'm no Jon Corzine," I warned Steve and Sheila. "I'm not moving any cots in here. If you guys close the government, I'll go outside and get into the big, black SUV with the state troopers, and they'll take me over to the governor's mansion in Princeton. I'll order a pizza. I'll open a beer. And I'll watch the Mets until you reopen the government. But I'm not raising taxes under any circumstances."

At three a.m. on July 1, we got the votes we needed to pass the budget and keep the lights on for another year—twenty-one in the senate (including four Democrats hand-delivered by Steve Sweeney) and forty-one in the assembly (including seven of Sheila Oliver's Democrats). We didn't raise taxes. We did things the right way, by matching our spending plan with our projected revenues. And I went home to my own bed in Mendham.

But I couldn't afford to doze for long. While I'd been fighting with the legislature over the budget, I'd also had my eye on property-tax reform. In the previous ten years, New Jersey property taxes had risen seven percent a year. That was unsustainable, and everyone knew it. So, two days after the successful budget vote, as the July 4 weekend approached, I called the legislature back into session to impose a 2 percent cap on property-tax increases. Why waste the momentum of the budget deal? "Our job isn't close to done," I informed the legislators.

They grumbled. But they came back and passed the cap.

And so it would be in the months and years ahead. Pension reform for police and firefighters. Gold health plans for teachers instead of platinum plus. The principles were simple. The vision was clear. New Jersey would always be New Jersey. Great schools. Robust government services. New Jersey will never be a low-cost or low-tax state. But there are limits, I said. Taxes and spending can rise only so much. Government pensions can be only so lavish. State employees should pay *some share* of their benefit costs, like almost everyone else in society does. Frankly, these were relatively modest changes, despite the howls of outrage. The free ride really did have to end.

I had cajoled the legislature. Now I had to sell my case to the public. My favorite way of doing that was at town hall meetings. I liked the face-to-face interaction. I didn't believe my every word needed to be filtered through the State House beat reporters. Unlike some politicians, I wasn't scared of mixing it up with my critics. And if a few loudmouths turned up to yell at me—well, I could handle the heat. In fact, I usually found the sharp exchanges invigorating.

I held town hall meetings all over the state. Many of them were quite convivial. But along the way I also got confronted by entitled teachers, angry police officers and firefighters, rattled environmentalists, misguided Yankee fans, and some hyperventilating people who had trouble marshalling any cogent arguments whatsoever. I almost always reminded everyone before we got started: "We are all from New Jersey, and you know what that means. You give it, you may very well get it back."

If people were civil, I answered civilly. If people were rude, they got rudeness in return. Most of politics is so phony. I think most people appreciated the fact that I wasn't phony at all. I explained what we were doing and explained the need to do it. I was happy to debate the alternatives. The people said what they were thinking, and so did I.

Soon Maria was posting four or five videos to YouTube each week. The feisty ones got by far the highest traffic. At a town hall meeting in Raritan, a teacher complained that I had disrespected her profession. As I began to respond, she tossed her head in disgust. I didn't let it pass. "I stood here and very respectfully listened to you," I told her. "If what you want to do is put on a show and giggle every time I talk, well, then I have no interest in answering your question." The audience erupted in applause, and the video got a million hits the first week.

Sometimes, people could be disarmingly nice. One woman stood up and said, "I think having a governor who is smart and that has the perseverance to do what's right is hot and sexy." When the laughter quieted, I responded, "Let me just say that I'm going to ask you, before you leave here, to write a note to my wife. Comments like that after twenty-five years will keep her on her toes. She won't take me for granted."

Maria made some logistical adjustments as we went along. The worst way to organize a town hall meeting, she figured out, was to put me on an elevated stage with people lined up at a microphone to ask questions. I was literally talking down to them. Also, if our time ran out before every last person had a chance to be heard, someone was sure to feel left out: "Hey, why won't you answer my question?"—even if I'd been fielding queries and comments for three hours by then. These events worked best in the round, where I could wander through the audience with a handheld microphone and speak to people face-to-face.

But as my reputation spread, some people were clearly itching for their YouTube moments with me, and not just in the town halls. They wanted to be able to say, "I got under Christie's skin." Mostly, I tried to ignore them. Sometimes I failed, like the night a man with a bicycle confronted the kids and me just after we'd stopped for ice cream on the crowded Seaside Heights boardwalk. "Hey, Christie!" he screamed in front of my children. "You fat fuck! Keep your fuckin' hands off the teachers' money!"

I lit into him.

"You're a real big shot," I yelled back to him, gesturing with one hand and holding my ice cream cone in the other. "You're a real big shot, shootin' your mouth off."

"Nah," he fumbled, before turning his bike and starting to hustle away. "Just take care of the teachers."

"Keep walkin' away," I called out at him. "Really good. Keep walkin'."

As he headed across the boardwalk, struggling to keep his bike wheels straight, I took a couple of steps in his direction until I heard one of the state troopers behind me.

"Governor, no!"

I felt totally fine about the encounter. The guy was a being a total jerk while my kids were there. I didn't mind that I had called him out. The encounter never turned violent or got out of hand. It was only the next day, while I was relaxing on the beach, that Maria called.

"I'm about to say a sentence that I hoped to never have to say to you, sir. There's some video of you on TMZ."

I guess I should have expected that.

"Well," Maria continued, "the good news is—and I'm shocked by this—the good news is you didn't swear at the guy. So, I don't have a swearing governor on video. But it's already becoming a bit of a sensation."

"Anything else?" I asked Maria.

"No," she said. "That's all for now." She wished me a peaceful rest of the vacation, and I said I would try not to fall into any more boardwalk debates.

———

With so much attention focused on my governing style and the meteoric rise of social media, it was inevitable, I suppose, that my reputation would spread beyond New Jersey. Invitations were coming in from across the country. Would I give a speech in California? Could I appear at a fund-raiser in Illinois? How 'bout one of the Sunday shows? Most of the invitations I ignored. But Terry Branstad, the legendary Iowa governor who'd been out of office for twelve years, had decided he was making a comeback, and I agreed to keynote his October 4, 2010, fund-raiser in West Des Moines. "Governor," he promised, "I will never forget it if you come and do this for me."

I knew political reporters would read significance into the visit. They'd say I was testing the waters for a possible 2012 presidential run. Iowans, after all, get to cast the first votes for presidential nominees. This was wildly premature. I had been governor of New Jersey for less than nine months by then. The presidential election was two years away. Branstad introduced me as the governor of a state that had been "mired in deep, deep doo-doo" before going on to tell the crowd, "since he was elected, he has done exactly what he said he would do." I was touched when he concluded his words by saying I was "the model of what a Republican leader and a Republican governor can do." Later he told me that he'd raised more than he'd ever raised in one night. After that, the invitations really poured in, and I started saying yes to more of them.

I campaigned in Roswell, New Mexico, for Susana Martinez, who was then running for governor. I did a get-to-know-Governor-Christie breakfast in Los Angeles. I was helping Republicans and promoting New Jersey, which was inevitably promoting me, too. I got a call from Facebook founder Mark Zuckerberg, who had been wooed by Cory Booker to help transform Newark schools. I met with Mark and his girlfriend, Priscilla Chan, in the lounge at Newark Airport. He called a few weeks later and said, "Priscilla and I have decided to put up a challenge grant. Every dollar you raise up to $100 million, we will match." Mark, Cory, and I—a young tech entrepreneur, a young Democratic mayor, a young Republican governor—announced our joint campaign September 24 on the *Oprah* show, in Oprah's example of how people can come together to solve tough problems. John Legend came out and sang a song from *Waiting for Superman*. When Mark was asked why he chose Newark for his Startup:Education initiative, he pointed to Cory and me and answered: "Because I believe in these guys."

The pace was becoming overwhelming. But the momentum outside the state was contributing to the momentum inside the state, and things were getting done. I campaigned in Ohio for John Kasich. I was profiled on *60 Minutes*. It was one thing after another after another. I wanted to use every bit of this national attention to help what we were doing in New Jersey. With so much wind at my back, it was getting harder for the legislature to say no.

By the end of 2010, my first year in office, we capped increases in police and fire salaries at 2 percent after an enormous fight with their unions. In June, we got pension and benefit reform, increasing the amounts that the public-sector workers contributed and eliminating the cost-of-living adjustment. The numbers were adding up. We'd saved $120 billion over thirty years. Steve Sweeney became a key ally in this. So did George Norcross. So did Joe DiVincenzo. And by my side as always were my Republican allies in the legislature, men like Tom Kean Jr., Jon Bramnick, Kevin O'Toole, and my campaign chairman, Joe Kyrillos. A Republican governor, a Democratic Senate president, and a Democratic businessman from South Jersey who had no official position but a lot of influence, working with Republican legislators to secure the long-term future of the state. No one ever thought that was possible. It was something to behold.

When it came time to deliver my State of the State address in January 2011, I wasn't just some quirky Republican who'd gotten elected because Corzine was such an awful candidate. I was a genuine national force.

By the middle of that year, the 2012 presidential talk was really heating up. I did my best to squelch it. I really did.

"I'm not running," I said.

"I'm not ready."

"What part of 'no' don't you understand?"

The questions kept coming from local and national media alike, and my answer was always the same.

Mitt Romney, the former governor of Massachusetts, had already announced. He was a good guy, and he seemed to have the inside track. I was already thinking I would probably endorse him. Texas governor Rick Perry was inching toward entering the race. Newt Gingrich had quit Fox News to run. There were others, too. Ron Paul, Tim Pawlenty, Michele Bachmann, Rick Santorum, Herman Cain. But it's fair to say there was a feeling among many Republicans that they hadn't yet found the right candidate to challenge Barack Obama's reelection.

In September 2011, Kenneth Langone, the billionaire cofounder of Home Depot and a major Republican donor, asked me to meet with a group of business leaders at the Racquet and Tennis Club on Park Avenue. "Just a small group of people," he said, "who want to talk to you about how they might be supportive in you running for president."

I reminded Ken I wasn't running for president. But when he pressed, I agreed to show up.

I walked into the meeting along with Mary Pat, our son Andrew, Mike DuHaime, Maria Comella, and Bill Palatucci. The room was already packed with about fifty billionaires. Despite Langone's billing, nothing was small about this crew, most especially not their aggregate net worth. A couple of people who couldn't make it in person were patched in by speakerphone. The CEO from Morgan Stanley. Industrialist and megadonor David Koch. One by one, about a dozen people stood and explained why they were convinced I should run for president. The party needed me. There was no one else. My brand of commonsense, across-the-aisle Republicanism was the only route forward. Then Langone stood and said, "We have one other person who wants to speak to you, Governor." He looked into the front row, where Henry Kissinger was pulling himself up on a cane.

"Governor," he said, "I have known eight presidents in my lifetime. And for the great presidents, there have only been two consistent characteristics: courage and character. You have both. Your country needs you."

Then, Kissinger sat down.

This was all so overwhelming for a kid from Newark who'd been governor for all of twenty months. These masters of the universe were begging me to run for president. "Governor," Ken said, "the floor is yours."

I think Ken was secretly hoping that I would stand up right then and say, "I'm announcing my candidacy right here."

Instead, I stood and said, "I'm still inclined not to run, for all the reasons I've been saying for months now. But obviously, all of you being here this morning was a huge, huge surprise to me, and I'm incredibly gratified. Because of the seriousness of all the men and women in this room, I think Mary Pat and I have an obligation to go back and rethink our position." And that's where I left it. On the way out the door, Mike DuHaime, my political adviser, leaned over and said to me, "I've never seen that before in my life, and I doubt I'll ever see that again. That was unbelievable."

For the first time, I really did start to question whether I should change my mind. As I was reflecting on that, another event was already waiting on my calendar, a September 27 speech at the Ronald Reagan Presidential Library in Simi Valley, California. I'd agreed to speak back in the spring when I got a handwritten note from Nancy Reagan. By the time Mary Pat and I flew out of New Jersey and got to the Reagan Library, I'd done fifty-six town hall meetings in twenty months. Did this count as number fifty-seven?

A huge crowd turned out. The people couldn't have been nicer to us. Before I spoke, Mrs. Reagan walked me over to the podium and said, "You know, this podium you're standing at, it was Ronnie's last podium at the White House."

"That's a lot of pressure," I told her. "I hope I'm not boring tonight."

I spoke about American exceptionalism, a topic Sarah Palin had brought into the 2008 presidential election. Then the questions began. Someone asked about immigration. Then a man stood and said: "Governor Christie, you're known as a straight shooter, one not given to playing games." I could feel the setup. I knew what was coming. "Can you tell us what's going on here? Are you reconsidering or are you standing firm?"

People cheered at that.

"Listen," I said, as people laughed nervously. "I have to tell you the truth. You folks are an incredible disappointment as an audience. The fact that it took you until the second question to ask that shows you people are off your game. That is *not* American exceptionalism."

The audience roared with laughter.

The questions continued—about school funding and public employees and the high cost of benefits and the future of Medicare and Medicaid. The last question came from a woman in the balcony.

"Governor Christie," she said, "all kidding aside. I've been listening to you tonight. You're a very powerful and eloquent speaker, and you know how to tell the American people what they need to hear. And I say this from the bottom of my heart, for my daughter who's right here and my grandchildren who are at home. I know New Jersey needs you, but I really implore you. I really do. This isn't funny. I mean this with all my heart. We can't wait another four years, to 2016. I really implore you, as a citizen of this country, to please, sir, to reconsider. Don't even say anything tonight. Of course, you wouldn't. Go home and really think about it."

People began applauding. Wildly.

"Please," she said. "Do it—do it for my daughter. Do it for our grandchildren. Do it for our sons. Please, sir. We need you. Your country needs you to run for president."

Applause went on and on.

What do you say? I had no idea what to say.

Mary Pat looked at me from the front row, petrified. There was another standing ovation. I was completely overwhelmed. I thanked the people, and we flew back to New Jersey.

———

It was hard not to be moved by outpourings like this—the billionaires in New York, the Reagan crowd in California. But I had to settle this fast. I didn't ever want to come across like Mario Cuomo—God love him, Hamlet on the Hudson—who could never seem to decide if he was or he wasn't running for president.

"Why wouldn't I run?" I kept asking myself, followed by: "Why would I?" I couldn't do both. I talked to my political people. I talked to my family. If I ran, I thought I would have a shot at winning the nomination. Romney would be serious opposition, but he didn't scare me. We'd be a good contrast on the campaign trail.

I never thought I would beat Obama. Most incumbent presidents get reelected. Despite his shortcomings as a president, he had sharp political skills. That wasn't what made the decision for me, but it was a factor. In the end, the biggest reason was that I just didn't feel ready. Not yet.

Since Obama and Trump, that may sound like a quaint proposition, the idea that being governor for twenty months wasn't enough experience. But to me, that really mattered. Someone said something to me—I don't remember who—that was bouncing around in my head: "The only thing worse than running for president and losing is running for president and winning when you're not ready."

The final decision came down to Mary Pat and me.

"What do you want to do?" she asked me.

"In my career," I said, "when I can't see it, I can't do it. I can't see myself winning. I do not think I am ready. And if I can't see myself winning and being president, then I have no business asking people for their money or for their vote. So, I'm not going to do it."

And that was it.

TEN

BLOWN AWAY

I endorsed Mitt Romney for president on October 11, 2011, seven days after I announced my final decision not to run, three days after Mitt and his wife, Ann, stopped by our house in Mendham and asked for my support. I didn't seek anything in return. I was happy to help Mitt's campaign any way I could.

If you are going to endorse someone, come in early, I say.

After Mitt clinched the Republican nomination with a victory in Texas the following May, his campaign vetted me as a possible vice-presidential nominee. I turned over all the information his people asked for and answered every question they had. Though Mitt ultimately chose Wisconsin congressman Paul Ryan, I was honored to be considered and happy to say yes when Mitt asked if I would deliver the keynote address at the Republican National Convention in Tampa on August 28.

I thought my speech was good, though it got mixed reviews. Some of Mitt's aides grumbled that there was too much Chris in there and not enough Mitt. The "Me-Note Address," they called it.

Clever. But the complaint was silly. These speeches are supposed to be a mix of the speaker's vision for the future and a rallying cry for the nominee. That's what Barack Obama did in 2004 for John Kerry. I'd submitted the text a week before the convention. The campaign approved it without changes. Where were the staff suggestions then?

When I spoke to Mitt immediately after I stepped away from the podium, he sounded thrilled. The only hiccup that night came when one of the show's producers made a last-minute decision to kill my video introduction, which Maria had been diligently assembling for weeks. I told the guy that if he yanked the video, he should be prepared for me to walk out onstage and drop a couple of F-bombs on prime-time TV. After several counterthreats and much yelling into wireless headsets, the producers decided I meant it and the video was aired as planned.

I never understood how Mitt tolerated so many backstabbers on his staff. Through all of September and most of October, I balanced my duties as governor with a heavy campaign schedule for Mitt. Other than Paul Ryan, I was his busiest surrogate. With less than two weeks to go, things were about to get even busier, as I'd agreed to join Mitt on his mad dash to the finish line.

Then a storm blew in.

———

When forecasters from the National Weather Service arrived at the State Police Emergency Operations Center in West Trenton to brief me on an Atlantic hurricane called Sandy, they brought color-coded "splash maps" that showed hundreds of square miles of New Jersey underwater.

"No way," I said. "Take these maps off the wall and come back with the real maps, okay? You're just trying to scare the crap out of me so I'll make preparations that are super aggressive, and then I'll look stupid when none of this stuff comes true."

This was Saturday afternoon, October 27. Hurricane Sandy was still 1,540 miles away, pounding Kingston, Jamaica. The forecasters sheepishly packed up their maps and left—only to return half an hour later with the exact same maps. "You may not want to hear it," one of the forecasters said to me. "But this is what's going to happen. It could be catastrophic."

That was enough to make me take a closer look. The likely track of the storm, the low-lying topography of New Jersey, the necklace of fragile barrier islands along the shore—I could see the risk. They predicted the storm would slam into New Jersey sometime Monday.

As soon as the forecasters left, I declared a formal state of emergency, invoking special powers under the New Jersey Disaster Control Act. Then I pulled on the blue fleece I'd gotten from Steve Adubato the day after I was elected—CHRIS CHRISTIE, GOVERNOR—and headed to the Jersey Shore, where I held the first two of countless Sandy press briefings.

There are people who, to this day, swear that I did not take off that fleece for the six months that followed, that the blue material eventually melted into my skin and had to be removed with battery acid and a metal wallpaper knife. Mary Pat and my children have voiced such claims, as have many of my staffers, members of the media, and Seth Meyers on Saturday Night Live's Weekend Update. All I will concede is that, while my team and I confronted the many challenges of Hurricane Sandy, I wore that blue fleece a lot. It was comfortable. It was practical. It was visible. And I liked it. So there.

"Let me be real clear," I said that Saturday afternoon before the storm in Monmouth County. "We should not underestimate the impact of this storm, and we should not assume the predictions will be wrong. I'm not trying to be an alarmist here. I want your families to be safe."

Early Sunday morning, I called in Kim Guadagno and state Homeland Security director Ed Dickson to West Trenton, along with representatives of every other state agency that would somehow be involved in preparing or recovering for the storm. If this thing was going to be as devastating as the forecasters were warning, we would need everyone. Then I called Mitt Romney and told him I had to cancel my final nine days on his campaign plane. "Chris, I completely understand," Mitt said with his usual grace. As soon as I got off the phone, his staffers started pestering my staffers: *Can't he at least do this event? Can't he do that event?*

No! Our state's about to get slammed by a killer hurricane!

We set up emergency shelters in the most vulnerable areas. We shared constant advisories with the media and the public. We positioned people and equipment as strategically as we could. We opened lines of communication with first responders, local officials, the Federal Emergency Management Agency, and the state's utility companies. I asked Mary Pat to bring our kids to the governor's mansion in Princeton. "Might as well," I said. "The schools will all be closed."

As the storm bounced up the Atlantic coast, I ordered evacuations up and down the Jersey Shore. I made the Garden State Parkway one way—all lanes heading north. Most people took the warnings seriously. A few refused. The mayor of Atlantic City, a moron named Lorenzo Langford, told his people they could ignore the mandatory evacuation. We had to send in Jersey Transit buses with state police escorts to pull seniors out of the high-rises.

Sandy roared ashore on Monday. By Monday night, the largest Atlantic hurricane on record, with tropical-storm-force winds, spanned nearly nine hundred miles. Sandy was so massive and damaging, the National Weather Service designated it a superstorm, actually two storms in one that would end up killing at least 233 people in eight countries and causing nearly $70 billion in damage, the second-costliest hurricane on record in the United States. New Jersey got kicked right in the teeth. I monitored the storm from Drumthwacket. My cell phone rang Tuesday at two a.m., just as I was finally drifting off to sleep. It was President Obama, saying he had signed an emergency declaration to smooth the state's way to federal help.

"How bad is it?" the president asked.

"Bad," I told him. "But I've only got anecdotal reports so far." He promised he'd call again.

At daylight, I climbed into a state police SUV. So many roads were blocked, the trip from the mansion to the emergency ops center, which should have taken ten minutes, lasted more than an hour—across parking lots, peoples' lawns, and every imaginable kind of debris. It was still too windy for the state police helicopters, but reports were coming in. A fifty-foot chunk of the Atlantic City boardwalk was missing. Half the city of Hoboken was underwater, cut off from hospitals and firehouses. On the New Jersey Turnpike north of Newark Airport, heavy metal cargo containers had been washed onto the elevated roadway. At nine thirty, I summoned my cabinet commissioners and department heads back into the conference room and got an earful from each of them.

"Two-thirds of the state's residents are without power," said Bob Hanna, president of my Board of Public Utilities.

"Every hospital in the state is on emergency backup power," said Health Commissioner Mary O'Dowd. "We're getting to the point where many of them are going to run out of fuel."

"Every water treatment and wastewater treatment plant in the state is inoperable," said Bob Martin from the Department of Environmental Protection. "You're going to have to decide pretty soon whether we permit these treatment facilities to dump raw sewage into the waterways."

"We're running out of shelter space," said Human Services Commissioner Jennifer Velez.

"If we're opening more shelters, we need more supplies," said Ed Dickson from Homeland Security. "And there's so much debris on the roads, how will the trucks get through?"

"Every major highway in the state is obstructed," added Jim Simpson, my transportation commissioner. Jim was especially concerned about Route 35, a barrier island roadway in northern Ocean County. "It's been breached completely. Barnegat Bay is running through it."

And so it went, agency by agency, commissioner by commissioner. Attorney General Jeff Chiesa reported scattered looting in evacuation zones. Brigadier General Michael Cunniff of the New Jersey National Guard said his people were staffing shelters and backing up local law enforcement. It got very quiet, and everyone in the room was looking at me. They wanted to hear my plan. I came up with something on the spot.

"To get back to some semblance of normal, we need four things," I started. "We need to restore power. We need to make fuel available. We need to clear the roadways. And we need to reopen schools." We'd be digging out for a good, long while. I knew that already. But those four steps would put us on the path to normal—the new normal.

By midday Tuesday, the state police had their first helicopter in the air, beaming back live video from northern Ocean County, a beach community where I had vacationed my entire life. "The governor wants to know, 'Where are the houses? Where are the stores?'" a state police colonel radioed to the crew in the air.

A crackly voice came back: "We'll show him in a minute."

They flew over Barnegat Bay, where a number of two-story houses were bobbing in the water. On the beach, there was hardly any evidence of life except for some empty foundations and some swimming pools. A few minutes later, I caught my first glimpse of what would become one of the iconic pictures of Superstorm Sandy: the Seaside Heights roller coaster, which I'd ridden since I was eight or nine years old, the pier beneath it now fully collapsed. As the coaster fell into the ocean, some of the metal had twisted— but the structure stood mostly erect.

As the helicopter tour continued, I saw flames and smoke rising from one of the barrier islands. "Why are the houses on fire?" I asked. I was told they'd been knocked off their foundations. Busted gas lines were igniting.

"What can we do?" I asked.

"Nothing," I was told. "We can't get fire equipment onto the barrier island. Those houses are just going to burn."

To me, that was the definition of helplessness.

———

The president called back late on Tuesday, this time from Air Force One. We were now one week from the presidential election, barely twenty-four hours after Sandy made landfall.

"Chris, it's Barack. Give me an update on what's going on."

I told him what I knew.

"I want to come see for myself tomorrow," he said. "Are you okay with that?"

No one had to tell me how politically loaded these two sentences were. A Democratic president, running for reelection in less than a week, flying into my state to express concern for the victims of a highly publicized natural disaster. And who would be greeting him? Mitt Romney's highest-profile surrogate. Me. Of course, this was a political land mine. From the way he asked the question, Obama understood that. New York mayor Michael Bloomberg had already laid out the unwelcome mat, telling White House staffers that a visit from the president would be too disruptive. I took precisely the opposite approach.

"Mr. President," I said. "You tell me what airport you're landing at, and I will be there to greet you."

"Are you sure?" he asked.

"Yes, sir, I'm sure," I said. "And on behalf of the people of New Jersey, we appreciate your willingness to come and see this for yourself."

Tuesday night, I held a press conference in West Trenton where I had real trouble keeping my emotions in check. I spoke about what I had seen already, knowing that most of the people of New Jersey could hear my words using only a battery-operated radio. "I just never thought I would see what I saw today, ever," I said, my voice carrying all the weight of everything I had witnessed.

———

A state police helicopter dropped me off at the Atlantic City airport on Wednesday at noon. When Air Force One landed at 12:55 p.m., I was waiting to greet the president when he reached the bottom of the stairs. The plan was for the two of us to take a ride on Marine One, the presidential helicopter, with me as the devastation tour guide.

As the president stepped onto the tarmac, I extended my hand to him. He shook it, and asked me, "How are you doin'?"

"I've had better days," I said.

He nodded. "I don't always believe what you tell me," he said with a smile, "but I believe that one."

I chuckled, too. He reached out with his left hand and patted me twice on the shoulder. Then we both turned around and, together, boarded Marine One.

That was it. That was the "Obama hug," as some agitated Republicans would soon be describing the way I greeted the arriving president.

I'm half Sicilian. I know hugs. That was no hug. It was receiving a friendly pat on the shoulder during a handshake. But describing the greeting as a hug played into a precooked political narrative that, six days before a presidential election, was impossible to dodge. I was the Republican governor of New Jersey. He was the Democratic president of the United States. Mix. Stand back. Watch the politics explode.

The Republican uproar didn't come only from that airport greeting. It also came from the fact that when I was asked by reporters about the political impact of Obama's visit I answered, "I don't give a damn about the election. I've got people dying here. What I care about is doing my job and helping my people. The president deserves great credit because he's done everything I've asked him to do."

I'm sorry, but that was the truth.

What was I supposed to do? Wear a Romney button? Shake GOP pom-poms? I had no basis to insult the man. He'd done everything I asked him to do. And we were going to be asking him for a whole lot more. What was the sense of jeopardizing that assistance, especially since the president didn't deserve the attack?

As a Mitt Romney surrogate, I'd spent most of the year making harsh comments about Barack Obama. I'd said, "He's like a man wandering around a dark room feeling the wall for the light switch of leadership, and for four years he hasn't found it." But now, the whole state of New Jersey was counting on me. I did what was right, and I'm glad that I did.

One final note: We invited Mitt Romney to come to New Jersey on Friday, two days later—to tour the devastation, to visit first responders, maybe even to make a contribution to the victims' fund. His staff called back and turned down the invite. That's all you need to know to understand how poorly Mitt was served by some of the petty, vindictive members of his team.

———

Getting back to normal called on everything we had. My four initial goals—power, fuel, roads, and schools—were still a work in progress for much of the state. We'd never had a disaster like this in New Jersey, natural or otherwise.

Amid so much struggle, my heart was lifted to witness the enormous acts of kindness, neighbors helping neighbors, people from around the country and around the world happily pitching in. Sandy brought out far more good in people than I ever would have expected—more good than many of us knew we had inside ourselves. I am so proud of my state for the grit we showed and the recovery we achieved.

I also had flashes of anger and frustration, which were utterly justified. The day after Obama visited, I was feeling deeply dissatisfied with the state's utility companies, which I thought were being ridiculously slow in getting the power back on. How long was this supposed to take? I was even angrier—*livid* is the word—that houses were still catching fire because of open natural gas lines, and all we could do was watch helplessly. "If we can't put the fires out," I said, "there's got to be a way to turn the gas off."

I was told that officials at New Jersey Resources were reluctant to turn the gas off because condensation would seep into the pipes and turning the gas back on would be costly. I summoned Larry Downes, the company's CEO.

"I understand you won't turn the gas off," I said to Larry.

"Oh," he told me, "it will be a huge expense, and we think most of the damage has already happened."

"You understand I've invoked my powers under the Disaster Control Act," I said.

"Yes, Governor, I'm aware of that."

"Larry," I continued, leaning right into his face and speaking as plainly as I knew how, "you've got three minutes to decide. Are you turning the gas off or am I turning the gas off? But the gas is going off."

I stepped into another meeting and quickly returned.

"So?" I asked when I got back into Larry's room.

"I'm turning the gas off," he said.

"Thank you, Larry," I answered, then got up and walked out of the room.

———

There was just so much that had to be done and done urgently. We had to coordinate with FEMA, which was a bureaucratic nightmare. We had to coordinate with New York governor Andrew Cuomo, whose state also had been badly battered by the storm. Working with Andrew actually worked out great. We spoke constantly. There was no time of the night that he didn't feel comfortable waking me with a phone call.

An event like Sandy pushes people to work in ways they never imagined. It became clear to me that my chief of staff, Kevin O'Dowd, and counsel Charlie McKenna were overwhelmed. I asked Kevin about Michele Brown and Regina Egea, who had recently taken over as director of the authorities unit in the governor's office. "Where are they?"

"They don't have direct responsibility here," Kevin said.

"We need as many smart people around this table as we can get," I told Kevin. "Get them in here." I put Regina in charge of getting the schools reopened. I put Michele in charge of gasoline. None of them had ever worked in those areas before. "You're smart," I told them. "You'll figure it out." And they did.

I called John Hess of Hess Oil to help with the gasoline. He said the refinery had shut down. He offered some gasoline he had ready. President Obama patched us in with Defense Secretary Leon Panetta, who got us a shipload of gas from the Defense Department. Michele assembled a list of key gas stations across the state to distribute it, and the gas started flowing again. John Hess called back and said to me, "I'm sure you have a relief fund. I want to write a check for three million dollars. Who do I give it to?"

Actually, we didn't have a relief fund—not yet. I told John I would get right back to him.

I phoned Mary Pat and said, "Okay, you want to know what you can do? You're chairing the Hurricane Sandy New Jersey Relief Fund. I'm going to send a lawyer over to execute the paperwork. You're going to put together a board. Run the names by me first. John Hess is going to start you off with three million bucks. Call John right now and tell him how to make out the check. And you run the fund, okay?"

Mary Pat was eager to help, but she expressed the same concern that Regina and Michele had: "I've never done anything like that before."

"Don't worry," I told her. "Everybody's doing stuff they haven't done before. This is your thing. You're in."

Mary Pat took a leave of absence from her position at Angelo, Gordon & Co., the investment-advisory firm. She set up the Sandy fund from scratch. Jon and Dorothea Bon Jovi wrote a million-dollar check. The United Arab Emirates underwrote a big project. By the time Mary Pat was done, she would collect $43 million in donations, 97 percent of which would go directly to Sandy victims. She did an amazing job for the victims and their families.

———

Given how massive Sandy was, a full recovery was going to take massive federal aid. That was obvious from the beginning. I negotiated hard with Barack Obama for the most generous package I could get. At Andrew Cuomo's request, I negotiated for New York State as well. Obama's first offer was $50 billion for the two of us. After much pushing, he inched up to $53 billion, which he insisted was absolutely as high as the federal government could go. When I kept pushing, he finally called and asked exasperatedly: "Chris, if the number had a six in front of it, would that work?"

"You know it would, Mr. President."

We settled at $60 billion. Now, all we had to do was get Congress to sign off. The Democratic-controlled Senate was agreeable, approving the $60 billion on December 28 by a vote of 62 to 32. Washington, after all, had approved large aid packages after Katrina, Andrew, Isaac, and all other major hurricanes regardless of which party was in charge. Surely, the Republican-controlled House of Representatives would step up this time, too—right?

Speaker John Boehner promised me explicitly that Congress would act on the Sandy-recovery package before the members left the capital on New Year's Eve. Then, just before midnight, he sent everyone home for the holiday without even taking a vote, sixty-six days and counting after the storm.

This was disgusting. I was angrier than I had ever been in my life. I called the Speaker's cell phone immediately. He didn't answer. I kept calling, each time leaving progressively rougher messages about what a wimp he had been.

On January 2, I called a press conference at the State House in Trenton. "There's only one group to blame for the continued suffering of these innocent victims," I told reporters. "The House majority and their Speaker, John Boehner."

How much more explicit could I be? "This is not a Republican or Democratic issue," I said. "National disasters happen in red states and blue states and states with Democratic governors and Republican governors. We respond to innocent victims of national disasters not as Republicans or Democrats but as Americans— or at least we did until last night. Last night, politics was placed before our oath to serve our citizens."

It was disgusting.

"New Jerseyans and New Yorkers are tired of being treated like second-class citizens," I said. "New York deserves better than the selfishness we saw on display last night. New Jersey deserves better than the duplicity we saw on display last night. America deserves better than just another example of a government that has forgotten who they are there to serve and why. Sixty-six days and counting. Shame on you. Shame on Congress."

The New Jersey storm toll was still being added up: 346,000 homes severely damaged or destroyed. Seven million people who'd lost power, some for up to fourteen days. Nearly 600 state roads impassable. More than 125 shelters housed 7,000 evacuees. All regional mass transit and Hudson River crossings had been closed. All New Jersey schools closed, some for weeks. Tens of thousands of businesses damaged or destroyed.

"Thirty-one days for Andrew victims," I reminded Boehner and his enablers. "Seventeen days for victims of Gustav and Ike. Ten days for victims of Katrina. For the victims of Sandy in New Jersey, New York, and Connecticut, it's been sixty-six days, and the wait continues."

Right after I finished talking, John Boehner called. "I thought we were friends," he said.

"Yeah," I answered. "So did I. But you promised me something."

"Well, circumstances changed, and I made a political judgment," he said.

To me, that wasn't remotely good enough. "If you made that judgment, you should have picked up the phone and called me and explained why. You could have avoided today. You just stuck it to me and made me look stupid and hurt my people. I can't have that."

The vote finally came on January 15, tortured with political machinations until the very end. I think even John Boehner came to believe I had a point.

ELEVEN

HEAVY STUFF

I was late for dinner, and Donald, always punctual, was not amused.

This was in 2005, back when I was still US Attorney. Donald and Mary Pat had been waiting at the table for half an hour, Mary Pat nursing a glass of chardonnay, Donald with his usual Diet Coke. Melania was elsewhere that night. As soon as I breezed into the restaurant at the Trump World Tower across from the United Nations, he told the waiter, "Quick with the menus. We have to order now."

He proceeded to berate me—half-joking, half-seriously—for being so late. "Only you would leave me waiting for dinner," he said, brushing off my pleas of Manhattan gridlock. "Only you."

He then spent most of the meal directing the conversation toward Mary Pat. "Tell me what's going on in *your* life, because you were here for me on time." Finally, as the entrée plates were being bussed away, he turned to me.

"I want to tell you something because I'm your friend, and I love you, and someday I want you to be governor," he said. "You have to lose weight."

What did *that* have to with my showing up time?

"Forget about whether you're going to die of a heart attack or a stroke," he said. "Forget that. You gotta look better to be able to win."

A friend of his, he said, had just gotten a new kind of surgery. "It's the greatest thing. It's perfect for you."

"Okay. What's that?"

"It's called lap-band surgery."

"What the hell is lap-band surgery?" I asked.

"Quick surgery. Takes forty-five minutes to an hour. They go in. They put a band around the top of your stomach to create a smaller stomach on top of your other stomach so you can only eat that much. My friend has lost ninety pounds. He looks fabulous, and he's in better health."

I was forty-three years old. I had already tried every diet that was ever invented. Atkins. South Beach. Weight Watchers. Nutrisystem. Sugar Busters. I'd been to the famous weight-loss clinic at Duke University. I dropped pounds with almost all of them—and soon enough packed those pounds back on, plus a few extra to grow on. But when Donald first broached the subject, I wasn't yet to the point in my own head where I felt I needed surgery.

If he could hear my reluctance, it certainly didn't slow him down. "I'll get you the name of the surgeon," he said. "He's at NYU. Wonderful guy. Did a great job. I'll let you talk to my friend."

I appreciated the suggestion. Or maybe I didn't. I don't know. But I never thought seriously about following it. "You can send me the information," I told him that night. "But I doubt I'm going to do it."

Donald doesn't give up easily. He held his finger in the air, and he said to me, "Don't be stubborn. I have your best interest in mind. I understand this stuff." At this point, Donald was a legitimate TV star with the success of *The Apprentice*. He had a feel for public appearance.

"Okay," I said. But I was only humoring him.

He sent me the information. I glanced at it and put it immediately aside.

——

Late in August 2012, barely a week before I turned fifty, I got a call from Rex Ryan, the head coach of the New York Jets, whose team played its home games at the Meadowlands in New Jersey. I had read in the papers that Rex had gone in for lap-band surgery and had lost a bunch of weight. That wasn't the purpose of his call. I don't think it was anyway. He was calling to bullshit about the upcoming football season and to arrange a dinner for us and our wives. We picked a night to meet, and I asked him, "By the way, how have you found the surgery?"

He got quiet on the other end of the phone.

"I'm so glad you asked," he said, "because ever since I had it, all I've been thinking about is you and that this would be perfect for you."

Rex described the procedure to me more or less the same way Donald had. It changed my life," Rex said. "The surgeon is a guy named George Fielding. He's at NYU." That must have been the doctor, I figured, who did Donald's friend. "I'm not pushing you," Rex said. "But Chris, I really think it would be good for you."

I have to say I was more open to the idea this time around. In the seven years since Donald had first floated the idea, my weight had continued to fluctuate. But it was up more than it was down.

Being this heavy was becoming an undeniable factor for me. My feet hurt when I stood for an hour or two. I still had plenty of energy. Actually, I felt okay, though a quiet voice kept telling me, "All this weight can't be good for you."

Or was that Mary Pat?

She threw a surprise party at the governor's mansion for my fiftieth birthday. I was genuinely surprised—not an emotion that comes easily to me. Family and old friends filled the music room and the library. Everyone seemed to have a blast. After the guests all left, Mary Pat and I stayed the night at the mansion. But I couldn't stop thinking about the phone call with Rex Ryan. I was lying on my back in bed, pitch dark in the room. I just kept going over what he'd said.

"You awake?" I whispered to Mary Pat.

"Yeah," she answered.

"I'm thinking about doing this lap-band surgery. What do you think?"

Mary Pat sat straight up in bed. She rolled over and put an arm on either side of me. She pressed her face right up to my face and said:

"Please. Do it. Please."

I don't think I really understood until that moment how much she was concerned about my health. The weight. The stress of being governor. The fact that I'd just turned fifty. So that next week I called Dr. Fielding and asked if I could make an appointment to see him.

"I don't want you coming over to the office," he told me. "Too many eyes here." He offered to meet with me and Mary Pat at my office in Newark. I knew Mary Pat would have questions. I definitely wanted her there.

Dr. Fielding described the procedure, officially known as laparoscopic gastric banding, and why he thought I was an ideal candidate: How heavy I was. The fact that I was generally healthy. My age. He showed us some charts and graphs indicating that 75 percent of lap-band patients shed substantial weight and, more important, managed to keep it off. No diet I've ever heard of comes close to that. Everything Dr. Fielding said sounded totally sensible. But the more he talked, the more skittish I got. As he was wrapping up his short presentation, I took a deep breath and said to him, "Yeah, you know what, Doc? I don't think so. I probably won't do it."

The doctor didn't argue or push. He just said, "No problem," and slid his charts and graphs back into a folder as he stood to leave.

"Just one thing before I go," he said. "What if I came in here today and, instead of obesity, you were dealing with cancer? And I told you that I had a forty-five-minute surgery that gave you a 75 percent chance of survival? What would you do?"

I knew the answer as well as he did. "I'd do it," I said.

"Let me tell you something," he continued. "This is going to kill you just as sure as cancer will. So you should give it some thought." He shook my hand, shook Mary Pat's hand, and said goodbye.

As soon as he left, I turned to Mary Pat and said, "Okay, let's do it."

———

We scheduled the surgery for November 10, the Saturday after the presidential election. I planned to be campaigning for Mitt Romney until then. Things would be relatively calm, I figured, right after the vote. Wrong! On October 29, when Hurricane Sandy slammed our shore, all bets were off. Along with all the other damage caused by the superstorm, the NYU Langone Medical Center, which backs up to the East River, had floodwaters up to the fourth floor. Dr. Fielding called and said we were going to have to postpone the surgery. "We're literally underwater," he said. But if the hospital flooding hadn't delayed us, I would have had to wait anyway. For weeks and weeks after that, Sandy would be my life.

I rescheduled the surgery for February 16, the Saturday of President's Day weekend. I was finally ready to do this—ready in my body and ready in my head. Then I got a bright idea for a last hurrah. For a very long time, David Letterman had been trying to get me to come on the *Late Show*.

I have always loved Dave. I think he's a brilliant performer and a supersmart guy, even though he did keep hammering me on the show, about my weight in particular. He'd been merciless with the fat jokes. He got more mileage out of my ballooning torso than anyone else on television, and some of the jokes—*some* of them— were actually funny. I also knew that Dave had become a bit of a health fanatic, especially since his own quintuple heart-bypass surgery. But post-Sandy, he really wanted me to come on. He even had our mutual friend Brian Williams call me. Brian said, "Dave has given me his word that he's going to be okay with you."

I was open to it. My reelection campaign was revving up. People were tossing my name around as a 2016 presidential candidate. I'd gotten a lot of national attention because of Sandy. As anyone could see, I was bigger than I had ever been. I wanted a fresh way to diffuse the weight issue. Going on Letterman was the best idea I'd heard.

We settled on February 5, less than two weeks before the surgery.

After I got to the green room at the Ed Sullivan Theater I asked my body man, Dan Robles, if there was a Dunkin' Donuts nearby. He looked at me funny, then looked at his phone and located a shop nearby.

"Get over there right now," I told him. "Buy two cinnamon jelly donuts. Don't let anybody see you. Two cinnamon jelly donuts. Bring them back right away."

"You serious?" Dan asked.

"Just do it," I snapped.

Dan bought the donuts. He raced back to the theater. I put one donut in one pocket of my jacket, the other donut in the other pocket. Then I was called out onstage to visit with Dave.

I settled onto the comfy beige chair, and Dave asked his opening question: "How do you feel about me?" He pointed out, "I've made jokes about you, not just one or two."

That's when I reached into my pocket and retrieved a donut. I took a good-size bite.

"I didn't know this was going to take this long," I deadpanned to Dave.

He handed me a tissue and urged me to wipe my mouth. By then, he was cracking up so hard, he almost looked like he was in pain.

He kept me on for three full segments, an eternity on late-night TV. We talked Sandy, New Jersey politics, the Super Bowl in New Orleans, the 2016 campaign for president, and my weight, age, and health. He expressed deep concern for people and businesses suffering from Hurricane Sandy, putting the website for Mary Pat's Hurricane Sandy New Jersey Relief Fund on the screen. He even endorsed my reelection.

Dave really delivered, even better than he promised he would. When I told him he was my favorite late-night host, he reminded the audience, "The governor is not under oath."

"I'm basically the healthiest fat guy you've ever seen in your life," I told him at one point.

He shot back, "There's your campaign poster right there."

It was a great night. My appearance on Dave's show accomplished everything I hoped it would, and even he had no idea what I was planning to do eleven days later. Hardly anybody did.

I told the state troopers I had to go to New York City for a medical procedure, and I wanted to go alone. The head of my executive-protection unit didn't like the sound of that. "You are too high profile," he insisted. "We cannot allow you to go anywhere without us." We compromised. Mary Pat would drive me. My brilliant cardiologist, Dr. Rachana Kulkarni, would come, too. A trooper would follow. "He'll be there in case anything happens." I would check into the hospital under an assumed name that Dr. Kulkarni dreamed up. We cleared all this in advance with the insurance company. I didn't want anything leaking out.

———

We left New Jersey on Saturday at 4:45 a.m. The city was about as dead as I had ever seen it. Dr. Fielding was waiting outside NYU Medical Center in a peacoat with a wool cap pulled over his head. I got out in sweatpants and a baseball cap. No one recognized me. He and I looked like a couple of homeless men walking into the hospital.

We rode up in the elevator, and then he led me into the surgery suite. There the nurses prepped me. The anesthesiologist pumped me up with knockout drugs. Dr. Fielding did what he was famous for and did it flawlessly. The band was secure. My stomach was smaller. All the plumbing was flowing like it was supposed to flow. I was out of surgery in less than forty-five minutes. I was out of the hospital by midafternoon.

———

I had to learn a whole new way of eating. That's a crucial part of it. The band and the smaller stomach make you feel less hungry. The weight comes off because you consume fewer calories. There were foods I used to eat—foods I loved to eat—that I couldn't eat anymore. No steak. Only shredded chicken. No bread. Much smaller portions of pasta. No large portions of anything. Sorry, Dave, no cinnamon jelly donuts. Not even one.

But you know what? All of it was doable.

I kept this to myself for the next three months. My family knew. That was it. Not Kevin O'Dowd. Not Maria Comella. Not Bill Palatucci. I wanted to be sure the surgery was doing what it was supposed to, and I wanted to be confident I could really do my part. I wanted to drop some pounds and have them stay off. I had lost about forty pounds at this point.

Finally, I gave an exclusive interview to the *New York Post*. After the story—which, naturally, ran with the headline "Weight Is Over"—appeared on May 13, just about everyone else in the media followed. The other papers. Cable and broadcast TV. The blogs and websites. Talk radio. I knew my girth was a topic of national interest. This confirmed it.

"For me, this is about turning fifty and looking at my children and wanting to be there for them," the *Post* quoted me as saying, and that really was the most important part. But that didn't stifle the media debate and speculation. Was this the proof the pundits had all been waiting for? That I was really serious about running for president in 2016? Most of them seemed to think so.

When the story appeared in the *Post*, I heard from lots of people, almost all of them wishing me well. But two of the well-wishers stood out from the rest. One was Donald Trump, the first person who'd ever mentioned lap-band surgery to me and the first person to reach me by phone when the *Post* piece came out. Of course, Donald took credit, even if I hadn't executed his suggestion as promptly as he would have liked. "So, you finally took my idea?" he said to me. "I'm so excited for you. This is so smart. Don't forget who told you to do it."

The other special well-wisher was David Letterman.

"Is it true what I'm reading in the paper?" Dave asked. "That was right around the time you came on, wasn't it?"

I told him it was. "In fact," I added, "my appearance on your show was my last hurrah. Those were my last donuts ever. No more donuts for me."

Dave let out one of his famous Letterman chuckles. Then he said, "Way to go!"

I've shed one hundred pounds since that last donut with Letterman and, except for some weight I gained during my presidential campaign, kept all those pounds off. I'd be lying if I didn't say I am happy about every one of them.

TWELVE

RED LANDSLIDE

Getting reelected as governor of New Jersey was a whole lot easier than getting elected the first time.

Instead of taking on a well-financed sitting governor like Jon Corzine, I faced a Democratic state senator from Middlesex County named Barbara Buono, who had served two years as Senate majority leader. I was politically formidable enough by then—high poll numbers, campaign contributions in the bank, an undeniable list of genuine achievements—that no first-string Democrats would jump into the race. Barbara took the expected shots, saying I'd been mean to the teachers, stingy to state pension holders, and too nice to well-heeled taxpayers. She called my assertive style a threat to good manners and public civility. None of it stuck.

Barbara's fellow party members were abandoning her in droves. We picked up dozens of endorsements from Democratic elected officials, based on our political strength and the strong constituent work we had done over the past four years. Our biggest day was on June 11 when Essex County Executive Joe DiVincenzo engineered an endorsement event that brought together Democratic mayors and African American clergy and Sheriff Armando Fontoura to endorse a Republican governor for reelection. This had been preceded the day before by the endorsement of Union City mayor and state senator Brian Stack. In retrospect, I believe this was the day the Buono campaign officially lost its heartbeat. Within twenty-four hours, the two most influential figures in the biggest Democratic counties—Essex and Hudson—had endorsed her Republican opponent.

In a mid-October burst of TV commercials, she slammed me for refusing to promise that, if reelected, I would serve all four years and skip the 2016 presidential race. "I'm Barbara Buono, the only one running for governor," she said in one of the ads. "He wants to be president. I want to be your governor."

I wasn't about to rule anything out. I'd skipped 2012, believing I wasn't ready to be president. But who knew how I might feel as 2016 drew near? As I campaigned for reelection, I ran on my record and asked New Jersey voters if they wanted more of the same. My campaign slogan couldn't have been more concise: "The Governor." I had filled and defined the job.

One question lingered, not in an especially damaging way—not at first. But it was there. It involved the George Washington Bridge. For those who don't know, "the GW" is the world's busiest bridge—fourteen lanes of traffic in total, carrying more than one hundred million vehicles a year over the Hudson River, between New Jersey and New York. On the Jersey side, three of those lanes had long been set aside for local traffic entering from Fort Lee, a suburb that hugs the bridge and the river it crosses.

As the story unfolded, the facts often got misreported by everyone from Rachel Maddow to Donald Trump. Here are the real facts: On the morning of Monday, September 9, not quite two months before Election Day, two of those three local-access lanes were shifted to traffic entering the bridge from busy Interstate 95. This shift caused massive backups on the streets of Fort Lee.

The bridge wasn't *shut down*, as some reports had it. No lanes were *closed*, not even for a second. Two lanes were redirected from local traffic to interstate traffic. Believe me, that was bad enough. If you've never driven in rush hour traffic in the New Jersey–New York area, take my word for it.

There'd been no advance warning of the lane realignment. No one at the Port Authority of New York and New Jersey, the bistate agency that operates the bridge, had alerted local officials or the public. Not surprisingly, complaints poured in. Officials at the Port Authority responded that they were conducting a traffic study to see if Fort Lee really needed all three lanes. The morning gridlock didn't let up until Friday, when the two diverted lanes were returned to local traffic. The Port Authority's executive director, Patrick Foye, who'd been appointed by New York governor Andrew Cuomo, put out a statement, apologizing for what he called a "hasty and ill-informed decision" that could have endangered lives.

Now you have a clearer picture than almost everyone in politics or the media. Those are the facts. Where things get murky is in the motives.

Just to be clear: I didn't know about any of this. I didn't order it or encourage it. I didn't hint in any way that I would tolerate anybody using traffic on the George Washington Bridge for any improper purpose.

Some people began suggesting that the traffic jam might have been punishment for the mayor of Fort Lee, Mark Sokolich, for not endorsing my reelection. That didn't make any sense to me. What would be the point? How would causing a traffic jam help our campaign, which was already cruising toward a large victory on November 5? If you wanted to punish a mayor, why would you do that but not speak to him after day one and say, "Here's how you can make the traffic stop. Endorse the governor tomorrow"? That never happened. As an act of political retribution, none of this made sense. It was stupid. It was ill conceived. It was everything our administration had not been about for four years. We were the reach-out people. It was not an idea of mine or one I would ever approve.

In a meeting at the start of October after a story ran in the *Wall Street Journal*, I asked my two top aides, chief of staff Kevin O'Dowd and chief counsel Charlie McKenna, what they knew about the bridge issue. They said they didn't know much. I asked them to talk to the folks involved and find out what was going on with this story.

Charlie went right out and started asking questions. He came back and told me that it was a traffic study and that Bill Baroni, the deputy executive director of the Port Authority and my top guy at the agency, acknowledged they could have handled it better with New York. Okay, I thought. Just another immature turf battle at the Port Authority. On to the next of the dozens of issues I was dealing with every day as governor and a candidate for reelection. I didn't lose a minute of sleep over what some of my political opponents were starting to call Bridgegate.

—

On November 5, I defeated Barbara Buono, 60 to 38 percent. It was a smashing victory, especially when you consider that Barack Obama had won New Jersey twelve months earlier by 18 points. That was a 40-point turnaround by our party in a state with 750,000 more Democrats than Republicans. It also made me the first Republican gubernatorial candidate to win more than 50 percent of the vote since Governor Tom Kean's landslide in 1985. I got 25 percent of the African American vote and 51 percent of the Latino vote, numbers nearly unheard of at this time in our nation's history for a Republican in a solidly blue state. The year before, Mitt Romney had gotten 8 percent of the African American vote. He was in the low 20s with Latinos. We celebrated at the Asbury Park Convention Hall, which was crawling with local and national media, then with an after-party at the legendary Stone Pony with a raucous performance by Southside Johnny and the Asbury Jukes. From a 4-point win in 2009 to an 18-point rout in 2013, we had a lot to celebrate long into the morning hours.

Time magazine put me on the cover November 18 just as I was heading to Scottsdale, Arizona, to take over as chairman of the Republican Governors Association. "The Elephant in the Room," the cover line said. I counted at least three levels of meaning there—my party affiliations, my weight (which, thankfully, kept declining), and the outsize role I might well play in the 2016 presidential race. Whatever. I loved the Alfred Hitchcock–style photo and the message of the piece: I was that rare Republican who could reach beyond the party's usual base and attract diverse voters. That was precisely my intention since I'd gotten into politics.

I was a rising force in my party. But my Democratic opponents in Trenton and in Washington weren't about to let up just because the governor's race was over. I understood that. In fact, the higher my profile, the more they would target me. Not surprisingly, committees in the state senate and the assembly both launched bridge-lane investigations. On November 25, Bill Baroni testified under oath, consistent with what he had repeatedly told us. At a public hearing of the General Assembly Transportation Committee, he told lawmakers that the lanes were switched around, as had already been reported, as part of a study to determine whether Fort Lee needed three dedicated access lanes.

As everyone was still in the glow of our fresh reelection victory, I assembled my senior staff. "You're all enjoying the spotlight," I said. "The big victory. *Time* magazine. Don't forget the spotlight can turn into a searchlight—just like *that*."

I snapped my fingers.

I wasn't talking about the George Washington Bridge. I just sensed the team was having what I described that day as a case of "senioritis." "Okay, we won," I said. "It's time to get back to work. And by the way, the first order of business is cleaning up this mess with the George Washington Bridge. So, tell me what you all know."

I asked point-blank whether anyone had any information about the traffic study or the bridge. Anything we didn't already know. Any emails. Any phone calls. Any background information. Anything. "The confessionals are open," I said. "Go see Kevin or Charlie. Tell them what you know."

No one offered up anything.

At a press conference on December 2 to discuss plans for the second term, one of the reporters asked if I'd had anything to do with the four-day bridge-traffic realignment. The question struck me as so ridiculous that I answered sarcastically, "I moved the cones, actually, unbeknownst to everybody." That got a few laughs and a few groans. I went on to say, "The fact is, I didn't know Fort Lee got three dedicated lanes until all this stuff happened, and I think we should review that entire policy."

I went into 2014 thinking about my inauguration, my agenda for New Jersey for the next twelve months, and the thirty-six governors' races across America.

The last thing on my mind was Fort Lee and the George Washington Bridge.

THIRTEEN

JAMMED UP

My day was already jam-packed.

I'd just finished working out with my trainer. I was about to jump into the shower and get out of the house. I had interviews scheduled with the *Wall Street Journal*, the Associated Press, and the *Star-Ledger*, and then a Sandy-recovery announcement in Ocean County. But at 8:50 a.m. on January 8, 2014, my phone rang. It was Maria Comella, my communications director.

"Have you been online this morning?" Maria asked.

I told her I hadn't.

"We have a big problem," she said.

"Okay," I said. "So, what's the problem?"

The fact that I had to ask that question makes clear just how blindsided I was by what Maria was about to tell me. It wasn't like I'd been sitting around worrying about what was coming next on the George Washington Bridge. At that point, I still believed that an ill-advised traffic study had been implemented by my people at the Port Authority and that those responsible had apologized—for the rotten timing and for their failure to keep people informed. Democrats in Trenton had gotten some mileage out of the story. But no one had contradicted Bill Baroni's sworn testimony to the assembly committee, and the issue had pretty much faded. In fact, I'd met that Monday with Steve Sweeney and Vinnie Prieto, the senate president and the incoming assembly speaker, who told me that they were not going to renew the subpoena authority of the joint committee that had been looking into the matter.

"We want to start clean with your new term," Steve said to me. "There doesn't seem to be anything else here," Vinnie agreed.

Well, Maria was about to throw fresh light on that.

"The Bergen *Record* has posted emails between Bridget Kelly and David Wildstein," Maria told me. Wildstein was Baroni's handpicked deputy at the Port Authority and also his best friend, overseeing capital projects. Kelly was the deputy chief of staff in the governor's office, responsible for constituent service and inter-governmental relations. In the key email, Kelly wrote to Wildstein on August 13 with those soon-to-be-famous words: "Time for some traffic problems in Fort Lee."

And Wildstein wrote back: "Got it."

I understood immediately how damaging those ten words were. Whatever had happened at the Port Authority—and it was looking less innocent by the moment—was now inside the governor's office.

I had already announced that Baroni was not coming back as the Port Authority's number-two official for my second term. That meant his buddy Wildstein was leaving, too. I knew they weren't happy about that, but I'd made that decision in September—nothing to do with the George Washington Bridge and everything to do with the fact that Baroni had been in place for four years, holding a plum position that paid $290,000 a year plus a housing allowance. I was replacing him with my policy chief, former assistant US attorney Deb Gramiccioni.

"Okay, anything else?" I asked Maria in that first, rattling call.

"Yes," she said. "Stepien is copied on one of the emails. Not the time-for-traffic-problems one. He's copied on another email between Kelly and Wildstein."

The presence of Bill Stepien, no matter how tangential, made things even worse. Though Wildstein and Kelly were part of the administration, I wasn't personally close to either of them. Wildstein was a former mayor of Livingston who'd briefly been the statistician on my high school baseball team. But I was never friends with him, then or now. As governor, I hadn't had a single phone call or a one-on-one meeting with him. In fact, he admitted later that he had not had a one-on-one conversation with me since 1995. His contact information wasn't in my phone. He was Baroni's guy. Kelly had been an aide to a Bergen County assemblyman and a volunteer on my 2009 campaign. When Stepien came into the governor's office, he'd hired her as part of his regional constituent operation. As Stepien left the governor's office in April 2013 to reprise his role as my campaign manager, he recommended Kelly replace him as deputy chief of staff. I asked if he thought she was ready. "I'll keep an eye on her," he said. "She'll be fine."

"If you think so," I said.

Bridget Kelly seemed like a nice person. She'd basically be a functionary and run every decision by Stepien. And this was all temporary, I told myself. Once the new term began, we'd read-dress the lineup. The main contact I'd had with her in her new job was that she handled invitations to the governor's box at the Prudential Center and at MetLife Stadium, coordinating with politicians, union leaders, and businesspeople we were courting for help in the reelection campaign.

Bill Stepien was a different case entirely. I was close to Step, as most people called him. Not only had he managed both my campaigns for governor, he had created my government-relations and constituent-service operations. He was a key member of my team.

"Stepien's calling right now," Maria said that morning on the phone. "Do you want me to take the call?"

"Take the call," I told her. "Find out what he knows."

I immediately called Kevin O'Dowd, my chief of staff. He hadn't heard anything, either. "The State House is going to be a loony bin," he said after I gave him a quick rundown. "Let's meet at Drumthwacket. I'll tell the core people to get there as quickly as they can."

As I showered and dressed, my mind was racing. If "time for some traffic problems in Fort Lee" meant what it felt like, how could anybody be so monumentally dumb? To torture the Democratic mayor of Fort Lee for not endorsing my reelection, as some people were suggesting? That still didn't make any sense to me. And if Bridget Kelly knew in advance, who the hell else did she tell? I had to get the facts—*all* the facts and *now.*

On the ride to the governor's mansion in Princeton, Bill Palatucci called. "I don't know anything, either," Palatucci said. "But I'll guarantee you one thing. This is Wildstein."

I also heard from Steve Sweeney. "I just have one question," he said to me. "We've been friends now for four years, and you'd better tell me the truth. Did you have anything to do with this?"

"No," I said without hesitation.

"That's good enough for me."

By the time I got to the mansion, my informal crisis team was already gathering around the dining table on the second floor. Kevin O'Dowd. Bill Palatucci. Maria Comella. Michele Brown. My brother, Todd. Chris Porrino, who'd just come over that week from the attorney general's office to be my chief counsel. Paul Matey, Chris's deputy. Mike DuHaime, my longtime political adviser. The only one missing was Mary Pat, who was at work in New York. I wanted to open the meeting with just the right mix of toughness and determination. But when I started talking, my eyes welled up. That was a side of me most of these people had never seen. We'd been down this road before, and I wanted to be sure we got it right this time.

When I'd asked about the bridge after my reelection, not a single senior staffer spoke up. Bridget Kelly was at that meeting. She didn't say a word. Not to me. Not to Kevin or Charlie. Not to anyone. Clearly, her silence had been a lie. That email she'd sent to Wildstein in August was ironclad proof of that.

Here we were a month later with most of the same people in the room, minus Bridget Kelly. "I can't take another moment like this," I said to the team. "So, if there's anybody around this table who has anything they need to tell me about this mess, you need to tell me right now. You owe it to me to tell me right now. I cannot get sandbagged again."

No one said a word.

"That's not good enough," I said. "We went through this in December. Everybody sat there and just stared at me. I took that silence as assent that there was nothing here. But Bridget Kelly had been sitting at that table. As we now know, her silence was not the truth. I want to hear from every one of you verbally. Look me in the eye. Tell me, 'I know nothing about this'—unless you have something to say."

One by one, O'Dowd, Porrino, Palatucci, and the others—they all said they had no personal knowledge about the purported traffic study on the bridge.

Already, Democrats in the legislature were revving up. Senator Loretta Weinberg and Assemblyman John Wisniewski, who cochaired the George Washington Bridge committee, had announced a press conference for later that day. Who knew what they—or the reporters—had managed to dig up. A few of my regular critics were already saying maybe I should resign. I couldn't take too many more surprises.

"We have to decide what personnel decisions to make," I said. "I think it's obvious that Bridget Kelly needs to be fired. She lied to me. We asked her if she had any emails with anybody at the Port Authority regarding the traffic study. She said she did not. Now we're reading them. Does anybody disagree with the decision to fire Bridget immediately?"

Nobody disagreed. Chris Porrino was given the job of calling Bridget and telling her she was being terminated for being dishonest with the governor.

"Okay," I continued, "who else needs to be fired?"

David Wildstein—who'd answered Kelly's email with, "Got it"—was out the door already. So that was taken care of. Bill Baroni was gone as well. Everybody around the table, except for Mike DuHaime, said Bill Stepien needed to be fired. No one could say exactly what Stepien knew about all this. We knew he'd been copied on one of the emails, and he'd also been the one who ushered Bridget Kelly into her current job. But fired from what? Step had been the campaign manager and now the campaign was over. He had no government job. A week or so earlier, I had announced his appointment as chairman of the Republican State Committee and a major consultant to the Republican Governors

Association, where I was now chairman. I couldn't see him continuing in either of those roles.

We called Phil Cox, the association's executive director. After asking if I was involved in any way—I wasn't, I assured him—he agreed that Stepien's consulting gig could not go forward. Phil also said he would talk to the other governors on the executive board and make sure they weren't looking to bounce me as chairman. "I think you're safe, but let me see," he said.

I still didn't really know what Stepien knew. "But how can I trust his judgment anymore?" I asked the crew. "He brought Bridget Kelly in. He promoted her and promised to keep an eye on her." At the very least, his gaze had drifted. He had to be held accountable.

Step had to go. I told his friend Mike DuHaime, who'd brought Stepien in and vouched for him, to fire him. DuHaime was reluctant but did what I ordered. Stepien was like a brother to him. He was heartsick as he left to deliver the news.

"Okay," I said, "is there anybody else who anybody thinks needs to be fired?"

Someone mentioned Mike Drewniak, my longtime press secretary. "He's had a lot of contact with Wildstein," Maria said. "We'd better find out what he knows." Porrino and Matey summoned the press secretary to the governor's mansion and grilled him for three hours. They came out saying they didn't think Drewniak had done anything wrong or had anything to do with the lane realignments or the emails. He stayed on.

"I think we have to fire David Samson," Maria said.

David was the chairman of the Port Authority and perhaps the most prominent lawyer in New Jersey. He had been a real mentor to me. When I was US Attorney, he was state attorney general, and that's how we got to be friends. He had been the chairman of my transition when I first became governor. "I don't know whether David knew anything or not," Maria said. "But it happened on his watch. Cleaning out the entire Port Authority in one fell swoop is the way to go." I summoned Samson to Drumthwacket that afternoon.

I brought him into the kitchen and said to him, "You know how much I love you. You know how close we are. But I've got to know. Did you have anything to do with this? Did you have any knowledge of it?"

He looked me in the eye. "Absolutely not," he said.

"David," I said to him, "if it turns out that's not true, our professional relationship will be over. And our personal relationship will be over."

"Governor," he said, "I swear to God I don't know anything about this."

I went back in to the dining room and said to the others: "David assures me he didn't know anything about it. I believe him. Unless someone has something else specific to say, we're not going to fire David."

That night, the story was all over the national news. I told Chris and Maria that I thought I needed to hold a press conference the next day and address all this directly.

"Absolutely not," Chris said. "You have no idea what all the facts are. You could wind up stepping all over yourself. You can't do it."

They left for the night. It was just me and Jeff Chiesa. I'd hired Jeff right out of his clerkship into our old law firm. He'd been with me at the US attorney's office. When I became governor, he was my first chief counsel. He went on to serve as attorney general of New Jersey and interim US senator, filling the seat of the late Frank Lautenberg that Cory Booker had just won. Of all the people around me, Jeff was the one I trusted the most.

"What the hell do you think really happened here?" I asked Jeff.

"I really don't know, Guv," he said. "But I can tell you this. I think there's a bunch of people who have been lying to us. And I think you've got to gird yourself up for a long fight."

I had an emotional ride home. Rick Scott, the governor of Florida and a member of the Republican Governors Association executive committee, called to see how I was doing. "As long as you tell me you didn't do anything wrong, I'm with you," he said. I got a similar call from Susanna Martinez, the governor of New Mexico. "Don't give in to all the pressure," she said.

After those calls, I had about forty-five minutes to be alone with my thoughts. I had never felt so betrayed. My political career, which I had salvaged from the ashes of my defeats in 1995 and 1997, was now threatened with extinction. After all the successes of the US Attorney years, the upset win over Corzine, the huge bipartisan successes of the first term and our landslide reelection victory, was my career really going to be ended by this type of ridiculous stunt? How did this happen? How could I have trusted Baroni and Kelly in light of what was now so clearly their lies to me and the public? I had blown it, I thought. After being so careful and so successful with the power of this office, how could I have missed this? After giving New Jersey Republicans, Democrats, and independents reasons to like and trust me, how did I let this happen? All my life I'd had a plan—how to move forward, how to succeed, or how to work my way out of tough situations. As my forty-five minutes ended and I pulled up my driveway in Mendham, this time I felt lost and very much alone.

I had spoken to Mary Pat throughout the day, but I was surprised to see Andrew when I got home. My older son had left his classes at Princeton University to come home and check on me.

"Are you okay?" he asked when I walked in.

"I'm okay," I said. "What are you doing here?"

"I just wanted to make sure you were okay."

"Go back to school and worry about school. Don't worry about me. I'll be fine."

"Yeah," he said. "But I've got to ask you something."

"Sure. What?"

"Did you do it?"

Even now the question sends a chill up my spine and brings tears to my eyes, my son asking me that question.

I looked at Andrew, and I said, "Of course not."

"I just needed to hear it from you," he said. He gave me a hug, and he left. I went up to bed and didn't sleep all night. I just lay there thinking, *I've got to do a press conference tomorrow.* If my own son needed to look me in the eye and hear me say that, then I needed to look the people of New Jersey in the eye and say it to them, too.

At daybreak, I called Maria and Chris and said, "We're doing a press conference."

———

Even before I stood in front of the media, Paul Fishman, the man who had replaced me as the United States attorney for the District of New Jersey, took his first of many cheap shots.

It was one of the worst-kept secrets in New Jersey legal circles that Fishman actively resented me. Nearly thirty assistant US attorneys had left his office to join me in Trenton for less money and a longer commute. He complained bitterly about that to me and to anyone else who would listen. He had wanted this job since he was passed over for the same position in 1994 by President Clinton in favor of future federal judge Faith Hochberg, even though Fishman had the support of Senator Frank Lautenberg.

Hochberg exiled him to Washington, DC, where he stayed for a time until he left for a New York law firm. Now Fishman finally had his dream job, but many of his best people were leaving him for one simple reason: they preferred to work for me for less money. It was a bitter pill he had to swallow nearly thirty times, administered by the man he had replaced, who now sat in the governor's chair.

Fishman was also an avid Hillary Clinton supporter. His ambition was rumored to be a return to DC in a Clinton Justice Department, perhaps as attorney general or deputy. What better way to increase his stock than by taking out her purported number-one 2016 rival? His combination of bitterness, imperiousness, ambition, and physical stature led to a nickname from the folks back at the office he once ran in Newark—Napoleon on Broad Street. Hearing that Paul Fishman was shoehorning himself into this was not good news for me or anyone around me.

Fishman announced that morning that he was launching a federal criminal investigation into what had occurred on the George Washington Bridge. That was outrageous for two reasons. First, it wasn't at all clear what federal laws might have been broken, even if the traffic study did have a political motive. And second, what was Fishman doing announcing anything? As I well knew, US attorneys aren't supposed to grandstand with media when they are opening investigations. They just go ahead and investigate, quietly and confidentially. These are the Justice Department rules. If and when the prosecutors turn up serious criminality that can be proved in federal court beyond a reasonable doubt, they bring charges to a grand jury, indict, and prosecute. That's how things are supposed to work. The loud and public way that Fishman jumped into this case raised suspicions from the start that he wasn't planning to follow the rules on this one. He had another agenda.

A massive crew of media showed up at the State House for my press conference. National, local, print, TV, online, you name it. They were there. I repeated what I'd said before: I didn't know anything about the traffic study being more than a traffic study. I had no involvement in any of it. Indeed, I still wasn't sure what the motive was, though Bridget Kelly's email was certainly troubling. I now had good reason to doubt the truthfulness of certain people who worked for me. "Prior to yesterday," I said, "I believed that if I looked someone in the eye, I would get an honest answer. Maybe that was naive."

One of the reporters asked if I'd spoken to Bridget about why she sent that email. I said I had not and didn't plan to. "She was not given the opportunity to explain to me why she lied because it was so obvious that she had," I said. "And I'm quite frankly not interested in the explanation at the moment." I said it did appear she had it out for the Democratic mayor of Fort Lee and was trying to retaliate against him. I emphasized how pointless that was. I couldn't pick Mark Sokolich out of a lineup, I said. I hardly cared whether or not he endorsed me. I had support from many Democratic politicians—mayors, county officials, state legislators, you name it. Others supported my opponent or, like Sokolich, didn't endorse anyone. To me, that was normal politics, not cause for an immature, ineffective, elaborate retribution scheme. I wasn't the hyperpartisan. I was the guy who'd spent the past four years reaching out to the other party to get things done.

The questions kept coming—for forty-five minutes and then an hour—and I kept answering them. "Don't call last question," I told Maria. I stood up there for an hour and forty-eight minutes without a note in front of me and answered every question that every reporter had. The press conference was carried live, every minute of it, on CNN, MSNBC, Fox News, and C-SPAN. By then, the Democratic National Committee had rented an entire floor at the Woodbridge Hilton for a Bridgegate war room, feeding baseless rumors and allegations to a very willing media. The story didn't develop organically. A propaganda machine was working the other side. The Democrats saw an opportunity to stick the knife in me.

When the press conference was finally over, I went back into my office by myself. I took my jacket off. My shirt was wet with sweat. A moment later, my phone rang. It was a Dallas number. Against my better judgment, I said hello.

"Is this Governor Christie?" a woman asked.

"It is."

"Could you please hold for President Bush?"

George W. Bush came on the line. "You did a great job today," he said.

"Thank you, Mr. President," I said. "I can't tell you how much it means to me to hear from you."

"You stood up there," he said. "You took all the incoming. You did really well."

"Mr. President," I said. "I was on TV for almost two hours. Don't tell me you watched the whole thing."

"Buddy," he said. "I'm retired. I watched the whole damn thing. You're my guy. You know that. Don't you worry about it. I've just got one question for you."

"What's that?"

"Did you do it?"

I couldn't believe he was asking me that. "Mr. President," I said, "I just spent all that time on national television saying I didn't."

"Yeah, I know," he said. "Now it's just me and you, Chris. Remember, I'm the guy who made you US Attorney."

"Mr. President," I said. "I did not do it."

"Well, then, you're going to be fine," he said. "You know, I've been through shit storms like this one. As long as you did the right thing, then it will all come out okay. Have faith and know there's a lot of people out here like me who believe in you."

As soon as I got off the phone with President Bush, I called Debra Wong Yang, who had been US attorney in Los Angeles while I was US Attorney in New Jersey. She was now at Gibson Dunn & Crutcher, where she cochaired the national law firm's crisis-management practice. "I need to hire you guys to come in," I said.

"To represent you?" she asked.

"No," I told her. "I need you to come in and do the internal investigation. I need to know what the hell happened here. I can't have my people do it. It wouldn't have any credibility. I need an outside firm to do it. No restrictions. Your people can have access to whatever they want."

FOURTEEN

SLOW WALK

And so, the Bridgegate investigations began.

Investigations, plural.

The two main ones got going almost simultaneously in January 2014, one conducted by the attorneys at Gibson Dunn & Crutcher, the other by my replacement as US attorney, Paul Fishman. At the same time, the state senate and assembly were also holding hearings and seeking documents. And then there was the media. There was no forgetting the media. The local and national print reporters, the local and national TV news, the cable news channels, plus assorted magazines, bloggers, and political activists masquerading as journalists. All spurred on by the opposition-research attack machine that was the Democratic National Committee.

Never in the history of automotive traffic had a four-month-old backup gotten this much coverage. Seventeen times more than the Obama IRS scandal in the first six months, according to the Media Research Center. A truly unprecedented feeding frenzy.

The competing media outlets didn't need fresh developments or new facts. Wild speculation and crazy theories were more than enough. An hour-long Rachel Maddow special on Kevin O'Dowd? Really? Segment after segment highlighting the ravings of the lunatic Hoboken mayor Dawn Zimmer as if they were proven facts? Apparently so. During the height of it, there was no allegation too flimsy, no claim so tangential, that it couldn't somehow be tied to Bridgegate. I ran into Jon Stewart on the street in New York one day in early 2014 as the front-page stories were flying and the cable channels were wall-to-wall me.

"Are you doing okay?" he asked me.

"I've had better days," I told him.

"The coverage of this is crazy," he said. "I didn't know that you were already the President of the United States of New Jersey."

As far as the media was concerned, I guess I was. But I still needed to figure out what had actually happened here. The Gibson Dunn attorneys were total pros. Led by Randy Mastro, a former federal prosecutor who is widely considered one of the top litigators in America, they interviewed seventy witnesses and reviewed 250,000 documents, including all of my personal texts and emails, which I handed over immediately, along with my cell phone, which they submitted for thorough forensic review.

Mastro and his people didn't grandstand. They didn't leak. They gathered every scrap of evidence they could find. Kelly, Wildstein, Baroni, Stepien, and Samson all refused to be interviewed, citing the Fifth Amendment privilege. We had no power to force them. But with two months of focused digging, the Mastro team managed to piece together a remarkably clear picture of exactly what had occurred.

Their final report, released March 27, fully exonerated me, concluding that I had no advance knowledge of the lane realignment and no other involvement in it. There was no credible evidence to the contrary. Blame was placed squarely on three people—Bridget Kelly, David Wildstein, and Bill Baroni—and nobody else. According to the Mastro report, Kelly and Wildstein dreamed up and executed the phony traffic study to exact political revenge against the mayor of Fort Lee, and Baroni knew about some of it in advance.

I was relieved, of course, though not surprised. Except for hiring Kelly and Baroni and allowing Baroni to hire Wildstein, I knew I hadn't done anything wrong. "Sometimes, people do inexplicably stupid things," I said when I was asked for my reaction to the Mastro report. To me, that pretty much summed it up.

The media and my political opponents derided the Mastro report as a whitewash. It had cleared me, after all. That wasn't the answer they were looking for. It certainly wasn't the answer Paul Fishman was looking for—and looking for and looking for. He had subpoena power. He had a federal grand jury. He had the cooperation of Wildstein, who agreed to turn on his former colleagues in exchange for the most lenient treatment from the federal prosecutors. With all those tools, he still wasn't finding anything criminal to pin on me. It wasn't just that he was a Democrat and I was a Republican or even that I represented a high-profile scalp for him to collect. His motives seemed far more personal. I was the successful predecessor who had not receded into private practice but had become more prominent as governor.

As Fishman's investigation crawled on, Chris Porrino came to me and strongly recommended that I hire my own lawyer. I knew a lot of good lawyers from my time as US Attorney. I wanted someone who was assertive but also someone Fishman would respect. I chose Christopher Wray of the King & Spalding law firm in Atlanta. A former assistant US attorney and chief of the Justice Department's criminal division, Wray would later be appointed

FBI director by Donald Trump at my urging. Paul Fishman knew he couldn't push Chris Wray around, as everyone in Washington has come to learn. Along with my decision to do the press conference in January, hiring Chris was the smartest Bridgegate decision I made. He kept me calm. He kept me focused. He gave me the space to devote myself to my many other duties in and out of New Jersey—and also plan for what might be coming next.

———

As 2014 chairman of the Republican Governors Association, I spent a lot of time traveling across America, working to elect Republican governors. I threw myself into the job. My team and I raised $130 million to fund tough races—including $3.5 million each from Sheldon Adelson and David Koch. I campaigned from Florida (Rick Scott) to Maine (Paul LePage) to California (Neel Kashkari, a tough one against Jerry Brown). The map was certainly challenging. We had twenty-two governorships to defend, compared with the Democrats' fourteen. But midway through the second Obama term, the wind was at our back. The results were better than almost anyone expected.

The Republicans Charlie Baker, Larry Hogan, and Asa Hutchinson replaced retiring Democratic governors in Massachusetts, Maryland, and Arkansas. In Illinois, the Republican challenger, Bruce Rauner, defeated the incumbent Democrat, Pat Quinn. We successfully defended every incumbent Republican governor but one. Tom Corbett lost in Pennsylvania to Democrat Tom Wolf. I was especially proud of the Massachusetts and Maryland pickups. Like New Jersey, those were solid blue states. As in New Jersey, Republicans showed how to win. Overall, we increased the Republican-governor count by two, to thirty-one. Along with winning a majority in the US Senate and expanding the party's majority in the House, this was one heck of a year for Republicans.

I made a lot of friends campaigning for Republicans and spreading that $130 million around. Some, I hoped, might repay their good feelings should I run for president in 2016, a decision I hadn't made yet but was definitely inching toward. If only Paul Fishman's interminable Bridgegate investigation would come to some kind of conclusion. At least the joint legislative committee seemed to be wrapping up. On December 5, the committee reported that I had no involvement in the George Washington Bridge scandal, placing the blame right where Randy Mastro had, on Bridget Kelly and David Wildstein.

Now I was two for two.

Fishman, moving even more slowly than a partisan state legislature, hardly seemed to notice. He just plodded on—figuring, I suppose, that if he kept looking long enough and interviewed the lying Wildstein one more time, he might find something, anything, to pin on me. All along, the federal prosecutors had been subpoenaing documents from us, and we'd been complying with the vast majority of subpoenas, balking only when the request was plainly beyond the scope of their inquiry. Fishman was also eager to quiz me. I was willing to answer his questions, as long as he and Chris Wray could work out some reasonable ground rules. The interview was finally scheduled for just before Christmas 2014. We agreed to a five-hour session at Drumthwacket, under oath and with a court reporter. The prosecutors could then read the transcript to the grand jury.

Fishman didn't conduct the interview himself. He preferred to stay back in his office, presumably coordinating the media leaks. He sent one of his assistants—and not one of his more talented ones—the assistant US attorney J. Fortier Imbert, who arrived with two younger assistant US attorneys, an FBI agent, and an official-corruption investigator. The agent and investigator had worked for me when I was US Attorney. That was incredibly awkward for all of us. During the course of the interview, they each pulled me aside to apologize for the way the US attorney was conducting the probe.

We sat at the same dining table on the mansion's second floor where, nearly one year earlier, I had questioned my top staffers when Bridget Kelly's explosive email first came out.

Being interrogated under oath by an assistant US attorney was definitely one of the more disquieting experiences of my life. In his questions, Imbert offered no credible evidence that I had done anything improper. He fumbled a lot with the pages in a thick binder he had in front of him on the table. He seemed nervous questioning me, hopping inexplicably from topic to topic with no rhyme or reason.

He covered a lot of ground but didn't seem to be getting the answers he was hoping for. Finally, about four hours and fifteen minutes in, Chris Wray interrupted. "Jay," he said, "we agreed to five hours and I don't know what question you are on in that binder, but I can't imagine you're anywhere near finished."

"I'm not," Imbert admitted. "So, we're going to need to come back another day."

Chris frowned at that. "I have to ask my client to leave the room so you and I can have a conversation."

I left while my lawyer and the assistant US attorney had what I can only imagine was an unpleasant conversation about the interview terms we had both agreed to. After a few minutes, Chris came out to speak with me.

"We have two choices," he said. "We can let them come back another day and give them the opportunity to finish their questioning. Or we can say, 'Hey, you made a deal. You had your five hours.'"

I nodded.

"But, Governor," Chris continued, "you didn't do anything wrong. Their questioning is getting nowhere. I don't want there to be any way for them to imply you have something to hide. We have nothing to hide. You're prepared. You're doing great as a witness. I think you should tell them to come back and let them finish."

And that's what we did.

I went back into the dining room and told the federal prosecutor that I would meet with him a second time. "I'll see you when you come back," I said, then got up and walked out of the room.

He and Chris scheduled another session, which went about the same as the first one. I answered every question. J. Fortier Imbert never seemed to find the smoking gun Paul Fishman wanted him to find. How could he? It didn't exist.

—

While US attorney Paul Fishman was slow-walking his Bridgegate probe, the election calendar was racing ahead. If I wanted to run for president in 2016—even if I just wanted to leave that option open—I couldn't entirely sit still. On January 25, 2015, I opened a political action committee, Leadership Matters, so I could start raising money for what *Time* magazine called "a likely 2016 presidential campaign." Likely perhaps, but I wasn't close to formally announcing anything. It was still early, and Bridgegate still hung out there. I already knew the Republican field was going to be crowded. With Barack Obama term-limited and Hillary Clinton looking like the likely Democratic nominee, Republican names were already being floated, often by the individuals themselves, and dollars were already being raised. Governors Scott Walker of Wisconsin, Rick Perry of Texas, John Kasich of Ohio, and Bobby Jindal of Louisiana. Former Florida governor

Jeb Bush. US senators Rand Paul, Ted Cruz, Lindsey Graham, and Marco Rubio. There were others, too: former Arkansas governor Mike Huckabee, former Pennsylvania senator Rick Santorum, former New York governor George Pataki, the businesswoman Carly Fiorina, public speaker/neurosurgeon Dr. Ben Carson—I'm sure I've forgotten a few. There was even talk that Donald Trump might jump in, though he had flirted with presidential runs before and most of the pundits thought this was more of the same.

As the months rolled on, so did Fishman's investigation, sending out little blips that served to keep the bridge story in the news. On February 6, prosecutors subpoenaed records from United Airlines about "the chairman's flight," a weekly nonstop between Newark Airport and Columbia, South Carolina, near the vacation home of Port Authority chairman David Samson. In early March, Fishman's investigators leaked their interview of the members of the Fort Lee Borough Council. After that interview, they hit the Port Authority with a new subpoena. On April 7, Samson, who'd already left the Port Authority, announced he would also retire from his law firm.

With Fishman's investigation still unresolved, there were limits to how close I could get to launching a campaign, even as potential donors drifted away. Woody Johnson, the billionaire owner of the New York Jets, went to Jeb Bush. New York hedge fund manager Anthony Scaramucci went with Scott Walker. The *New York Times* ran a piece on February 19, complaining about "the Christie bubble," saying no one knew what I was thinking about the race. Meg Whitman, the chief executive at Hewlett-Packard, hung tough, as did my old friend and 2012 booster Ken Langone. "Some guys move from Christie to Bush? That's politics," Langone said to the *Times*.

I was planting what seeds I could. In early April, I got a clean bill of health from my doctor. He was pleased I'd kept the weight off from my lap-band surgery. On April 15, the NBC *Today* show ran a will-he-or-won't-he profile of me. "Mary Pat and I have not made this decision yet," I told Matt Lauer. "You don't rush that decision. You do that in the time that it takes." When Lauer asked about my health, I was ready. "Let me put it to you this way," I said. "My cardiologist has donated to my federal PAC. So that probably should tell you everything you need to know."

Finally, on May 1, 2015, nearly a year and a half after Fishman launched his probe, more than a year after Mastro's report, the US attorney announced his charges. Following Mastro's lead, Fishman unsealed federal indictments against Kelly and Baroni, charging that they had deprived the people of Fort Lee of their right to travel freely across state lines. Really, that was it. That same day, prosecutors also revealed Wildstein's plea bargain, saying he had agreed months earlier to plead guilty and testify against Kelly and his best friend, Baroni.

When I was US Attorney, I'd have been embarrassed to bring such a jerry-rigged charge—especially since Fishman could easily have referred the case to the state attorney general's office, which could have brought official-misconduct charges that would have actually fit the defendants' conduct. Then, however, he would have lost control of the case and his ability to inflict political damage on me.

Kelly and Baroni certainly deserved to be fired, and they were. They violated my trust and the trust of the people of New Jersey. They behaved reprehensibly. But this string-gum-and-spittle prosecution? In my mind, this wasn't how federal criminal law should be manipulated. Still, Fishman would ride the Bridgegate publicity train all the way to Election Day, keeping the story alive in ways that would still prove damaging to me.

PART FOUR

CAMPAIGN TRAIL

FIFTEEN

IT'S SHOWTIME

I was ready this time. So ready. As ambivalent as I had been four years earlier, that's how raring to go I was this time to run for president.

I had five and a half years as the Republican governor of blue-state New Jersey, preceded by seven as a corruption-fighting US Attorney. I had Hurricane Sandy and a boatload of fiscal reforms under my belt. My landslide reelection had proved I could attract Latinos, African Americans, and other voters Republicans seldom won. After all the partisan foot-dragging by Paul Fishman, I'd been fully cleared in Bridgegate. I had grateful governors across America and name recognition up in the stratosphere. Not all the way to the Trumposphere, but still sky high. And with Hillary Clinton looking like the likely Democratic nominee, I knew exactly how to take her on in 2016.

This time there was no family heart-to-heart or decisive lightning-strike moment on the way to my decision. I didn't need any of that. We'd all been talking about my running for president since my near run of 2011. There was never a time since then that I and everyone around me didn't agree that this would happen eventually. The only real question was when.

Our active conversation was briefly interrupted by Hurricane Sandy and my reelection, but the national attention that came with both of those only brightened my national prospects. Though my Democratic opponent and some reporters had pounded me for it, I had been careful in the 2013 governor's race not to promise I would definitely serve all four years of my term. Nothing was stopping me now.

The political team I had in place was a well-oiled machine. They'd been with me on my two campaigns for governor. A number of them were with me on thirty-six other Republican governors' races across the country. Maria Comella wrote a detailed "Path to Victory" memo, which Mike DuHaime and Bill Palatucci both signed off on. The only key piece still missing was a campaign-manager replacement for Bridgegate casualty Bill Stepien. We hired Ken McKay, who had been political director of the Republican Governors Association.

As 2015 moved along, the national mood felt just right for a candidate like me. That far into Barack Obama's second term, people had grown weary of "No-Drama" Obama, who wouldn't enforce the red line in Syria, who was more nuanced than strong on terrorism, who often preferred to lead from behind. The economy was doing better than it had when he arrived in the White House, but it still wasn't where it needed to be. People weren't getting raises. Family expenses kept going up. Growth was stuck around 2 percent. The mood in the country, I believed, was ripe for a tough, decisive Republican with a history of shaking things up. Whoever the Democrats put up—Hillary Clinton or Bernie

Sanders or Joe Biden—would have a hard time beating a strong Republican candidate like that.

Stopping Hillary, the Democratic front-runner, from being president was one of the biggest reasons for me to run. I didn't think she could be trusted in the White House. To me, her judgment was suspect. So was her honesty. I was convinced she would take the country further left. She was no Bill Clinton. She certainly didn't have her husband's capacity for empathy—not to mention his ability to connect with other human beings. And you know what? I think a lot of Democrats secretly and not-so-secretly agreed with me. No way could I sit by and watch her win the presidency.

As for the Republicans—well, there were certainly *a lot* of them. More than a dozen were hinting, weighing, threatening, and, soon, announcing they would run. But most of those being mentioned in the press, including Donald Trump, didn't scare me at all. I knew we could compete in the debates and on the stump. As long as we could raise the money to be competitive, I was confident we would be in the thick of things.

As for the others? We would have to pay attention to Jeb Bush and his money. He could raise mountains of it, some from donors who would otherwise support me. We'd have to watch Marco Rubio. He was young and telegenic—the Republican Obama. Not much experience but attractive and articulate. You always have to keep your eyes on guys like that. The only other person who gave me any pause was Ted Cruz, who might be able to unite the Far Right of the party. He wasn't tough, but he had an edgy personality, and that might play. As the field began to crystallize, I figured it would eventually come down to a four-person race—Jeb, Marco, Ted, and me.

As for Donald Trump? I doubted he'd get in. And if he did get in, I doubted he would stay in. I assumed what everyone else assumed at the time: He'd hang around until the first debate or when his polls began to sag—then he'd be out of there. All the lessons of history said he'd move on to other things soon enough. For Donald, the experience of running would be plenty.

Boy, we were all wrong. So very wrong.

———

On June 30, 2015, sixteen months before Election Day, I stood in the old gymnasium at Livingston High School, my alma mater, where I had once been student body president and captain of the baseball team. The crowd was large and boisterous. I felt confident and loose. It was just my kind of political event—celebratory, unpretentious, and loud. "As a candidate for president," I said to the cheering people, "I want to promise you a few things. First, a campaign without spin, without pandering or focus group-tested answers. You're going to get what I think, whether you like it or not, or whether it makes you cringe every once in a while."

I got some knowing smiles at that last one.

"I don't seek the presidency for any other reason than I believe in my heart that I am ready to work with you to restore America to its rightful place in the world and to restore the American dream to each one of our children," I told the people that day.

"We are going to win this election, and I love each and every one of you," I declared before leaving the stage and signing the paperwork that made me an official candidate.

It is hard to describe that feeling to anyone who has not experienced it: to stand in the very spot you stood when you were fifteen, sixteen, and seventeen years old, all the emotions of a happy childhood filling your consciousness, as you announce you are running for president. It was an amazing moment for me and for so many of my family and longtime friends who had made that journey with me. From the gym at Livingston High out into the big world and back again to start the road to the White House.

Now, it was a fact, politically speaking, that I wasn't in the same position I'd been in four years earlier, when my path to the Republican nomination seemed scattered with rose petals and billionaires begging me to run. I had taken quite a beating in the preceding eighteen months, and I had the poll numbers to prove it. By the summer of 2015, as I launched my campaign for president, my job-approval rating among New Jersey voters stood at a bruised-and-battered 33 percent.

But none of that worried me. Polls went up. Polls went down. No one knew that better than I did. And I had a first-class team joining DuHaime, Palatucci, Comella, and McKay: Russ Schriefer, Larry Weitzner, Amanda De Palma, Matt Mowers, Phil Valenziano, and a few others, people I had known and trusted for years. The polling said Bridgegate wasn't much of an issue in Iowa and New Hampshire, where voters would cast the first ballots in early 2016. In fact, it was the Obama "hug" that seemed to be a much-bigger problem with Republican primary voters.

Our plan was to spend enough time in Iowa so no one could say I had skipped it but to devote most of our resources to famously independent-minded New Hampshire. If we did well there, the thinking went, we could ride that momentum into South Carolina, which had become far more urbanized in recent years with northeastern transplants and retirees. And we'd be on our way.

The Republican field was getting more crowded by the day. Rand Paul had his sights set on the party's libertarian wing. Scott Walker figured he'd be the darling of budget cutters and antiunion hawks. Ben Carson was pushing his personal-empowerment story.

John Kasich was still searching for a message. Frankly, I was a little surprised to find him there. In November 2014, he and his wife, Karen, had taken Mary Pat and me to a Republican Governors Association dinner and asked if I was likely to run for president in 2016—adding that if I did, he wouldn't have to. When I said I was leaning that way, he proposed a toast to me and Mary Pat as the next leaders of the Republican party. I never heard another word from him about it until I read he was jumping in.

And the list went on from there, stacked with dreamers who figured that, if lightning was going to strike, it might as well strike them: Bobby Jindal. Lindsey Graham. Mike Huckabee. George Pataki. Jim Gilmore. Rick Santorum. Rick Perry.

Donald Trump was in a category all by himself. He was the unpredictable celebrity businessman. No clear ideology. No previous office held. But he was famous beyond famous, having spent decades in the New York tabloids and on network TV, and all his opinions were delivered with a disarming conviction. People couldn't seem to turn away.

Donald had given me no heads-up that he was thinking seriously about making the race. And I hadn't recently discussed my plans with him. The last time we'd talked explicitly about my running for president was in 2014, when I was raising money for the Republican Governors Association. Mary Pat and I went to see him at Trump Tower, and he wrote a check for $250,000.

"Will me helping you help you run for president?" he wanted to know.

"Yes," I told him. "I can give more money away to other governors. They will appreciate that."

"Good," he said. "I want to help you."

He did issue one cautious note that day, though he didn't tie it directly to the presidential race. "This Bridgegate stuff is a bitch," he said to me. "I know you didn't do anything, but it's a bitch. These people won't let go of you. It's really unfair."

In retrospect, it is clear that Donald had been toying with the idea of running for president since 1988. Given his age, he knew that this was most likely his last chance. *The Apprentice* was no longer an impediment. If he was ever going to run, 2016 was the year. At the time, though, I thought it was just another dalliance, another tease. When the rubber met the road, he was unlikely to go through with it. I wasn't the only one who thought that. The entire Republican establishment, the media, and the Democratic Party did, too.

The next thing I knew, he was on television riding down the escalator in Trump Tower and announcing his own candidacy for president.

———

Sean Hannity showed up at the American Legion Dupuis Cross Post in Ashland for my first New Hampshire town hall and aired an hour-long interview with me on Fox News. Our ground team was led by Matt Mowers, who'd been executive director of the New Hampshire Republican Party. Everything was so personal. At times, I felt like I was running for governor of New Hampshire.

United had nonstop flights between Newark and Manchester. So, getting back and forth was pretty convenient by modern presidential-campaign standards. Some people complained in New Jersey, saying I was ignoring them. But with cell phones, email, and other digital technology, I never missed anything back home. I had no trouble negotiating the state takeover of Atlantic City in a series of phone calls with Steve Sweeney and Mayor Donald Guardian. Fund-raising was always hard. But we were raising enough, and my budget director, Amanda De Palma, who most recently had run the New Jersey Republican

Party, really knew how to squeeze a dollar. And I had first-string policy advisers. Bob Grady, my old friend from the Bush 41 White House, led the economic team. Brian Hook, a highly regarded lawyer, diplomat, and former assistant secretary of state, helped craft my foreign-policy positions. I was even receiving monthly tutorials from Henry Kissinger, who seemed happy to school me like I was one of his long-ago Harvard graduate students.

As in New Jersey, the loose town hall format would become my signature event. Between July 2015 and Primary Day in February 2016, I would hold more than one hundred New Hampshire town halls. It was hard to draw crowds at first. But word began to spread that our town halls were fun and spontaneous and people started showing up.

But I wasn't the only one drawing a crowd.

A lot of people underestimated Donald Trump as a presidential campaigner. I never did. Once he was out on the trail and rallying his people, his polls shot up and stayed there.

By the time we all met for the first debate, August 6 at the Quicken Loans Arena in Cleveland, he was standing at the center podium with nine of us flanked on either side of him. Seven other candidates were relegated to the warm-up stage.

For Donald, that night got off to a challenging start when Megyn Kelly aimed a barbed missile at him. "You've called women you don't like 'fat pigs,' 'dogs,' 'slobs,' and 'disgusting animals,'" the Fox anchor said. "Your Twitter account has several disparaging comments about women's looks. You once told a contestant on *Celebrity Apprentice* it would be a pretty picture to see her on her knees. Does that sound to you like the temperament of a man we should elect as president?"

"Only Rosie O'Donnell," Trump quipped. Then, he unloaded on Kelly: "What I say is what I say. And honestly, Megyn, if you don't like it, I'm sorry, I've been very nice to you, although I could probably maybe not be, based on the way you have treated me. But I wouldn't do that to you."

They weren't playing. Neither one of them.

When the first break came, the whole arena was buzzing. Donald walked over to my podium. "Can you believe she asked me that?" he said incredulously. "So biased."

He had a point. But I'd been around politics long enough to know there was nothing he could do about it. "That's what you have to expect in this business," I said. "Nobody's going to cut you a break."

"That's hugely unfair," he protested.

"I don't disagree with you," I told him. "But this is politics today—here we are."

But that was only one exchange. Watching the rest of Trump's performance that night, I really began to worry—not for him, for me. *He's enjoying himself too much*, I thought. To the extent that he was enjoying himself, I feared, he would stick around. As Mary Pat and I headed back to the hotel, I said to her, "We've got a problem."

"What's the problem?" she asked.

"Donald Trump."

From a stylistic perspective, he was everything I was—but on jet fuel. He was brash. He was direct. He was in-your-face. I was doing all the things I normally did and was good at doing. I was getting strong reviews from the pundits. Yet he was still dominating.

———

And so it was out on the trail with Donald and the other candidates.

After the CNN Reagan Library debate on September 16, he sent out a nice tweet about a comment I'd made on opioid addiction. I called to thank him. He answered the phone—typical Donald—and before I could even speak, he said, "Chris, was that a great tweet I sent out about you this morning—or what? Are you loving what I tweeted about you? Isn't it great?"

"Well," I said, "if you'd have waited five seconds, I was calling to say thank you."

"You know I love you," he said. "You know whether you win or I win, you and I are going to be together. I know that. I want to win, and you want to win. But we're friends. That's why I sent out the tweet."

"We have history," I agreed.

I couldn't afford to obsess about Donald. I was pursuing my own strategy, fighting my own battles against the other candidates, trying to fill my own niche and expand it. And as the temperatures began dropping in New Hampshire, things were heating up for me. On November 28, I won the endorsement of the *New Hampshire Union Leader*, the state's largest newspaper. "For our safety, our future: Chris Christie for President," the front-page headline read. The *Union Leader*, like most American newspapers, didn't pack the punch it once did—but this was still big.

Donald was not pleased. "You have a very dishonest newspaper up here," he told the crowd at his rally that night in Nashua. "It's also a failing newspaper. It's really going down the tubers." Yes, he said *tubers*.

The *Union Leader*'s publisher, Joe McQuaid, who'd compared Trump to the villain in the *Back to the Future* movies, had clearly gotten under the candidate's skin. "I've been friends with Christie," Donald said. "But McQuaid, he is Christie's lap dog."

Two things happened after that. I shot up in the New Hampshire polls to second place, right behind Donald. And my rise infuriated him, even more than the endorsement did. He was still livid on December 7 at a rally in Mount Pleasant, South Carolina, where his main agenda was sliming me. "The George Washington Bridge—he knew about it," Donald told the crowd.

Donald proceeded to lay out his own imaginative scenario for the two-and-a-half-year-old lane realignment. "They're closing up the largest bridge in the world. The biggest in the United States."

Of course, that wasn't true. The bridge hadn't been closed for a second.

He imagined my conversations with Kelly, Baroni, and Wildstein: "They're with him all the time, the people that did it. They never said, 'Hey, boss, ah, we're closing up the George Washington Bridge tonight'? No? They never said that? They're talking about the weather, right? He knew about it. He knew about it. Totally knew about it."

Totally invented. He was angry, and he made up every word of it.

"They didn't mention it at one of their meetings? I think they had breakfast, like, every day or every other day."

We didn't ever have breakfast together. But if we had, how would he know? That endorsement and my poll bump really got to him.

Donald went on to complain about the taxes in New Jersey and make erroneous claims about the state's credit rating. Then, to the delight of his rally crowd, he hit on the nonhug with Barack Obama after Hurricane Sandy. "You had Christie so friendly with President Obama during the flood. I actually called. I said, 'Let me ask you. Is he gonna vote for Obama?'"

That call? Never happened.

"I thought he was gonna vote for Obama," Trump said. "I don't know, I think he possibly did."

Another whopper. I voted for Mitt Romney.

Donald was coming at my skull with a rhetorical Louisville Slugger because I had snatched a prized endorsement and was advancing too close in the polls.

Donald's attacks were unfounded and, worse, he knew it. He had told me so on many occasions. I had no problem with hardball politics. I had some talent for that myself. But knowingly lying because you were pissed that someone else got a newspaper endorsement? To me, that was over the line. You don't do that to anyone, let alone a friend of long-standing. I was really angry about it but also excited. I knew I was getting under Donald's skin.

The good news, I guess, was that I didn't also get a caustic nickname like "Crooked Hillary," "Low-Energy Jeb," "Lyin' Ted Cruz," "Liddle Marco," "Pocahontas," or "Crazy Bernie" Sanders, not to mention media stars like "Sleepy Eyes" Chuck Todd and "Crooked H. Flunkie" (Maggie Haberman). Be thankful for small favors, I suppose.

Even so, as the year came to a close, I didn't want a war with Donald Trump. And apparently, he didn't want a war with me. Ken McKay, my campaign manager, took a call from Corey Lewandowski, who was Donald's, asking for a truce. We had other candidates to worry about—and no money to take on Donald directly yet—so we agreed. We'd square off with him in South Carolina. By then, we'd be in a position to really engage.

In January, the conservative *Boston Herald* endorsed me, another coup. By that point, Marco Rubio and Jeb Bush, who'd also noticed my surge, had spent millions on TV ads attacking me. I was not a real Republican, they said, running endless loops of the millisecond Obama "hug." I knew exactly how to respond to the double-barrel onslaught, but we didn't have the money to buy our own slap-back ads. I felt enormously frustrated as I watched my support slide from 19 percent to 9. For me, that was when the real concern began to seep in.

One brief ray of political sunshine appeared from Iowa, of all places, where I'd hardly been campaigning at all. I had been courting Iowa governor Terry Branstad since 2010. As chair of the Republican Governors Association, I'd given him an early $1 million in January 2014. I believed Terry was a friend and ally. Most of his political operatives were working for me.

One week out from the first-in-the-nation Iowa caucuses, I got a mysterious, unscheduled call from Terry summoning me to a secret meeting at the state capitol in Des Moines. He was clear: just me, Mary Pat, and one staffer.

We were ushered through a back door and into a basement conference room to avoid the Iowa press corps. As Terry walked in, he shook my hand, hugged Mary Pat, and sat across from us. After very few niceties, he got to the point. "I've made a decision," he said. "Chris and I will be caucusing for you on Tuesday night." Christine Branstad is Terry's wife.

I wanted to jump out of my chair. An endorsement from Mr. Iowa Republican? From the man who had served as governor for twenty years and was on his way to a sixth landslide win? "Governor," I said, "I am so honored by your support. When and where do you want to announce it?"

That's when the smile left his face.

"Oh, no, Chris," he said earnestly. "I promised the people of Iowa I would stay neutral, and I cannot break my word."

I was dumbfounded. We talked for the next thirty minutes about how game-changing his endorsement would be, not just in Iowa but also for my momentum in New Hampshire. He acknowledged my argument but refused to budge. I left the meeting flattered but frustrated. And to this day, I wonder how the results in

Iowa and New Hampshire would have been different if I'd gotten my picture on the front page of the *Des Moines Register* and papers across the country: "Branstad Endorses Christie."

So close. So very close.

With our dwindling campaign funds, we bought ads hitting Jeb and Marco. Those seemed to work to some extent. But as we flew out of Iowa on February 1 with our sad, 2 percent finish, I said to my team on the plane, "Starting tomorrow morning, we're on Marco every minute." We could survive finishing behind Jeb Bush in New Hampshire, I believed. But we had to beat Rubio.

I had already been labeling him "the Boy in the Bubble." Now I also made fun of the fact that, at his town hall meetings, he would answer only three, presubmitted questions. "We can't send an ill-prepared candidate into the fight against Hillary Clinton," I'd say. "We'll end up with a third Obama term or worse." I could see we were getting under Marco's skin. But my takedown of Marco, if it was going to be effective, would have to come at the final New Hampshire debate, Saturday night, February 6, at Saint Anselm's College in Manchester. In the green room beforehand, my campaign staffers wanted to know what exactly I had planned.

"Don't worry," I said. "I'll find the right moment."

I didn't have to wait long. The second question of the night gave Marco a chance to slam me. He took a halfhearted stab at the New Jersey credit rating, then shifted immediately into one of his canned lines. "Let's dispel with this fiction that Barack Obama doesn't know what he's doing," the senator from Florida said. "He knows exactly what he's doing. He is trying to change this country. He wants America to become more like the rest of the world. We don't want to be like the rest of the world. We want to be the United States of America."

And so I pounced, portraying him as a robotic creation of his handlers. "That's what Washington, DC, does," I said. "The drive-by shot at the beginning with incorrect and incomplete information and then the memorized twenty-five-second speech that is exactly what his advisers gave him."

I could hear a murmur of recognition in the room. I slammed Marco's poor attendance record in the Senate. "That's not leadership, that's truancy," I said.

Marco came back by attacking me for not having returned to New Jersey as quickly as he thought I should have during a recent snowstorm. But I wouldn't let him wiggle away.

When he repeated the canned Obama line, he gave me an opening that delighted the crowd.

I leaned on the podium and pointed across at him—"There it is, the memorized twenty-second speech"—and the crowd went wild. Unbelievably, he interrupted me again to repeat the Barack Obama line.

Now the audience was fully abuzz. I went right at him, and he repeated the line *again*. An incredible seven minutes of presidential-debate history.

At the first break, I walked to the edge of the stage. Mary Pat, Patrick, and Bridget had seats in the front row. "What did you think?" I asked.

"What did I think?" Mary Pat answered incredulously. "Oh, my goodness, you killed him. He should just go home now."

"Dad, that was wild," Patrick agreed.

Sitting behind Mary Pat was my number one donor, the hedge fund honcho Steve Cohen. Steve's not normally a highly effusive guy. By now he was flashing two thumbs-up signs. Right then, I felt a tap on my shoulder. It was Donald Trump. Donald put his arm around me and said, "God, you destroyed him. Do me a favor, Chris. Never get angry with me. You were Perry Mason on cross-examination. He's finished. You're the only one who could have done that. Just remember: I haven't said anything bad about you. Don't go after me."

The next morning, the *Boston Herald* carried front-page photos of Rubio and me. "CHOKE!" the headline read. "Just when he needs to be strong, Rubio wilts under Christie attack."

━━━

The final four days before New Hampshire voted, our crowds were enormous. People wanted to come out and see the guy who had decimated Marco Rubio. So many people showed up for our Sunday-brunch town hall, the Hampton fire marshal wouldn't let everyone inside. I turned to Mary Pat as I was being introduced and whispered to her, "Maybe we have one more comeback left."

Both of us were hoping, but we knew it was a long shot. We were buoyed again over the weekend when we won the endorsement of Massachusetts governor Charlie Baker. Our rally with Charlie was one of the most memorable of the campaign.

Monday night in Manchester, I told the story about my last conversation with my mother. It was a story I had told many times on the campaign trail and at our New Jersey town halls. "If you wonder who I am and why I am the way I am," I said to the people, "that's why. Because of her."

It's an intensely personal story, though months of repetition had drained some of its spontaneity. Not this time. As I looked across the crowded room, I wasn't talking to persuadable strangers anymore. I was talking to people I cared about and loved. My father was there. So were all four of my children and several members of Mary Pat's family. Most of my campaign staffers were also in the room. People weren't scattered between Iowa and New Hampshire anymore. All of us knew, depending on how the vote came in, this could be my last night running for president.

That was the one time in the whole campaign that I almost lost it. I looked out at Wayne McDonald, my New Hampshire chairman. Wayne had heard the story of my mother probably sixty or seventy times. But this time, Wayne was tearing up. I looked at Jeb Bradley, the state senate majority leader who had traveled with me for months and had introduced me that night. He was reaching for his handkerchief.

I did my very best that night, just as I had through the whole campaign. If I had to go out somehow, this was how I wanted it to be. There was nothing else I could have done. The political atmosphere that was so welcoming to me in 2012 was blocked in 2016. It was blocked by Donald Trump. If he hadn't been there, I had no doubt I would have won New Hampshire. But he was, and I didn't. That was the tough reality.

"We love your husband," people had been telling Mary Pat for months. "He's blunt. He's smart. He's real. But we're voting for Trump."

Rubio was clearly hurt by my debate-night pounding. But I didn't get enough of the votes that he shed. They ended up split among Jeb Bush, John Kasich, and me. Since no one had been attacking Kasich, he was the dark horse who managed to sneak up at the end.

Trump finished first at 35 percent when the New Hampshire votes were counted on Tuesday night. Kasich was second with 16 percent, followed by Cruz with 12 and Bush with 11. Rubio, who'd been gaining until that last debate, landed at fifth with 10.5 percent. I was in sixth place with 7.4 percent. Another ten candidates followed me.

I didn't drop out that night, not officially. I didn't want my New Hampshire volunteers to have to hear me say it. In my concession speech, I thanked everyone and said we were going back to New Jersey to reevaluate. Everyone knew what that meant, and so did I.

Back in the hotel suite, three people cried: my two sons and my old friend Larry Hogan, the governor of Maryland, who'd been battling cancer but was healthy enough to have come up the last two weeks and campaign. My daughter Bridget and I had both worn HOGAN STRONG bracelets for him throughout the campaign.

Then my cell phone rang. I glanced at the number. It was Donald.

"Well, this should be interesting, everybody," I said. "You all deserve to hear this." I put the call on speaker.

"I know it's a tough night for you," Donald said. "I know you're disappointed. You ran a great campaign. I so admire and respect you. I want you to know that. I hope you already do."

"I do," I said.

"There will always be a place for you with me," he said. "I know you're not ready to make any decisions now, but I hope that when you and Mary Pat think about it, you'll consider coming with me."

He was right. I wasn't ready to think about the future. Not yet.

He told me he loved me, told me to hug Mary Pat and the kids for him, and got off the phone.

The people in the room sat there slack-jawed. I think a lot of them were surprised to hear Donald Trump talk like that. So *human*.

I wasn't sure if they were suspicious or grateful or what. But all of them wanted to know what this might mean. What would I do next?

SIXTEEN

TEAM DONALD

Mary Pat and I returned home to New Jersey in a daze. The mood was quiet—not really despondent or depressed. We felt we had done the very best we could. We were beaten by two forces we couldn't control: Jeb Bush locking up so many of the donors who would have come our way and the total dominance of our political lane by Donald Trump.

Mary Pat told me something that I knew she'd been thinking for a while. She did not want to go back to work. She was ready to retire from Wall Street and stay at home to tend full time to Patrick and Bridget, our younger two, who were still at home. I was fine with all that. She'd certainly earned it. I still had a job I loved. I knew I'd be returning to the State House in Trenton, and life would go on.

Donald Trump wasn't the only candidate who reached out to me in my electoral disappointment. Several others also called, some bearing gifts. Jeb Bush said if I endorsed him, he would name me chairman of his campaign. "You'll be at the table," he said. "You'll be in the middle of everything." Marco Rubio didn't seem to hold a grudge over our encounter at the final New Hampshire debate. In fact, our public hostility would make my endorsement that much sweeter, he said. "I think it would be a great bit of theater," he told me, "us being the ones who are together."

I thanked them both but told them I needed time to think.

John Kasich called just as I was pulling up to our campaign headquarters in Morristown to draft my drop-out statement and commiserate with the staff. I had campaigned for John in Ohio in 2010 and helped him raise money. Back then, I considered John a friend. His promise over dinner not to run if I did had strained things a bit. But our post–New Hampshire phone call really sealed my view of him.

He asked how I was doing. I told him, okay, considering. "You know what happened to you, don't you, Chris?" he said.

I told him I didn't.

"God wanted you to play right field, and you insisted on playing shortstop. No matter how many times God told you to play right field, you insisted on playing shortstop. And last night, you went out to shortstop, and the ball went through your legs."

Right there, I understood why so many people in politics despised John Kasich, why only one of his thirty fellow Republican governors had endorsed his presidential campaign—and that was Alabama's Robert Bentley, who later resigned in disgrace and pleaded guilty in a messy sex-and-corruption scandal.

"And John," I asked, "what does God have in mind for you?"

He didn't hesitate. "I think you're going to see that very clearly over the next couple of months."

We sure did, didn't we?

The first thing I decided was that I wouldn't endorse anyone before the South Carolina primary. It was just too soon. My team was still shell-shocked. My feelings were still too raw. I wanted this to be an intellectual decision, not an emotional one.

Donald kept calling. He called more than anybody else. "We're here and ready," he said. "The only endorsement we want is Chris Christie . . . We've got to be together, you and me."

All the other candidates were serious in their pitches, emphasizing our shared visions for America and our policy overlaps. Donald was far more jovial. He knew I wasn't ready to make a decision, but he was having fun with the chase.

Marco Rubio got Nikki Haley's endorsement in South Carolina, but Trump still won big, with 35 percent to Kasich's 16. Mary Pat and I watched at home in Mendham with Meg Whitman on the speakerphone. Once the results were clear, the Hewlett Packard CEO, who'd been my national finance chair, said she couldn't believe the results.

"Meg, you've got to get real about this," I told her. "This guy is going to be the nominee. He won by double digits in South Carolina after winning two to one in New Hampshire and coming in second by a whisker to Cruz in Iowa. If it was any candidate other than Donald Trump, everyone on TV would be saying, 'It's time for the other candidates to start dropping out.'"

"I don't want to believe it's over," Meg said. "We've got to figure out who to get behind."

"Meg," I repeated. "It's a folly. The voters have spoken. No one else is going to beat this guy."

She was so upset, all she could say was, "I have to go. I have to try and absorb this."

Before Mary Pat and I got up from the couch that night, I put the question to her. "Okay, what do you want to do?"

"What do you mean?" she asked.

"Well, we've got two choices," I said. "We can sit on the sidelines and endorse nobody and not be involved in this presidential race anymore. Or we can be with the guy we know is going to win. He's been our friend for fifteen years. I know we can make him a better candidate. To me, it seems like a pretty obvious choice."

Mary Pat wasn't there yet. The campaign had been exhausting, for her especially. She was burned out on the whole thing. It took another day or two, but she agreed.

I called Donald right away and told him Mary Pat and I wanted to have a talk with him and Melania. "Just the four of us, okay? No fanfare. No publicity. Just us."

"Great," Donald said. "Come to the apartment for breakfast on Tuesday. Eight o'clock?"

———

On the morning of February 23, Mary Pat and I rode to Trump Tower on Fifth Avenue between Fifty-Sixth and Fifty-Seventh Streets in Midtown Manhattan, headquarters and command center for all things Trump. Donald and Melania live in a three-level penthouse that starts on the sixty-third floor. The Trump Organization, the family real estate, licensing, and entertainment business, occupies the twenty-sixth floor. And more recently, the Trump-for-president campaign had most of its offices on the fourteenth floor.

We slipped in the side, residents' entrance on Fifty-Sixth Street. I'd been there several times before. I knew that trick. Nobody seemed to notice us. We rode the elevator to sixty-three. Melania answered the door in black pants, royal blue heels, and a zip-up hoodie, her hair pulled back in a ponytail. She greeted us as always with hugs and kisses. "We're so excited for you guys to be here," she said. "Donald is coming downstairs."

She led us into the small dining room off the kitchen. The staff had prepared eggs and pancakes. Once Donald came down, we all sat, and he started in with the questions.

"What do you think of the campaign? What do you think about where we are?"

I told him I thought he was in excellent shape—that the party regulars were still adjusting, but they were going to have a very tough time denying him the nomination.

He cut that off quickly. "All right," he said, "so what do I have to do here? What do I have to do to get you on the team?"

"You don't have to do anything," I told him. "We're here this morning to tell you we're in."

A giant smile slid across Donald's face. He turned to Melania and tossed his hands in the air. "We're all back together again," he said. "Isn't this great? This is amazing. No one is going to expect this. It's going to be huge." Then he turned to me. "But if I win," he said, "is there something you're interested in doing with me?"

My support wasn't conditioned on anything. Truly, I hadn't come to discuss that. But he was asking, and I thought he had a right to know how I felt. "There are only two jobs I'm interested in," I said. "Only two. Vice president or attorney general. Other than that, I'm not really interested in anything."

He took that in for a second. "All right," he said. "That's really reasonable. Let's figure it out as we go along. But you know how I feel about you, and you'd be a great vice president, and you'd be a great attorney general. So, let's say either-or."

I told him again I wasn't negotiating. "I'm not asking you for a guarantee of anything," I emphasized. "You asked me if you won, what would I be interested in? Those are the things I'd be interested in."

"I understand," he said. "I just want to make sure you know I hold you in that kind of regard."

We went on to discuss the mechanics of how we would announce the endorsement. Donald said he wanted to break the news the day after the CNN-Telemundo Republican debate, which was set for Houston on February 25, the final debate before Super Tuesday, when nearly half the delegates needed for victory would be at stake in Texas and ten other states. "Can we keep this secret till then?" he asked me.

"Absolutely," I promised. I'd been a United States attorney. I knew how to keep my mouth shut.

We all got up from the table. Donald shook my hand. Melania hugged Mary Pat. He called downstairs to the campaign office. A few minutes later, Corey Lewandowski and Hope Hicks, his young campaign manager and even younger communications director, showed up. I had never met either of them before, though I knew who they were. Corey seemed a little manic—his default position, as we would soon discover. Hope was very poised as she questioned me about staffing. "Who should I reach out to?" she wanted to know. Both of them seemed competent, respectful, and very dedicated to their boss—and almost beside themselves at the news.

"This is a great day for us, Governor," Corey said. "Thank you so much."

——

I knew I was climbing out on a limb. When I made my decision to endorse, exactly zero governors had backed Donald Trump. Zero US senators. Not even Senator Jeff Sessions was on board yet. Trump's highest-profile backers at that point included Kid Rock, Ted Nugent, Jesse Ventura, Jerry Falwell Jr., South Carolina lieutenant governor Henry McMaster, New York congressman Chris Collins, and former Alaska governor Sarah Palin, whose wacky endorsement speech during the Iowa caucus was punctuated with so many *hallelujahs*, *you-betchas*, and *pussy-footin's*, even Trump looked pained.

What I didn't expect was how some of my closest advisers would react.

Bill Palatucci, the only one I called immediately, was supportive. He said I was making a smart move. I didn't tell anyone else until a few hours before I was flying down to Texas, when I called Maria Comella, my trusted communications director, and asked, "You want to come with me?"

"I really don't want you to do this," she said. "Why endorse anybody at this point? You ran a great race. You gained a lot of respect. I think this diminishes you."

I told her I appreciated her openness and tried to explain my thinking. "I know this guy. I can help him be a better candidate. And I don't want Hillary Clinton to be president."

It was a short conversation and an uncomfortable one. She didn't want him to be president, and I think she believed I really could help elevate him to the White House.

I got no further with Mike DuHaime, my chief political adviser. "I can't be with you on this," he said. I told both of them I understood. I loved and respected both of them. They had been through a lot with me. But I think I got over losing more quickly than they did.

Palatucci agreed to fly with me on one of Trump's smaller business jets. We took off from Morristown Airport in New Jersey and landed in Houston just as the debate was wrapping up. From there, we boarded the much-larger Boeing 757-200 that I would come to know as Trump Force One and waited for Donald to arrive. "This is so great," he said as we made the twenty-minute hop to Dallas–Fort Worth. "No one even knows you're here."

We sneaked into the side door of a hotel in Fort Worth. The next morning, we rode together to meet the media at the Fort Worth Convention Center. "Chris, you're so good at keeping secrets," he said again. "You, your people, nobody leaked. It's amazing."

Later in the campaign, when Trump's son-in-law, Jared, and Steve Bannon would accuse me of leaking, I would say to him, "You think I'm a leaker? Remember Fort Worth, Texas."

"That's a good point," Donald would admit. But that day in the car, I just said thank you.

Side by side, my prior rival and I walked down the convention center hallway and toward a room packed with national media. Just as we reached the open door, I heard a gasp and a female reporter's voice: "Oh, my God!" When we reached the podium, Trump said a few words about how well the debate had gone and how little stock he put in endorsements, something he'd said repeatedly, as he had gotten so few. But "this was one endorsement," he said, "that really meant a lot." Then he turned the microphone over to me.

I said how proud I was to be supporting Trump for president. "I guarantee you that the one person that Hillary and Bill Clinton do not want to see on that stage is Donald Trump." The Clintons, I added, "do not know the playbook of Donald Trump, because he is rewriting the playbook." I meant it.

—

Donald and I then headed off together to barnstorm the Super Tuesday states, starting with a massive noontime rally in Fort Worth. This was my first experience with Trump campaign events, which have no equivalent in American politics. Thousands, sometimes tens of thousands, were gathered at every stop, often in airplane hangars, yelling, screaming, eager to be a part of a movement that would make America great again. The rallies felt as much like rock concerts as political events. Even though I was Donald's warm-up act, the crowds roared their approval for my every syllable, from "Hello, Bentonville" to "I am so thrilled to see this packed airport hangar." I'd made a lot of speeches in my time, some in front of sizable audiences. I had never experienced anything like this.

Still, by modern campaign standards, we were an absurdly tiny road crew. Besides Palatucci and me, Donald's onboard entourage included Corey Lewandowski, Hope Hicks, social media director Dan Scavino, body man Keith Schiller, and the Secret Service agents, who, at that time, were traveling with the top candidates. That was it. At one point, Palatucci glanced at them and then at me and whispered, "We lost to *this*?"

We had.

The crowds weren't the only eye-opening aspect of traveling with Donald's campaign.

In the section of Trump Force One where Donald sat, there were two large seats, side by side, and two seats facing them. He had a console next to him with a three-button remote control that flipped the channels on the closest TV from Fox to CNN to MSNBC and back again. The seat beside Donald stayed empty unless he invited someone to sit with him. Every now and then, he called out to Schiller: "Keith! I need my paperwork from New York." Keith would gently place a stack of business reports in the seat.

Which Donald would then ignore. To him, the campaign was infinitely more fun. "Who could be interested in that shit anymore after what I'm doing here?" he said to me, nodding at the stack of papers beside him. "Who cares?"

He found it harder to ignore the onboard TVs. As Marco Rubio unleashed a last-gasp barrage at "con man" Trump with his tiny hands and spray-on tan, Donald yelled back at the TV, "Who is this guy? What the hell does he think he's talking about? He's nobody. Liddle Marco! Liddle Marco with the lifts in his shoes."

I tried to calm Donald. "It's two o'clock on a Saturday afternoon," I said to him. "Do you know who's watching CNN right now?"

"Who?" he asked.

"You," I said. "You're the only person in America watching CNN right now. Ignore it. Nobody gives a shit. Put on ESPN. Who cares what he says?"

Donald, who had no basis of comparison for anything, quizzed me constantly about his crowd size. "That looks pretty good, right?" he'd say at nearly every stop.

"It's amazing."

"Did you have crowds like this?" he'd ask me.

"No."

———

Donald choreographed every last detail, including where the pilot should park the airplane and where the camera risers should be. "I want the gold TRUMP letters on the plane directly over my shoulder in the shot," I heard him tell the pilot before we flew to Bentonville, Arkansas. "Make sure it's all lined up."

He picked the music: the theme song from *Air Force One* would blare as he came off the airplane, the Rolling Stones' "You Can't Always Get What You Want" as he waved goodbye. He produced me, too, or tried to.

"I want your tie to be longer," he said. "It's slenderizing."

"I'm not retying my tie," I told him. "My tie is fine. I think yours is too long."

"No, no," he shot back at me. "Mine is the perfect length. It makes you look thinner."

Donald stage-managed everything. The staffers executed his precise instructions—and good luck to the underling who deviated one inch. When we arrived in Florida the night before Super Tuesday to await the results, Donald was on a tear against what he called *pinhead microphones*, the long and pointy ones. He didn't think they were loud enough. Apparently he had mentioned his displeasure to George Gigicos, his senior advance man, but the pinhead mics kept turning up.

During a late dinner on the patio at Mar-a-Lago, Trump was still upset. "I'm straining my voice," he said, "because of those goddamn pinhead microphones." Near the end of the meal, Hope got a text from George, asking if it was okay if he came over and said good night to everybody—or should he just go up to bed?

"George would like to come over and say good night," Hope said to Donald.

"Yeah, yeah," Trump said. "Sure."

George appeared at the table. "Great trip, everybody," he said brightly. "Let's go get 'em tomorrow."

Trump looked up slowly from his plate. He took a breath and then he spoke. "George," he said, "you fuck up that microphone one more time, you're fired. Do you understand? One. More. Time. Your ass will be outta here."

"Yes, sir," George said before scampering off as quickly as he could.

Corey turned to Hope and shrugged. "Guess it was a bad idea for George to come over and say good night," Corey said.

———

Super Tuesday, March 1, lived up to its name for Donald Trump, draining more air from the Never Trumpers and pushing Marco Rubio to the edge of surrender. Trump took Alabama, Arkansas, Georgia, Massachusetts, Tennessee, Vermont, and Virginia. Ted Cruz won Alaska, Oklahoma, and his home state of Texas. Marco Rubio had to console himself with a win in Minnesota. John Kasich and Ben Carson, also on the ballot, won no states at all.

For days, I'd been pushing Donald to hold himself above the Republican fray. "Time to shift your fire toward Hillary," I kept telling him. But when Marco gave a Super Tuesday concession speech that was yet another Trump attack, Corey called my room at Mar-a-Lago, clearly agitated. "You need to come to the apartment to see the boss," he said.

"That's it," Donald said when he let me in. "I get punched, I counterpunch. I'm going after him."

"There's no reason to do that," I told him. "Not this time. He's baiting you. Don't take the bait. You're going to be the Republican nominee. Don't pay any attention to Marco."

"Then you do it," he said. "You go after him in the introduction."

"I'm not doing that, either," I told him.

"Why not?" he asked.

"Because a stupid strategy for you is also a stupid strategy for me."

He reluctantly agreed.

A few dozen members were waiting in the ballroom, along with the media. I gave Trump a rousing introduction. He came out, and I was turning to leave when he said to me, "Stay up here with me."

Big mistake.

As he spoke and answered questions, I was happy that he mostly avoided the Marco bashing—mostly. But this time, there was no Trump Force One fuselage strategically positioned behind him in the camera shots.

There was just me, standing alone on the empty stage behind him.

It's one thing to be with a group of people standing behind a speaker. You can play off each other. You can interact naturally. But standing all alone, it's very difficult to know what to do. Mostly, I just stood there. Every once in a while, I reacted to something Donald said, but mostly I just looked straight ahead. Even before Donald was finished, the pundits were saying on television that I looked like the star of a hostage video.

The pictures became a meme on social media. They were annoying. They were funny. They were everywhere. The suggestion was that I must have felt trapped having endorsed Donald Trump, which couldn't have been further from the truth. This campaign was going places, and I was now at the center of it. In a situation like that one, you can't look natural no matter what. If you hold a fake smile, you look like a phony. If you look away, people will say you are distracted or bored. Really, there's no winning this game. I should have known better, and I should have just walked off the stage even though Donald asked me to stay with him. I didn't do anyone any favors staying up there.

It was on to the Florida primary, where people were already asking if we could finally bury Marco once and for all. I was thrilled with how my candidate had done, but I definitely could have skipped becoming the hostage meme.

SEVENTEEN

PEER REVIEW

Donald Trump had already made it through ten Republican debates, winging it like he did almost everything. The last thing he felt like doing now was preparing for number eleven. But just five days later, winner-take-all primaries in Florida and Ohio could finally seal the deal for him. So Donald's campaign manager, Corey Lewandowski, had been pushing me to offer some pointers—not to change Donald's freewheeling performance style, but maybe just to focus him a little.

The day after Super Tuesday, I had what I thought was a clever idea. "I've never seen your golf course down here," I said to Donald. "Let's go have lunch at the golf club." He agreed immediately. Once the Secret Service agents drove us to the Trump International Golf Club in West Palm Beach, I figured, I could feed him my tried-and-true debate tips.

When we walked into the club, there was a large room on our right where a few dozen women were playing cards. We waved to them, and about two dozen came sprinting over, asking for pictures with the two of us. We accommodated all of them. As we walked away, Donald shook his head and said to me, "I've been coming in here for years with a hit TV show, and none of them would get out of their chairs. Now that I'm in politics, they all come running. This business of yours is too much."

Funny, he still saw it as *my* business.

We had lunch in the clubhouse, then Donald suggested we take a golf cart ride, just the two of us. I figured that would be the perfect opportunity for some uninterrupted and casual debate prep. As he drove to one hole and then another, with agents trailing us in their own golf carts, I began to talk with him about health care policy, trying to give him a more nuanced answer to the question, "What should replace Obamacare?" All he'd been saying in the debates so far was, "Obamacare is a disaster, and we're going to blow it up on day one." Which was fine. But there was an obvious follow-up: What should come next? Donald didn't yet have a clear answer. He had given the question some thought, but not enough to answer it crisply.

I tossed out a couple of concepts, and he listened—or pretended to. But by the time we reached the third hole, his mind was obviously somewhere else.

"Your kids are amazing," he said to me. "They're so well mannered. They're so together. How did you do it?"

Five minutes of debate prep was enough for him. Now he wanted to talk about fatherhood. That was Donald.

"I didn't do it by myself," I told him. "It was me and Mary Pat. And I think we got lucky, too."

"I got divorced, and it made things much harder," he said. "But I really tried to be there for my kids. I tried to be present in all their lives."

Here he was, on the verge of nailing down the Republican nomination for president, facing another grilling from the media and his increasingly desperate opponents. He had a personal debate tutor in the golf cart beside him. And all he wanted to talk about was fatherhood.

"I am always asking myself," he said, "am I doing the right things with them in the business? Am I giving them the right responsibilities so they can be successful? You don't have this problem, because you don't do business with your children. But I have to evaluate, as objectively as I can, each one of their strengths and weaknesses so I can put them in the right places. I want them to be successful for the business and successful for themselves."

This had all gotten more complicated, he explained. Now that he was running for president, he was busy with that. He had less time to focus on his business. And his children were also taking on new roles. It was, I thought, a fascinating glimpse into a side of Donald Trump that few people ever saw. It was also striking how objective he could be about his own life and family. The way he analyzed the situation, it was like he was on the outside looking in.

"This is getting real now," he said of his long shot campaign. "I might be president. What am I going to do? I've been the one who determined what my kids were doing and how they were doing it. I've tried to set an example for them. And I'm not going to have the time to do that anymore. What's going to happen if I'm not there?"

Off the top of my head, I didn't have any easy answers for him. But I loved the fact that he was thinking about all that. "Those are important questions," I told him. "Just the fact that you're asking them is good. You are getting ready to win."

We drove around to nine or ten holes having this conversation, leaving health care arguments in the rough somewhere.

He was starting to realize there was a genuine possibility that he would be president. He wasn't worried so much about whether he had what it took. He was confident about that. His concern was far more personal. What would it do to his family? If he was president, Donald knew he could not be the dominant daily influence in their lives that he was in New York. To him, that was far more important than a debate with Ted, John, and Marco at the University of Miami.

——

March 8, 2016, was my thirtieth wedding anniversary. Mary Pat and I had been hoping to get away somewhere, just the two of us. But things had been busy at home and on the campaign trail, and we really hadn't planned anything. As the day approached and Donald heard it was our anniversary, he insisted we both come down and celebrate at Mar-a-Lago.

I assumed I would live to regret this. What would begin as a well-intentioned gesture on Donald's part would morph inevitably into another "workcation," and I'd be explaining to Mary Pat why I kept getting dragged away from our romantic anniversary trip to Palm Beach.

"I'll give you the suite, I'll leave you alone—I promise," Donald said. "Come on down." We headed down for a three-day stay.

The second morning we were there, I got an early call from Donald. He explained that his son-in-law, Jared, was bringing a couple of guys down to Florida to work on debate prep, and Donald had agreed to sit with them for an hour. "Please come and do this with me," he said.

I asked if he really needed me. I reminded him it was my anniversary. I warned him I was in a T-shirt and gym shorts. He dismissed all of those objections and said: "Come in fifteen minutes."

I looked at Mary Pat. She nodded, and I said, "Okay."

When I walked into the meeting room, it was, as well as I can recall, my first face-to-face meeting with Jared Kushner. It had been eight years since I headed the office that sent his father, Charles, to prison. Jared and I shook hands. With him was Rich Zeoli, a talented political operative I knew from New Jersey who Jared said would be leading the debate prep. Rich had set a four-inch binder in front of Donald's chair.

"What is that?" I asked Rich.

He replied that it was Donald's debate-preparation materials.

"That's about to become the most extensively researched coaster at Mar-a-Lago," I said.

Right then Donald walked in and immediately asked for a waitress. He ordered pancakes and bacon, then added an order of bacon for me even though I hadn't asked for any. The waitress also brought him a glass of freshly squeezed orange juice.

Where did he put that glass? Right on top of that four-inch binder.

———

There was never any doubt on the Trump campaign who was in charge. Donald was.

That was clear from the moment I arrived as his first major endorser, and it would never stop being true. Donald told Hope Hicks and Dan Scavino what to tweet in the morning. With his fat, black Sharpie, Donald edited every press release that went out. He was the one deciding which slogans he wanted the crowds to chant at which campaign rallies. *Who's gonna pay for the wall? MEX-ico!*

Though Donald talked on the phone all day with old friends, new friends, New York business cronies, club members, and Fox News hosts—seeking opinions, trading stories, testing ideas—he always made the decisions himself. He was his own strategist, his own producer, his own spokesman, his own pollster, his own personnel manager, his own counterpuncher, and his own judge of how well things had turned out. "Amazing!" "Huge!" "So much better than Obama!" He had people assigned to all the usual positions. But whatever their titles said, they were all in support roles.

Corey, Hope, Dan, and the other aides—many of them were young enough to be his children. They were great, but they were hardly his peers. The family was the family. And he wasn't about to listen to outside consultants. What did they know, with their binders and their lesson plans? Hadn't most of them spent the past year and a half predicting he would never get this far? When he did get advice from people, he often found himself reluctant to follow it. Once Donald had his mind made up, he found it almost impossible to change.

This lack of peers was a problem for him, a problem I think even he was beginning to recognize. As he had demonstrated in the golf cart, he needed someone from the world of politics he could talk to. Really talk to. I was happy to help fill the void.

I was older and more experienced than even his most-senior staffers. I'd been around politics and government and law enforcement my entire adult life. I was the governor of New Jersey. I'd been US Attorney. And more important, he and I had a fifteen-year relationship. We'd spent a lot of social time together. I felt close to Melania. I could tell him things that most people couldn't. I could tease him in ways the staffers wouldn't dare. I could contradict or disagree, and he wouldn't blow up at me or freeze me out. I could tell him what I was thinking for real.

So as the campaign continued, being his peer was a key part of the role that I played.

———

The March 10 debate in Miami went well, even though Donald didn't trot out too many specifics on what might replace Obamacare. Primary night, March 15, went even better. As the results trickled in, I got a knock at my door at Mar-a-Lago. It was Hope and Corey. "We're winning Florida by double digits," Corey said. "Maybe twenty points. It's a huge, smashing victory."

That sealed it as far as I was concerned. It was finally time for the Republican establishment to get behind the clear front-runner and inevitable nominee. I picked up the phone and called my old friend Haley Barbour. The former governor of Mississippi and a well-wired Washington insider personified a large part of the Republican establishment. "Trump's going to win big tonight," I told him. "We've got to start bringing people around. People have to come to grips with the fact that Trump's going to be the nominee."

Haley didn't argue with my analysis. But like many, many other prominent Republicans, he wasn't offering to join me, either. "I have nothing against the guy," he said, "but I'm not ready yet." We'd had better luck with Maine governor Paul LePage, who'd endorsed Trump just hours after I did. We'd gotten our first US senator when Alabama's Jeff Sessions came aboard. Sessions wasn't a Washington powerhouse. But he was a genuine United States senator and a legitimate conservative. I didn't know Jeff, but he seemed like a cordial, nice guy. Given Trump's intense New York pedigree, Sessions's being from the Deep South was an added bonus.

Sessions brought along an intense young man who became an integral part of the Trump team. I first met Stephen Miller, who had been Sessions's communications director, on Trump Force One. Amid the banter of the campaign plane, Stephen could seem studious and quiet. But he was obviously bright, and he had strongly conservative views on immigration and government regulation. His stated job was issues director, but he quickly took on the role of speechwriter. His language was sharp and direct, and Donald seemed to like the muscular words that Stephen was crafting for him.

There were times when Donald wanted to say things that even Stephen considered over the top. In one of those moments, Stephen sought me out as an ally. "He listens to you," the younger man said as I boarded the plane one morning. "Please, see if you can get this section out of the speech." I went and sat down with Donald and explained why I didn't think we needed the section Stephen was worried about. After some cajoling, Donald came around and crossed it out with his black Sharpie. Stephen looked at me with the slightest of sly smiles. *Thanks*, his smile seemed to say. *Crisis avoided.* From the beginning, some people tried to demonize Stephen. To be sure, he and I didn't agree on every issue. But vilifying him was unfair, I thought. He was doing his best to provide the language that would help the candidate deliver a message. I couldn't help but like Stephen.

I kept trying to bring more and bigger people under the Trump tent, but I was still facing resistance, especially for a candidate who was doing so well. Politicians like backing winners. Losers can't deliver anything. I suspected most of them would eventually come around. But for now, it hardly seemed to matter that Trump won four of the five March 15 primaries. The only place he came in second was John Kasich's home state of Ohio.

I was getting my share of pushback. Meg Whitman, my own former national finance chair, had sent around a scathing statement calling my endorsement "an astonishing display of political opportunism. . . . Donald Trump is unfit to be president." The papers in New Jersey wouldn't let the subject drop. The *New Hampshire Union Leader* went so far as to retract the paper's big endorsement of me, though I didn't quite understand the point of that.

All this did hurt my standing inside New Jersey. My polls slipped even more. But I was taking what I considered to be the long view, which was that Donald Trump was going to be president, I could help him, and he needed me. The fact that I stood with him early would be good for me and good for my state. If he won, I'd have influence that other people didn't. I had confidence in my own political judgment. This was a practical decision by me. An election is a binary choice, and I did not want Hillary Clinton to be president.

———

At the very end of March, another grown-up arrived. At sixty-eight, Paul Manafort had certainly been around. A lawyer, lobbyist, and veteran political operative, he had advised the presidential campaigns of Gerald Ford, Ronald Reagan, George H. W. Bush, and Bob Dole. After that, he cofounded the Washington lobbying firm of Black, Manafort, and Stone along with the veteran capital insiders Charles Black and Roger Stone. It wasn't clear exactly what Manafort had been up to in recent years—a lot of international work is what I had heard. I had picked up the rumblings of some shady business, but I assumed he had explained it all to Donald. I obviously assumed too much.

Paul had an apartment in Trump Tower and had supposedly wandered into Donald's office one day and offered to work for free. The release the campaign put out said he was "volunteering his considerable insight and expertise because of his belief that Mr. Trump is the right person for these difficult times." I'd met enough Washington lobbyists to know there had to be more to it than that.

As the campaign's new convention manager, Paul would be in charge of corralling Trump delegates to the Republican National Convention, which was set for July 18–21 in Cleveland. We were on track to win a large share of delegates. But given the party's complex rules and the persistence of the Never Trumpers, who knew what mischief someone might try to cause?

Paul and I didn't click instantly. He saw me as a Corey guy, and Paul was clearly gunning for Corey. It looked to me like he and Corey were headed for a showdown. I kept hearing that the family had played some role in bringing Paul in, which probably gave him a leg up in any fight with Corey. All I knew was that when I traveled with Donald during that period, he was constantly praising Paul.

"See how smart he is?" Donald said to me more than once. "Look how he's managing the delegate situation." He believed that Manafort had the secret sauce for turning votes into convention delegates.

He did need someone who could watch his back with the party officials at the convention. But I got hints from the beginning that Paul might not be up to the job. He wasn't familiar with any of the latest campaign software. He conducted himself inconsistently on TV. Most of his contacts were people from bygone eras. At the presidential level, the game had passed him by.

One morning, when I was coming in for a ten a.m. meeting with Donald, Paul asked if he could meet with me beforehand to discuss transition issues. I arrived an hour early. Paul and I slipped into a conference room down the hall from Donald's office, just the two of us.

Paul literally fell asleep during the meeting. I was in midsentence, and I heard a snore. And then another one. He wasn't just dozing. He was *out*. I stopped talking. For a moment, I just looked at him. Then I banged the table hard—*bang, bang, bang*—three times.

"Governor," he sputtered.

"Paul," I said. "Go back to your apartment and get some sleep before the next meeting. Because if you fall asleep in a meeting with the principal, that's going to hurt you."

━━

I kept up my efforts to bring new people in. A couple of weeks before the May 3 Indiana primary, I got a call from Mike Pence, who was the governor of Indiana. I knew Mike from the Republican Governors Association. I had campaigned and raised money for him three times in 2012, including one date I still remember, September 15.

"It's Mary Pat's forty-ninth birthday," I told Mike when he asked if I could come out that day. "I really can't."

"Chris, please," he said. "This donor says he'll raise a huge amount of money if you're here. Please."

I went to Mary Pat: "Do you mind . . . ?" She said, "Go ahead. We'll celebrate the night before or the night after."

The fund-raiser went great. Mike raised a ton of money. Before I returned home to New Jersey, Mike's wife, Karen, gave me a beautifully wrapped present for Mary Pat.

But now, nearly four years later, Mike had a different request. "I've never met Trump," he said to me. "I'm trying to figure out who I want to endorse in this primary. Any chance that you could introduce me to Trump?"

I told him I would try to set something up.

I spoke to Donald. "The guy's looking for a horse," I said. "Why don't we fly out there and see him?"

Donald agreed immediately. We got on Trump Force One and flew to Indianapolis. We went to the governor's residence on North Meridian Street, where Mike and Karen were waiting for us. Mike and Donald had a nice though slightly stiff, very serious conversation, which Mike led, about the state of the country. They traded all the familiar platitudes. There weren't many flashes of personality or much joviality between them. It was very business-like. When it was time to leave, Donald and I both stood. "Well, there are things we have to do back at home," he said.

"Before you go," Mike said to Donald, "do you think we could just join hands and say a prayer?"

I looked at Donald. Donald looked at me. I had done this with Mike before, but I knew it was new to Donald. Karen, Donald, and I joined hands with Mike as he said a short prayer, asking God to protect the nation and to keep our travels safe.

"Does he do that all the time?" Donald asked as we walked out of the governor's residence.

"Yeah," I said. "I've been in a lot of meetings with him. He likes to end with a prayer."

Donald gave a one-word answer. I wasn't quite sure how to take it at the time.

"Interesting," he said.

Then we rode to the airport for the plane ride home.

The Friday before the Indiana primary, I was guest-hosting the *Boomer and Carton* show on sports radio WFAN in New York City when my phone started buzzing. First it was Corey. Then it was Donald. Then it was Donald again. As soon as I got off the air, I called Corey.

"Pence is endorsing Cruz," he said, even before *hello*. "Did you know this was going to happen?"

"No," I said. "I got no heads-up at all."

"He's really hot," Corey said, meaning Donald. "He's really angry. Then I heard Donald's voice in the background: "Is that Chris on the phone?" He grabbed the phone.

"Are you kidding me?" he said. "You take me out to see this guy and then the guy screws me? He stabs me in the back by endorsing Cruz? And how come he didn't give you any heads-up?"

"I don't know," I said. "Let me look into it. I'm sorry about this. I don't know."

I called Pence's cell phone. The call went straight to voicemail. A few minutes later, I got a call from Nick Ayers, a Republican campaign strategist I'd known from his days as executive director of the Republican Governors Association when I was chairman. He was working on Pence's 2016 reelection campaign.

"It's a very hard decision for Mike," Nick said, "but he did what he thought was right. He has nothing against Trump."

"How about picking up the phone and giving me a heads-up before you're going to do it?"

"I don't know why he didn't do that," Nick said. "I'm really sorry, but that's just kind of the way it is."

"Let me ask you a question. Are you telling me that Mike has staffed out this conversation? I mean, I love you, Nick. We're close, but he's staffing out this conversation? Tell him that's not good enough. I need to hear from him directly."

"I understand," Nick said.

Later that day, I got a call from Mike Pence.

"Mike," I said, "you endorsed Ted."

He started to say how tough a decision it was, but I cut him off. "You endorsed Ted. That's your business. But I'm the guy who brought Trump to you. Couldn't you at least pick up the phone and give me a heads-up so the guy hears it from me instead of on the news?"

He hemmed and hawed but had no real explanation. I had no idea at the time that Mike Pence would play any future role in the political life of Donald Trump. I'm pretty sure neither Donald nor Pence had any idea, either. But when Donald finally read the actual endorsement statement, he calmed down a bit. On his way to backing Cruz, Pence had said a lot of nice things about Donald. Trump, he said, "has given voice to the frustration of millions of working Americans with a lack of progress in Washington, DC. . . . I'm also particularly grateful that Donald Trump has taken a strong stance for Hoosier jobs."

"His endorsement of Cruz sounded like an endorsement of me," Donald said to me, shaking his head at Pence's language. "It's one of the nicest endorsements I've gotten, and he wasn't even endorsing me."

Pence had skillfully threaded the needle. Donald ended up winning Indiana.

No harm, no foul.

EIGHTEEN

JARED'S MELTDOWN

On the morning of April 20, 2016, an article in the *New York Times* caught my eye.

The piece described a new federal law designed to smooth the transition between outgoing and incoming presidents. The idea was a noble one: to make sure that whoever was elected in November would be ready to govern starting January 20, Inauguration Day.

Putting together a new government was such a mammoth undertaking, everyone agreed, it required serious planning and coordination starting many months prior to Election Day—long before anyone could say who was going to win. A nonpartisan organization called the Center for Presidential Transition had already begun the process for this election cycle, summoning representatives of Hillary Clinton, Bernie Sanders, John Kasich, Ted Cruz, and Donald Trump, the five presidential candidates whose campaigns still had a heartbeat. The Trump campaign, I learned from the story, was represented at the meeting by Michael

Glassner. I knew him to be a perfectly able political operative but not someone you'd put in charge of creating an entire government.

That afternoon, I got a call from Corey Lewandowski. "We're going to have to take this transition process seriously. Is there any way you'd be willing to chair the transition?"

Before I could answer, there was something I needed to know. "Is this coming from you or from Donald?"

"Both," Corey said.

"Well, let me think about it. I'll get back to you."

The more I thought about it, the more I liked the idea. I could help to organize a government for Donald. I was halfway through my second term as governor. I'd done transition for myself, in the governor's and US attorney's offices, so I knew the basics. Plus, I figured this would get me off Donald's campaign trail, out of the day-to-day politics and into the substance of the governing. I might really enjoy this.

I called Corey back: "If he wants me, I'd be willing to do it."

"I'll have him call you," Corey said.

Trump phoned that afternoon, reaching me at the governor's office in Trenton. "Corey says you're willing to do this transition thing," Trump said, sounding like a man who had been told to eat his vegetables. "I hate the transition stuff. It's bad karma to be talking about a transition, very bad karma. Mitt Romney wasted his time on a transition and forgot to win first."

"Bad karma," I said, tossing his words back at him. "But it's the law."

"Here's the thing," he said. "If you take this, I don't want it to preclude you from being considered for vice president or a member of the cabinet."

"Well," I said, "that's completely up to you. Nothing would legally preclude me from any of that."

"As long as that's the case, then why don't you and Corey work out the details, and we'll announce it."

"Great," I said.

Corey and I got on the phone again on May 5. "We're ready to do it," he said. "We'll launch the transition with an announcement next week. Can you come in tomorrow morning"—to Trump Tower—"see Donald yourself, and sign off on the press release? Then we'll be ready to go."

All fine by me, I said.

The next morning, I headed into the city to see Donald, to button down the announcement details, and to dive into this important new responsibility. No one had to tell me how huge a job it was. An almost-incomprehensible amount of work was waiting for me. Priorities to establish. Executive orders to draft. A whole cabinet to fill, and God only knows how many subcabinet and staff positions. Potential candidates to vet for all of them. And all of it could easily be for naught.

The polls showed that Hillary Clinton was handily ahead of Donald Trump. Even if we created the greatest transition in the history of transitions, it would be little more than a theoretical exercise if Donald didn't win. But I was all in. I would damn well make sure that he had everything he would need to start governing this country of ours.

———

Donald's office was always frantic and his door always open. People were constantly coming in and out. He would call out for his executive assistant, Rhona Graff, to get someone on the telephone or ask another assistant for a Diet Coke. Shovels from construction ground-breakings sat in one corner. Plaques and mementos hung everywhere. Endless stacks of papers. And on the desk, the couch, and almost every other flat surface—except for the executive chair Donald sat in and chairs for visitors directly in front of the desk—were magazine covers featuring Donald Trump, his favorite being the one of him on the cover of *Playboy* magazine (March 1990).

The views stretch down Fifth Avenue and up to Central Park. There is absolutely not one scintilla of doubt whose office this is.

By this point in the presidential campaign, I'd become a semipermanent fixture on the twenty-sixth floor. The Secret Service agents didn't bother me anymore. Everybody knew who I was. I didn't have to check in with Rhona or anyone else. On this particular morning, I walked past the receptionist—"Hello." I nodded good morning to everyone, and I breezed in.

"Hi, Chris—what's up today?" Donald said without looking up as I dropped into one of the chairs in front of his desk.

"I'm doing the transition stuff," I said.

"Oh, come on," he said with a sigh, finally glancing up at me and scrunching his face a little. "I hate that stuff. It's bad karma, Chris. You know that."

I just smiled. It didn't surprise me that he'd be back to that again. A thought once lodged in Donald's head never leaves until it's good and ready to go.

"I know, Donald," I assured him. "But you gotta do it."

"I know, I know," he admitted. "Let's get Corey in here, and let's finish this up."

He called to Rhona, who summoned the campaign manager. Half a minute later, Corey walked in. He handed me a draft of a press release announcing my appointment as chairman of Donald Trump's presidential transition team.

"Is this okay with you, Governor?" Corey asked as he sat in the chair next to mine.

I gave the release a quick glance. "Looks fine to me," I said. Then Corey handed the paper to Donald, who picked up a black Sharpie, made a couple of minor edits, and handed the sheet back to me. "I'm really happy you are doing this for me," he said. "And I think it's going to be good for you, too."

"Yeah," I answered cheerfully. "I think it will be good for both of us."

The meeting was over. Our business was finished. Or so I thought. Actually, the meeting had hardly begun.

Just as Corey and I prepared to stand, I heard a voice from behind. It was a soft voice coming from just inside the open office door.

"Good morning, everyone," the voice said.

As Corey and I both turned around, there stood Jared Kushner, Donald's thirty-five-year-old son-in-law and close campaign adviser. Since our handshake at Mar-a-Lago, Jared and I had spoken once or twice at Trump Tower. We didn't really know each other well by then, despite both of us being close to Donald and both of us working on the campaign. But given the role I had played more than a decade earlier as the prosecutor of his father, of course there was an added something between us.

"Governor, how are you?" Jared said.

"Good, Jared," I responded.

The two of us shook hands. He sat in a third chair in front of the desk. Looking at Donald, he asked, as if no one had told him: "So what are we doing here?"

"Great news," Donald said. "The governor has agreed to run the transition, and we're so lucky to have him. He's so smart. He's so good. This is going to be great for us, and then I don't have to worry about any of that. Chris will handle everything."

Jared's face remained stubbornly blank. But he filled in the picture soon enough. "I don't think we need to rush on this," he said. "I don't think we have to do this now. Let's take our time on this one."

That's when Corey jumped in. "Actually, Jared," he said, "we're already late on this. The law requires us to designate someone. Right now, we've had Michael Glassner. Michael shouldn't be in a role like that. We need to get somebody with the governor's experience. The person has to meet at the White House with the Obama people. We need somebody who can handle all that. The governor's the right guy."

Jared clearly wasn't sold.

"I think we're rushing on this," he said. "Donald, I'd like you to hold back and give us some time to talk about it. There are a lot of things to discuss about this."

I'd been around politics long enough to grasp what was happening. Jared was trying—and not so subtly—to derail my appointment as transition chairman. The issue wasn't the rushing. The issue was the guy. Donald didn't sound as convinced as Jared did.

"Jared," he said, "why do I have to wait on this? Chris is great. He's been my friend forever. He ran for president. He's a governor. Why would we have to wait on this? It's going to be a great announcement for him and a great announcement for us."

Jared let a beat pass before he spoke up. But when he started talking, he sounded like a person who'd been holding poison inside himself for a very long time. "You really want to know why?" Jared asked.

"Yeah," Trump said.

"Because I don't trust him to have this, and you know why I don't trust him to have it."

——

Corey and I hadn't said much since Jared arrived. But I looked at him, and he looked at me. Then Corey looked at Donald. "Do you want me to step out?" Corey asked.

"No," Trump shot back. "You stay right there."

And Jared began to detail his ancient grievances against me. "He tried to destroy my father," Jared said.

"There was a dispute inside the family," Jared reminded Donald, severely underplaying the sordid details of the felony indictment of Charles Kushner and subsequent guilty plea and imprisonment. In Jared's version of the tale, his uncle's lawyer brought the matter to me, and I collected damaging evidence from members of the family who already hated his father. He implied I had acted unethically and inappropriately but didn't state one fact to back that up. Just a lot of feelings—very raw feelings that had been simmering for nearly a dozen years. Those feelings were now, finally, coming to a boil in front of the man who had brought all this heat on the Kushner family—me.

"My father made those people rich, and they did nothing," Jared said. "They just benefitted from my father's hard work. And those are the people who turned him in."

As Jared spoke, he never raised his voice. But some strong emotions are not dependent on volume. Jared delivered his in a soft quiver. As he continued, his voice began to crack.

"It wasn't fair," he said.

He said I had worked with a bookkeeper who'd stolen private information. He said that once I got involved in the case, I said false things about his father and, after the guilty plea, I made his father stay in prison longer than he was supposed to. He had it down to the exact number of additional days, according to his story, that I made his father stay in jail. Jared said I did all this because I was vindictive and ambitious and untrustworthy.

"You don't know what it was like for me," Jared said to Donald. "Almost every weekend, I flew to Alabama to visit him. He didn't deserve to be there." All these years later, Jared still carried a wallet that his father made for him in a prison workshop.

"This was a family matter," Jared said, "a matter to be handled by the family or by the rabbis"—not by a hard-charging federal prosecutor.

Jared glanced at me, then fixed his gaze on his father-in-law, Donald. "How can he be trusted to handle the transition?"

As Jared plowed through this litany, I didn't dignify his decade-old rantings with a response of any kind. I just didn't speak. Not to correct his version of the record. Not to add crucial details. I didn't say a word. I looked right at him. I kept thinking to myself, *What is this?*—and shooting perplexed looks at Corey and across the desk at Donald. *How long are we going to let this go on?*

Finally, Donald spoke up.

"Jared," he said. "Listen to me. Chris was just doing his job. What do you expect? The people you should be really angry with are your own family who gave all this information to Chris. Once they gave the information to Chris, what was he supposed to do with it? Ignore it? He couldn't ignore it. He had to do it."

Jared wasn't having it.

"You don't understand all the circumstances," he said, the emotion in his voice rising, though the volume did not. "He didn't have to do what he did. He chose to do it. This is wrong. You don't want to be associated with him."

Donald pushed back again. "Jared, if you were in Chris's position, you would have done exactly the same thing. It was a big case against a famous person who had done something wrong, and he did what he had to do. You're a lawyer. You would have done exactly what Chris did if you would have had that job."

Trump stopped there for a moment, letting his words sink in. Then he said one more thing that I didn't expect to hear: "And your other problem was you didn't know me at the time. Maybe if you would have known me, maybe I could have helped."

I wasn't entirely sure what Donald meant by that. But as I sat there and soaked it all in, the thoughts in my head had more to do with Donald than with Jared.

Okay, we're going to find out right now. Is Trump going to defend me and do the right thing? Or is he going to side with Jared and his ancient grudge?

I knew this was a crucial test for what this new phase of our relationship was going to be.

Donald continued to defend me. Corey and I were really just bystanders to the conversation. Jared and Donald did all of the talking, and Donald was hanging tough for now.

"I think you're wrong about this," Jared said finally. "I'm not saying I couldn't agree to him chairing the transition. I'm just saying I want you to wait."

Corey took that as his signal. "Jared," he said, "we don't have time to wait. We have to make a decision. We have to designate someone. We're already past the time the campaign is supposed to do that."

"Here's an idea," Trump said. "We should be able to resolve this. How 'bout if the four of us go out to dinner?"

That came out of nowhere for me. But it was classic Trump. Hammer it out over dinner. And who exactly would be there?

Donald laid it out. "Me and Chris, you and your dad. What if we all go out to dinner and just try to resolve this?"

I have to say I breathed a small sigh of relief when Jared refused to bite on Donald's deal. I could hardly imagine a tenser gathering. "I don't think there's any way that my father is ready to have dinner with the governor," Jared said.

"Are you sure?" Trump asked. "Maybe you want to talk to him about that first."

"No chance, not now," Jared insisted.

With that idea off the table, Donald leaned back in his large leather chair. "Chris," he said to me, "do you have anything to say here?"

"Just this," I answered. "This is your decision, Donald. Whatever you want to do. I didn't ask for this job. You guys approached me."

Then, I turned to Jared, feeling like I should probably say something to him. The whole thing was just too surreal.

"You and I are both burdened with things that are difficult for the other person to understand," I said to him. "You're burdened with a love for your father that I can't possibly understand, because he's not my father. And I'm burdened with facts about your father that even you don't know, that I can never tell you, because if I did I would break the law." Then I turned away from Jared and looked back at Donald.

"I've made my decision," Donald said. "Jared, I know you're not happy about it, but Chris is the chairman of the transition. Corey, put out the press release."

Jared looked at Donald. "Fine," he said. "I understand." Donald looked back at him. Then Jared turned toward me.

"Good to see you, Governor," he said before getting up and walking out of the room.

After Jared walked out and Corey also left, I lingered behind to talk alone with Donald. I was pissed. Pissed that Jared would dare to lecture me for doing my job as US Attorney—holding his father responsible for the crimes he admitted he had done. Pissed that I'd been set up like this.

After such a bizarre confrontation I felt like I needed a moment alone with Donald to clarify the lines of authority here. I could tell he was itching to leave the office. He had a meeting with Sheldon Adelson, the Las Vegas casino magnate and influential Republican donor. "I've got to get out of here," he said when he noticed I wasn't leaving too.

I shut the door and walked around to the side of the desk. He was still sitting. I stood.

"I don't need this job," I said. "I didn't ask for this job. But I need to know right now who I'm answering to. Because if I'm answering to you, I'll do the job. If I'm answering to Jared after what he just did, I don't want the job. You can see how he feels about me."

"Absolutely not," Donald said. "You answer to one person and one person only. That person is me. And that's the way it will always be."

That was the assurance I wanted. "Okay, then," I said. "I'll do it."

Donald said thank you, shook my hand, and added just before I turned toward the door: "If there's ever a problem with that, you let me know."

I promised I would.

As I rode the elevator down to the lobby, I had two thoughts. I was impressed with how firmly Donald had stuck up for me. I definitely felt good about that. It gave me confidence that I would actually be permitted to do this job. In addition, I no longer had to speculate about Jared's lingering resentment. It was all out in the open now. Jared was still deeply upset about his father's prosecution and imprisonment. As he'd made clear, his father was still upset, too.

Whatever was said from that point forward, I knew I couldn't afford to overlook one fact: I had an enemy here who would still be gunning for me.

———

I hit the Midtown sidewalk by 11 a.m. At 5:41 p.m., a story popped up on the website of the *New York Times*. The piece was obviously a leak from Jared, attempting to undercut Donald's big decision and me. "Trump Asks Son-in-Law, Jared Kushner, to Plan for Transition Team," the headline read.

Really? Jared is planning the transition? Where the hell did that come from? Hadn't Donald just decreed precisely the opposite, handing that assignment to me?

Citing "a senior adviser" to Trump—*Hi, Team Jared!*—the *Times* reporter Ashley Parker did her source's bidding right in the lede: "Donald J. Trump has asked his son-in-law, Jared Kushner, to begin quietly working to put together a blueprint for a transition team should he win the White House in November."

It was as if our meeting that very morning had never even occurred. And in case there was any doubt about who was behind the story, the *Times* reporter went on at some length about the "close relationship" between Donald Trump and his "very successful" son-in-law, who is "very good at politics." The two are "often in contact, talking informally about the campaign," the writer oozed, even noting that Jared, aided by the *New York Observer* editor Ken Kurson, "wrote a closely watched speech Mr. Trump delivered to the American Israel Public Affairs Committee in March."

This wasn't journalism. This was stenography.

Jared's little game didn't scuttle the official announcement. That Monday morning, just as planned, the campaign put out the press release exactly as Donald had edited it, quoting him as saying: "Governor Christie is an extremely knowledgeable and loyal person with the tools and resources to put together an unparalleled transition team, one that will be prepared to take over the White House when we win in November."

I did get an odd call the next day, one of many I would receive in the coming months.

It was Jared, asking if I could stop in to see him. I told him sure. I didn't know exactly what he wanted to add to our showdown with Donald. But I didn't see any purpose in ducking him. I was perfectly satisfied with how I had handled our encounter. I liked where Donald had come down. The official announcement had discredited the leaked story in the *Times*.

Jared couldn't have been more pleasant when I stopped into his office.

"You and I should put all this behind us, Governor," he said as soon as I sat down. "It's all in the past as far as I am concerned. We have to do what is best for the campaign. We have to work together here. The most important thing is that Donald Trump is elected president."

Now all he had to do was prove his intentions through his actions.

Things didn't quite turn out that way.

NINETEEN

SELF-INFLICTED

Like most of us, Donald Trump hates to be criticized, only more so. But of all the attacks he has weathered over the years, few got under his skin quite like the ones surrounding Trump University.

The issue had been around a while, and Mitt Romney had happily piled on, calling the Republican front-runner "a phony" and "a fraud" and cracking: "His promises are as worthless as a degree from Trump University."

Donald countered that the vast majority of Trump University students rated the curriculum favorably and said he wasn't worried about a class-action suit making its way through federal court in Southern California. "I could settle it right now for very little money. I don't want to do it out of principle." But it wasn't until May, when Hillary Clinton gave the issue fresh oxygen in a TV ad buy, that Donald really exploded.

"I have a judge who is a hater of Donald Trump," he roared at a rally in San Diego on May 27. "His name is Gonzalo Curiel." At the rally and on Twitter, Trump said Judge Curiel "happens to be, we believe, Mexican" and had been "very hostile" because of Trump's support of a wall at the US–Mexico border.

This was unfortunate on several counts. For one thing, Judge Curiel had been born in East Chicago—not Mexico—had earned his law degree at Indiana University, and once ran the narcotics-enforcement division at the US attorney's office in San Diego, prosecuting alleged drug smugglers. The issue played terribly with Latino voters. It gave new life to the complaints about Trump's real estate school. And most glaring of all, Judge Curiel had ruled in Trump's favor more often than not, even agreeing to delay the trial until after the 2016 election.

Several times, I pleaded with Donald to drop the judge talk. "This makes no sense," I said. "You're not going to win anybody over."

I got exactly nowhere with him.

He was upset about the lawsuit. He was upset about the media coverage. He kept spouting off. Finally, I got a call from Corey Lewandowski. "I really need you to speak to him," Corey said. "Try and convince him to put a statement out and end this Judge Curiel stuff."

I told Corey I'd already tried, several times. "He is not responding very well. I don't know what you want me to do."

"Think of something," Corey urged, "because we're dying here. We do not want to be talking about Judge Curiel."

"I hear you," I said noncommittally. Then Corey brought in reinforcements. I got a call from Ivanka. "Governor," she said, "will you please come up to New York and help me write a statement that we can convince my father to put out?"

I told Ivanka I'd try again if she would join me in leaning on her dad. "Maybe together we can get him to listen," I said.

As soon I got to Trump Tower, I huddled with Ivanka. Together, she and I drafted a written statement for her father to release. It made two basic points: that he was sorry if anybody took offense at things he'd said about Judge Curiel and that he wouldn't be talking about Trump University anymore. The matter was in the hands of his lawyers. That is where it would be resolved.

This was Politics 101, a standard, damage-control press release, the obvious way to quiet a controversy that had dragged on too long. Two or three paragraphs, really tight. Ivanka and I were both happy with the approach. Together, we walked into Donald's office on the twenty-sixth floor and made our pitch. "This issue is hurting you," Ivanka said as soon as she and I sat down. "There's no upside," I added. "Just put out a statement and end it."

He resisted at first. "I don't want to put out any statement," he said. "I'm right about this."

I kept pushing. Ivanka pushed, too. We said it didn't matter if he was right or wrong. What mattered was that the issue was damaging him. Finally he seemed to soften. "Okay," he said, "let me look at the statement."

Ivanka handed him the paper. He picked up his fat, black Sharpie even before he'd read a line. There is no language Donald can't edit. Ivanka and I traded glances, wondering what was coming next.

He changed a couple of words in the two paragraphs we'd drafted. Then he drew an arrow from the front to the back of the page. I could see him writing furiously. "I'll put it out if we can do it this way," he said.

Actually, the edits weren't bad. He inserted a couple of paragraphs between the two we had drafted, defending the honor of Trump University. It was A rated by the Better Business Bureau.

The students received valuable information. The vast majority of them were satisfied.

I was asking myself, *Why do you want to add all that? No one is going to read it.* But before the words came out of my mouth, it struck me: *No one is going to read it, so why are you fighting with him about this?*

"You're right," I said. "Let's just put it out just like that."

"Are you sure, Governor?" Ivanka asked.

"I am," I said.

"Looks good to me," she said.

She walked the paper down to Corey, who passed it on to Hope Hicks. The statement went out June 7, and the story about the "unfair . . . Mexican" Judge Curiel finally faded away.

The only question I had was why we couldn't have done it a week earlier and saved us all a lot of grief.

———

I knew Mike Flynn was trouble from the first day I met him.

He looked great on paper. A retired lieutenant general who had spent thirty-three years in the US Army, he had dismantled insurgent networks in Iraq and Afghanistan and helped shape counterterrorism strategy around the world. In 2012, President Obama appointed him to direct the Defense Intelligence Agency, a highly sensitive position he'd held until his retirement in 2014. Flynn was the first general to endorse Donald Trump for president, which Donald certainly appreciated.

But whenever I saw Flynn in Donald's presence, he struck me as a dangerously loose cannon. At first it was just passing comments, views that sounded odd from a high-ranking military man—and which certainly wouldn't help the Trump campaign. That the Turkish strongman Recep Tayyip Erdoğan was someone the United States should cozy up to . . . *really*? That Russia's Vladimir Putin was a trustworthy ally . . . *really*? I wasn't sure where Flynn was getting this stuff, but I hated the prospect that he had sway over Donald Trump's foreign-policy views.

One day in June, I got a call at the transition office from James Clapper, the White House director of national intelligence. Clapper asked if I would help arrange a series of classified, multiagency intelligence briefings for the candidate, now that he was the presumptive Republican nominee. Hillary Clinton would be getting similar briefings, Clapper said, adding that Trump could bring no more than two people with him to the sessions. I told Clapper I would be happy to coordinate.

When I called Donald and asked when he would like his top-secret briefings, the first thing he said to me was: "Are you sure I'm cleared to get these?"

"You've been cleared by the members of the Republican Party who have decided to make you their presidential nominee," I answered. "That's your clearance process."

"All right then, I'm ready," he answered. "I want to bring you and Flynn."

I got General Flynn's cell phone number from someone at the campaign and left a message on his voicemail. The general didn't call back. His son, Michael G. Flynn, did. The son had to be one of the haughtiest young people I'd ever spoken to. "The general's schedule is very busy," he informed me, referring to his father as "the general." "We're going to have to see what days we can give you."

I couldn't let that pass. "I can't imagine that the general is busier than the candidate," I said to young Flynn, "and the candidate has already given me dates. The general has to work within these dates."

"I'll talk to the general," Junior said, committing to no more than that.

Somehow, the general was able to clear his schedule. And so, the three of us took a ride from Trump Tower to 26 Federal Plaza, the FBI headquarters in New York, to meet with top-level briefers from the FBI, CIA, the Defense Intelligence Agency, the National Security Agency, the Department of Homeland Security, and various other agencies.

As we were led through the office past the agents' desks, Donald was greeted like a conquering hero. Dozens of people stepped out of their carrels and came out of their offices to shake his hand and ask for pictures and autographs. This was definitely Trump country. He accommodated everyone.

We eventually made our way into the secure meeting room, known as a "sensitive compartmentalized information facility," or SCIF. Trump, Flynn, and I sat on one side of a long conference table. On the other side, fifteen briefers were waiting for us, each with a different geographical focus or subject expertise. I can't talk about the classified details of the briefing, but I can describe the atmosphere in the room. It was somber and formal.

The briefing began with a history of ISIS, how the terror network was founded and grew so rapidly. "Wait a second," Trump said, trying to lighten the mood with some humor at his own expense. "You mean Barack Obama didn't create ISIS?"

That claim had become a perennial at Trump campaign rallies. His critics descried it as a crazed falsehood. He saw it as vivid but truthful hyperbole, and the crowds always ate it up.

I don't believe anyone at the table cracked a smile.

"Fellas," Trump piped up, "I'm kidding. But I'm going to be very disappointed if I have to amend my stump speech now that I know this."

When that produced just a couple of nervous chuckles, he turned and whispered to me, "They're a barrel of laughs, aren't they?"

But that brief exchange was immediately overwhelmed by the bullheaded Michael Flynn. As the briefing began in earnest, Flynn kept interrupting the briefers. He lectured them. He challenged their intelligence.

"No, no, no," General Flynn kept interjecting. "That's ridiculous..." "Don't try to sell us that crap..." "Who told you that?"

There was hardly a comment he didn't amend, ridicule, debate, or contradict. Partly, he seemed to be showing off for Trump. Partly, he seemed to be settling scores with his old bureaucratic competitors. The more Flynn talked, the more he sounded like an ignorant blowhard.

In this setting especially, his behavior was highly adversarial and simply inappropriate.

Donald, of course, had relatively little foreign-policy experience compared with Flynn. But the questions he asked were on point and intelligent. I think the briefers walked away with a grudging respect for him. He was really good. Unfortunately, the briefing was dominated by the unguided missile, Michael Flynn.

Once we got back to Trump Tower and Donald and I were alone, I broached the subject of Flynn. It would be the first of many times.

"That performance was embarrassing," I said.

"He does talk too much," Donald conceded.

"It's more than just talking too much," I said. "It's what he's saying and how he's conducting himself. He and I were there to be staff to you, to provide support. Our job isn't to ask questions and show off. Our job is to take notes, talk to you afterward, and make sure you get the most out of the briefing. Figure out what was missing. Make sure you hear that next time. Help you get a briefing that's useful to you. This guy is settling scores on your time."

Donald wasn't convinced. "You just don't like him," he told me.

"It's not that I don't like him," I said. "It's that I don't think what he's doing is helpful to you."

"He was with me early," Trump said. "He's my first general. He's a smart guy. He's got a lot of experience."

"All of that may be true," I said. "But he's trouble for you."

Soon everyone at Trump Tower was talking about new palace intrigue, this time between Corey Lewandowski and Paul Manafort. Who would get fired? Who would survive? I had a sinking feeling on Corey's behalf.

I had no idea why Corey needed to be fired. I never thought he did. But that's how things often worked on the Trump campaign—for everyone but members of the family: One day you were in favor. Then you were not. No real explanation. No chance to explain or defend. Everyone could feel it happening and still not know why. There were theories. There were always theories. Corey was getting too much publicity, never good on this campaign. He was fighting with the shiny new penny, Manafort. The family didn't like his closeness to the candidate. Those were all suppositions. But they were the most educated guesses I had.

The ax began to fall on Corey in the second week of June, when I got a call from Jared Kushner. "I'd like your support in moving Corey out," Jared said.

I flatly refused.

"I think Corey needs to be supplemented," I told Jared that day. "We need to get some people around him who have run presidentials before, people who have experience that he doesn't have. But Corey's very important to the candidate's psyche. The candidate trusts him and likes him, and we need that."

Jared wasn't having any of it. "That's not the case anymore," he insisted. "Donald doesn't like some of the stuff he's been doing. Donald knows Corey's in over his head. I just need you to be supportive with Donald on this."

I didn't budge, and Jared didn't like it. But I wasn't able to back him down. He asked me about potential replacements. Ironically, given his later over-the-top anti-Trump commentary the campaign veteran Steve Schmidt even met with Team Trump as a potential replacement.

Monday morning, June 20, Hope put out a statement, which she gave first to the *New York Times*, saying that Corey "will no longer be working with the campaign." "The campaign is grateful to Corey for his hard work and dedication and we wish him the best in the future," she added.

Hope delivered the announcement, though I had no doubt who'd done the deed. Jared had, in coordination with its chief beneficiary, Paul Manafort.

The afternoon Corey was fired, I got a call from Donald asking me to come up to the office to discuss next steps in the campaign. As soon as I stepped into the office, Trump expressed what sounded like mixed feelings to me: "They fired Corey, you know. I don't know if it's the right thing or not, but I like Manafort. I think he'll do a good job. He'll do a great job with the delegates. We need him to do that. Manafort is good at that. Maybe it's for the best for Corey. We're going to bring Corey back later, another time. I know you like Corey."

Clearly, he hadn't overruled the decision. But Trump wasn't celebrating, either.

"I do like Corey," I said. "I think Corey is incredibly loyal to you. I think he's talented. And I think he's probably got to be pretty hurt."

Trump let that sink in.

Right then, we heard from Hope: "Corey's on television."

People are often surprised to hear that Donald Trump does not have a TV in his command center of an office in New York. Everyone just assumes he does. The modern media communicator. The longtime *Apprentice* host. The avid Fox watcher. But he doesn't. When he wants to look at something on television, he gets up from his desk and walks out to where his executive assistants sit. A large flat-screen TV is hanging on the wall, almost always turned on.

Others must have heard Hope, too. People started gathering near the TV. All of us were standing around, watching Corey being interviewed by Dana Bash, live on CNN. And Corey was being the gracious, good soldier. He wasn't dumping on anybody, including Jared, Paul, or Trump.

"Things change as a campaign evolves," Corey said without a hint of rancor in his voice. Despite his fresh firing, he made clear he would do everything he could to help get Trump elected. "If I can do that from inside the campaign, I will make that happen," he said. "If I can do that from outside the campaign, that's also a privilege."

Even when the CNN anchor pressed him on whether he'd been fired *Apprentice* style, he remained gracious and cool. "I had a nice conversation with Mr. Trump," Corey said. "And I said to him it's been an honor and a privilege to be a part of this, and I mean that from the bottom of my heart."

As Corey spoke on the television, Trump kept turning to me. "Chris, isn't Corey doing a good job? . . . Isn't Corey doing great on

TV? . . . Look how great he is. I think when he gets off we should call him. You and I should call him."

To me, this all felt a little bizarre.

"Didn't we just fire him?" I asked.

"Yeah, yeah, yeah," Trump answered. "But we've got to call and tell him he did a great job."

I knew Donald liked Corey and respected him. Donald still did. It was clear to me that this was a decision he had real misgivings about, even as it had just been made.

And soon as Corey got off the air, Trump called him. "You were super on TV," Trump said. "You did a great job. Keep calling me. Let's keep talking about things."

Then he said, "Chris is here. You know how much Chris loves you." Trump looked at me and said, "Corey says he loves you too, Governor."

"Thanks, Donald," I said.

As soon as I got out of the building, I called Corey myself. "I know it's Jared who did this to me," he said. I had no basis to disprove that, so I didn't say anything. "Manafort is a bad guy and that's going to come out," Corey said. "And when it does, then I'll come back."

He had half his prediction right.

TWENTY

RIGHT WAY

I fully understood the magnitude of the assignment I had taken on.

At that late juncture of a competitive presidential campaign, being chairman of a transition was the second-biggest job in American politics, right behind being the candidate. As transition chairman, I had to oversee the creation of an entire federal government seventy-three days after the vote came in.

First, I knew I needed guys at the top I could trust. Those choices were easy. My first chief of staff in the governor's office, Rich Bagger, is a man of nearly incomparable organizational skills and competence. He had left me after two years to take a senior executive position at Celgene, but I knew he would be perfect as the executive director of the transition. After talking to him and his CEO, Bob Hugin, he came on board and committed to being in Washington four days a week. Next, I needed a lawyer who was tough, with uncompromising ethics. I turned to my old law partner Bill Palatucci. After securing buy-in from his law partner

Patrick Dunican, Bill committed to making Washington his home until after Election Day at least. His long relationship with Donald was also a big plus. Adding Rich and Bill was a very good start.

All of us were volunteers, as were 80 percent of the 125 lawyers, accountants, government retirees, and others who came aboard to help. That number would ultimately grow to 140.

The job of organizing the 2016 transition was especially daunting due to the candidate in question. At that point, despite the tightening polls, the conventional wisdom was still that Hillary was going to pull off a win on Election Day. And there weren't a lot of go-to Republicans raising their hands to join the Trump team. Almost all the usual suspects, biding their time in think tanks, law firms, activist organizations, lobbying outfits, and on Capitol Hill had long since aligned with one of the other presidential campaigns. Many of them had said nasty things about Donald Trump, vowing never to join a Trump administration. Especially in the foreign-policy realm, the Never Trump movement was still going strong, even as the plausible alternatives kept hitting the dirt one by one. So it was crucial, I thought, to recruit a highly credible foreign-policy or intelligence leader who could run that part of the transition for me and show everyone else in the politics-and-government world that this was going to be a first-class operation.

Mike Rogers was at the top of my list

A former FBI agent, a former Republican congressman, and a well-respected figure in establishment Washington, Mike had been chairman of the House Intelligence Committee and still had excellent relations on Capitol Hill. He was the first call I made. "The candidate has guaranteed that I will be answerable only to him," I told Mike. "I need you to come on board."

Mike was reluctant at first. He wasn't thrilled with some of the positions Trump had been taking on the campaign trail. "Come on,"

I pressed. "The guy's going to be the nominee. You're going to vote for him. You can either help inform his growth as a foreign-policy figure or sit on the sidelines carping on CNN." Mike agreed.

Another big addition was Ed Feulner, the veteran leader of the Heritage Foundation, to run domestic policy. This gave us great credibility with the conservative think tank world.

This helps put the lie to the story in *Fear*, the Bob Woodward book, claiming that my position as transition chairman was merely "honorary." If so, why would people of the caliber of Mike Rogers, Ed Feulner, and former attorney general Ed Meese (not to mention 140 other employees and volunteers) join the effort under my leadership? Steve Bannon was the obvious source of this gratuitous nugget. It was not surprising to find Bannon lying once again. The surprise was that a reporter as seasoned as Woodward would fall for such self-interested drivel without even calling me to fact-check or reviewing the impressive lineup on the transition team. Hardly the "meticulous" reporting Woodward claimed on his endless promotional tour.

———

Rich and Bill spent all week in Washington, supervising everyone. I came down Tuesday nights, worked all day Wednesday, and was back in the governor's office every Thursday morning. We divided the sprawling federal government into subject areas and worked out from there. Our job, as I saw it, was to provide the incoming president with all the tools he would need to govern *his way*.

We devised what I considered an almost foolproof approach. It didn't matter what our personal agendas or pet peeves were. We were there to be guided by Trump's vision, as defined by the promises and pronouncements he was making as he campaigned. If he meant what he kept saying out there—and we had every indication that he did—our mission was to put his words into action. With a George W. Bush or a Barack Obama, you might have been able to look at their records as governor or senator and learn a lot from that. Since Donald had never held public office, his entire résumé was what he was saying on the campaign.

We were writing a detailed operator's manual for the United States government. Our people drew up policy rollout plans and laid down strategies for dealing with Congress. We had an entire operation drafting executive orders. We had another crew focused on landing teams that could go into each department on day one. We had a day-one plan and a 100-day plan once the administration started. We had a 200-day plan after that. Whatever the time frame we were focused on, we kept asking ourselves: What are the hot issues in this or that department? What is likely to be pending in January 2017? Based on the candidate's campaign promises, what policy initiatives should we prepare for him, and how should they be implemented?

If Trump won in November, he'd have thousands of appointments to make, including 1,212 senior leaders—cabinet secretaries and their deputies, the heads of independent agencies and far-flung ambassadors, who would need to be confirmed by the US Senate. And that was just the top tier. He would need legions of staffers. He would need advisers, assistants, and aides. All manner of leadership and policy-making positions would have to be filled. Heads and members of commissions and boards. The list was nearly endless. Finding so many qualified people—and vetting them to make sure they were what they seemed—was daunting at first. But our team dove in. We couldn't fill all the positions, but we could certainly get a running start.

The immediate goal was to make high-quality short lists of four to six pre-vetted candidates for dozens of major posts. We

did all our background checks with public sources and commercial databases. We didn't contact anyone directly. We were
extremely careful not to let anything leak out. Spearheading this
effort were a dozen former presidentially appointed US attorneys from my time in the Bush 43 administration, all of whom
knew how to build a case. Now they were toiling away in a locked
room, where all our personnel binders were kept behind swipe
card security. Their computers were kept separate from the transition network. In fact, nothing ever leaked out. Everything was
confidential. Rich, Bill, and I made sure it stayed that way.

These were just short lists. The final picks would always be up
to the incoming president. In some cases, he might choose someone we hadn't suggested. We understood that. But at least this way
the president-elect would have a six-month head start.

And every step of the way, everyone had to understand: if Hillary Clinton beat Donald Trump, her transition plan would be the
one that mattered. That was motivation.

▬▬

Losing Corey Lewandowski in late June was a big blow to the
transition team, bigger than any of us realized. Corey had understood how important the transition process was, especially for an
outsider candidate like Donald Trump who didn't have a ready-
made administration to step into. Corey always tried to get us
what we needed from Trump Tower. He was also there to protect our independence from the larger campaign. Lots of people, it seemed, had a friend or a colleague or a brother-in-law
who would be just perfect for some plum Trump administration
appointment, should a Trump administration ever materialize.
The more we were insulated from the attempted cronyism, the
better off I knew we'd be.

Paul Manafort was not nearly as committed to the whole idea of a professional transition. I got a call from Paul soon after Corey left. "I need to talk to you about the transition," he said. I stopped by his office the next time I was in New York.

"The family doesn't trust you to run the transition," he said.

I knew the code words by now.

"Do you mean the family," I asked. "Or do you mean Jared?"

"I mean Jared," Paul said.

I figured as much.

"So, here's what we're going to do," Paul said, as if he were on my side in the showdown that suddenly sounded inevitable. "I'm urging you not to fight this with the candidate. You can if you want to. You have your own relationship with him. But we're going to set up an executive committee that you're going to report to once a week on all the hiring you're doing, on any of the policy stuff that you're doing, on any vetting of potential cabinet, sub-cabinet, and staff people."

That sounded like a lot to me.

"It's going to be good for you in the long run," Paul said, "because you're going to be able to say everything you've done has been approved by this executive committee."

I was definitely skeptical.

"Who's on the executive committee?" I asked.

"The executive committee will be Jared, Ivanka, Eric, Donny, Steve Mnuchin, and Jeff Sessions," Manafort said. "And me."

I told him flat out I didn't like the idea. It went against the explicit promise Donald made to me, that I would report to him and nobody else. This was just the latest attempt by Jared to under-cut the crucial work that I was getting done.

Manafort insisted I was overreacting. "Think about it," he said. "These are all busy people. They're not going to have the time to micromanage you. And if you fight this, it's a fight I think you'll lose. Take my advice on this. Just say yes."

I still didn't like the idea, but it was probably good advice. So I told him okay. After that, our rhythm changed a bit. Every Friday, Rich would send a package to the executive committee—the names of proposed hires and other moves we had identified. The committee members would review that over the weekend. Monday morning Rich and I would meet with them at Trump Tower and get their sign-offs. And Tuesday night, I'd head back down to Washington. It was a little cumbersome, but we made it work.

I was the person making the presentations at those executive committee meetings. But it was clear that the real chairman—unnamed—was Jared Kushner. The others—Donald Jr., Eric, Ivanka, Mnuchin, Sessions, and Manafort—deferred to him. Mostly they seemed impressed by the strategies we were laying out and the people we were vetting. And, once in a while, Jared raised a question that didn't quite compute. Out of the blue one day, he objected to Mike Rogers overseeing the foreign-policy and intelligence transition.

"Why wasn't he cleared with us?" Jared asked.

"Well," I explained, "there was no executive committee then, and I was told by the candidate that the only person I had to report to was him. He said, 'Fine,' so I don't know what we are arguing about."

"I want to review this," Jared said. "I want to meet with Rogers, and I want to approve it before it's final."

"If you want to meet with Rogers, that's fine, but we've already publicly announced that Michael Rogers is the national defense/intelligence chair of the Trump transition. He's already doing the job."

Eventually, Jared did meet with Mike. Apparently they got along fine. Jared signed off on the choice, though he continued to bring the topic up from time to time. He would finish a sentence by saying, "Like when you picked Rogers without telling any of us."

On the vast majority of decisions, however, everyone seemed aligned. In the course of four months, there were maybe half a dozen serious disagreements, which mostly involved people not policies, some version of, "I don't want that guy. I don't like him."

So we found another guy.

When Manafort left the campaign in mid-August and Steve Bannon came aboard, he took Paul's role on the transition executive committee. As Jared got busier, Jeff Sessions often filled in for him, adding his longtime aide Rick Dearborn to the mix. My firm impression was that, essentially, Sessions and Dearborn were Jared's in-house spies, reporting back to him on everything.

Sessions and I were usually able to work things out between us. Dearborn's relationship with Bagger was more problematic. Dearborn was constantly carrying the water for people inside the campaign but wouldn't say so. That left Bagger always wondering, "Where is this coming from?"

I still thought things would have run more smoothly if Donald had stuck to his word: "Chris is handling the transition. I don't have to worry about it. I'll talk to Chris the day after we win." But there was one advantage to this alternative approach that I came to see over time: Once we assembled a final road map—with all the names and all the strategies—I would already have gotten sign-offs from all the major players in the campaign. By keeping the executive committee closely engaged, they'd all have a hand in creating the plan. How could they object to it later, right? Or so I thought.

———

Then there was Jared.

Jared never deviated from his pleasant demeanor, though he always seemed able to get his licks in. He would ask questions at the executive committee meetings as if he was seeking neutral information, still managing to pick apart whatever was being proposed. Little things, mostly. "Do we have enough information on this? . . ." "Are you being careful enough with that?" And his favorite: "It's a Jersey operation," as if the Trump transition team were a wholly owned subsidiary of *The Sopranos*. He didn't say that directly to me, but I kept hearing that he was saying it to others around the campaign.

Though Bagger, Palatucci, and I were from New Jersey, we were in fact the only people on the transition team from the state. This pissed me off. We were scrupulous about carrying out the candidate's agenda, not our own. None of us was being paid. What was he talking about? From what I was hearing, Donald was one of the people Jared was saying this to: "Christie's down at the transition office feathering his own nest." Despite all his promises to the contrary, Jared was still trying to sabotage me with the candidate.

One day when I was speaking with Donald, he used Jared's exact phrase. "It's a Jersey operation," Donald said to me.

I flinched at that. "I know who you're hearing that from, and it's wrong," I said emphatically. "You want to hear the facts?"

"What are the facts?" Donald asked.

"The facts are that, of the 140 people who are there, only three are from New Jersey."

"Really? That's not what I'm being told."

"I know," I said. "Bagger, Palatucci, and me. You want to see the roster?"

He backed off immediately. "All right, all right, I trust you," he said.

I know he did. But it was also clear to me that however supportive Jared was sounding in my presence, he was still constantly trying to undermine me with his father-in-law.

It didn't always work. I could often reverse his efforts. But he definitely wasn't giving up.

TWENTY-ONE

VEEP STAKES

One day in May, Donald called me in my Trenton office and asked straight-out, "Are you willing to be considered for vice president?" I don't think he was surprised by my answer.

"Yes," I told him without hesitation.

From the day Mary Pat and I showed up at Trump Tower for our endorsement breakfast with Donald and Melania, I'd been open with him about my interest in the job. Vice president and attorney general. Those were the two positions I had my eye on. As the presumptive Republican nominee for president, he needed to start thinking seriously about who he'd want in the first one.

"Okay," Donald told me that day. "A. B. Culvahouse is running the vetting for us."

Arthur B. Culvahouse Jr. is a legendary Washington lawyer. A former aide to Senator Howard Baker and senior counsel in the Reagan White House, he had vetted Anthony Kennedy for the US Supreme Court and handled the aftermath of the Iran-Contra scandal for Ronald Reagan. I knew him to be a total pro.

Having been on Mitt Romney's short list in 2012, I had some idea what to expect. I'd have to provide a giant stack of paperwork—tax returns, investment statements, speech transcripts, campaign-finance reports—detailing every imaginable aspect of my personal and professional life. Then, if I got through the paper review, I might be invited in for an in-person grilling by A. B. and his team. It would be a time-consuming process. Luckily, I'd kept my Romney files in a safe at the State House. I still had to update some things, and the questionnaire was a bit different now. I knew the vetting this time would be focused on Bridgegate.

From the start, I said to myself: *He's never going to pick me.* It just didn't make sense. We were a couple of in-your-face north-easterners whose states were next-door neighbors. What kind of ticket balancing was that? Then again, Donald was an unconventional candidate. He and I were personally close. And I'd endorsed him when almost no one was signing on.

He and I did not discuss who else he was looking at.

On May 10, Donald told the Associated Press that he was considering "five or six people" from the world of politics and government, though the reporters weren't immediately able to pin down just who that might be. In mid-June, *Politico*'s supposed short list included Senator Jeff Sessions of Alabama, former House Speaker Newt Gingrich, Oklahoma governor Mary Fallin, and me. Two weeks later, the *Washington Post* tossed four more US senators onto the pile: Tennessee's Bob Corker, North Carolina's Richard Burr, Arkansas's Tom Cotton, and Iowa's Joni Ernst, and also Indiana governor Mike Pence. For a minute, John Kasich was being hyped, but that faded quickly when Kasich said he didn't want to be considered and refused to endorse Trump. Along the way, Trump mentioned retired general Michael Flynn.

After I submitted all my material, Donald started inviting people to join him on one-day campaign swings, what the media called a "beauty contest." The idea was to test Trump's personal chemistry with his possible running mates. Corker, who chaired the Senate Foreign Relations Committee, came out. So did Ernst, the first female combat veteran elected to the US Senate, and the stubbornly hard-to-shake General Flynn.

When a couple of weeks passed and I hadn't been summoned to the beauty contest, the New Jersey press started saying I wasn't a serious candidate for vice president. But I wasn't worried. I had campaigned with Donald plenty of times, long before any of the others had. He already knew me. I couldn't imagine he had any doubts about our chemistry.

Then Culvahouse called. "I'd like two things if you're willing," he said to me. "I would like to meet with you."

"Okay," I said. "What else would you like?"

"I would like you to give me permission to talk to your lawyer about Bridgegate," he said.

I told him that was fine, too, as long as he wasn't expecting Chris Wray to breach the attorney-client privilege. "I don't want to waive the privilege for anybody," I told Culvahouse. "Still, I'm sure there's plenty Chris can tell you about his own evaluations or impressions that don't involve the communications between the two of us or his advice to me."

That seemed to satisfy Culvahouse, and Chris was okay with it too.

It was June by now. The convention would be held from July 18 to 21. Trump would probably want to announce his choice the week before the convention. Apparently I was still a real candidate.

I had a grueling, four-hour meeting in the governor's office with Culvahouse, two of his partners, and my chief counsel, Tom Scrivo. The Washington lawyers asked me general questions about my tax returns, Mary Pat's career, and my time as US Attorney. All that stuff was easy. It had been closely scrutinized by the national and New Jersey media. Then we got into Bridgegate—not just what happened but what I expected might come out when Bridget Kelly and Bill Baroni finally got to court. The criminal trial was set to begin right smack in the middle of the fall presidential campaign. A coincidence? I certainly didn't think so.

"Do you expect someone to implicate you?" Culvahouse asked me.

"No, I really don't," I said. "If anyone had anything incriminating, they would have brought it up already and gotten a deal for themselves. As David Wildstein showed, the US attorney was eager to make deals."

I felt like I had answered all their questions.

Chris Wray had his own conversation with Culvahouse after they got done with me. "Your conversation must have gone very well," Chris said to me afterward. "He was very positive and upbeat about you. I gave him my impressions and filled in a few blanks he had. I don't see any further issues here."

At that point, I figured it was all in Donald's hands.

———

Two weeks out from the convention, Donald called again. "Why don't you come and campaign with me Friday in Miami?" he said.

"I can do that," I told him. "But is this one of these audition things? Do you think you need to do this to make it look like you're serious about me? If that's it, don't bother. I don't care."

He got really quiet. Then he said, "I want you to come."

"All right," I said. "I'll come."

That was always how I spoke with him. Without much sugar-coating, I told him what I thought.

Word leaked of our plans to campaign together in Florida. But around nine o'clock on Thursday night, shots were fired at police officers in Dallas, killing five and injuring nine. This was no time to be campaigning. Donald tweeted: "Prayers and condolences to all of the families who are so thoroughly devastated by the horrors we are all watching take place in our country." But since he still wanted me to join him for a campaign rally, we flew to Virginia Beach on Monday. I introduced him to the raucous crowd saying "law and order needs to be once again the first priority in our country."

The coverage was wall to wall. The supporters were totally psyched. Ivanka was on the trip, which kept her father in a good mood. We had a fun day together. I spoke with Steven Mnuchin, the campaign's finance chairman and a longtime friend of Trump's, about the vice presidency. He was very encouraging and waved me off when I said I would not be asked. "He is very serious about you," Mnuchin said. That meant something coming from Steve.

When I got home, I told Mary Pat: "I still don't think he's going to pick me, but this is starting to feel weird."

"I think you're probably right," she said. "He's probably not going to pick you. But who knows?"

The trip did quiet the grumbling in New Jersey. The reporters there decided I might be a serious contender, after all. By then, most of the national media seemed to agree that Trump had a short list, and it was down to three: Former House Speaker Newt Gingrich. Indiana governor Mike Pence, who seemed to have overcome his lukewarm Ted Cruz endorsement.

And me.

Tuesday night, I headed down to Washington as I had been doing every Tuesday night, to work on the transition. I checked into the Willard hotel near the White House. After I got to my room, I saw that the *Wall Street Journal* had posted a story online about the kind of person Trump wanted in a veep. "Donald Trump Wants an Attack Dog as His Running Mate," the headline said. He wanted somebody combative. He wanted someone who was tough. He wanted "a fighter skilled in hand-to-hand combat."

Hmm, I thought, *who does that sound like?*

I never thought of Gingrich as a serious player. He was too much the Washington insider. As soon as I read the *Journal* piece, I forwarded it to Mary Pat, who called about five minutes later.

"That doesn't sound like Mike Pence to me," she said.

"I know."

Half an hour after she and I hung up, my phone rang again. It was Donald this time, calling from Indiana, where earlier in the evening he'd been introduced by Pence at a rally in Westfield. "I've got a question for you," he said.

"What's that?"

"Are you ready?"

"Am I ready? Ready for what?"

"You know what."

"Are you *asking*?" I said to him.

"No, no," he said emphatically. "I just want to know before I make my final decision, are you really ready to do this? Because you know, Chris, there will be a lot of bullshit. There will be a lot of stuff you have to put up with. There will be a lot of scrutiny. And I just want to make sure that you and Mary Pat are ready for that."

"We're fine," I said. "Don't you worry about it. We've been through plenty of scrutiny. This won't bother us."

"Is Mary Pat ready to campaign? I want Mary Pat to campaign."

"If you and I ask Mary Pat to campaign," I said, "she will. I've spoken to her about this. She's ready to be a full partner in all this."

"All right," he said. "Well, I'm going to make my decision tomorrow. Where are you going to be?"

"I'm in DC," I said. "I'm working on your transition."

That rung a familiar bell with him. "What are you wasting your time on that for? It's ridiculous. Bad karma."

I started to laugh. He couldn't help himself. Every chance he got, he was dismissing the transition.

"Don't bother yourself with it," I told him. "This work has to be done, and it is getting done. I'm in Washington if you need me."

"Good," he told me before saying good night. "I'm glad to hear that you're ready."

As I got off the phone with Donald, the vice presidency didn't feel like an exercise anymore or some theoretical possibility. It felt real. It felt likely. It felt like something I had better prepare myself and my family for.

———

After my late-night conversation with Donald, I called Mary Pat one last time and recounted what he had asked. "When the kids wake up in the morning, you need to tell them this is a real possibility now. Not that it's going to happen but that it's now very possible. I don't want to get the call tomorrow and just spring it on them. That's a lot to spring on them."

Mary Pat said she would.

It was after I said good night to Mary Pat that I got a call from a high-ranking Trump staffer. This person had just been around for a discussion with family members about the vice-presidential decision.

"The family is very upset that he says it will be you," this person said. "They are getting on a plane and flying to Indianapolis tomorrow morning to meet Donald and get him to go see Pence again. If you've got any cards to play, you should play them now."

Wow. I had no doubt that what I was hearing was the 100 percent, honest-to-God truth. This person had real credibility with me. But what should I do about it? That was the question. My answer? Nothing.

"I haven't played any cards this whole time," I said. "I'm not playing any cards now. If he wants to pick me, he picks me. If he doesn't want to pick me, he doesn't pick me. I'm not playing games here."

When the media learned the next morning that Trump was meeting with Pence again, Sean Hannity lent Newt Gingrich his plane to fly to Indianapolis and make his own pitch. I knew some people who had airplanes. "Do you want my plane?" one of them called and asked after hearing the Gingrich news.

I said no thank you. "I'm not going out to Indianapolis to audition for this job," I told this person. "That's not who I am. Donald knows me. If he wants to pick me, he picks me. But I'm not going to get into this."

I was definitely curious about all the back-and-forth.

People I trusted told me that my tipster was exactly right. Family members, Jared and Ivanka especially, were upset that Donald seemed to be on the verge of choosing me. They flew into action in an eleventh-hour attempt to block that. Joining them in the effort, I heard from several sources, was Paul Manafort. Stories were starting to appear, citing unnamed sources, saying Paul was pushing for Pence and against me.

Soon, Paul called. "What you're hearing is complete bullshit," he insisted. "I'm not pushing against you. I'm neutral in this. I'm agnostic. This is the candidate's choice. This is the way to get yourself in trouble if you're an operative. I don't do that. If he picks you, I will be working my ass off for you. You know I like you."

But from the tone in his voice, I didn't believe a word he said. I couldn't forget something he had said to me after he'd been with the campaign a few weeks: "You know why I'm beating out your friend Corey here? Because I'm smart enough to agree with Jared, and he is not." If my tipster was on target, it helped explain Manafort's action.

"Paul," I told him. "I don't bother with that stuff. It doesn't matter to me. Donald will choose whoever he's going to choose, and I will support whoever he chooses."

"Governor," Manafort said, "I'm glad to hear you say that."

I took an early-afternoon train back to New Jersey. The whole way I was thinking, *I don't know what's going on in Indianapolis, but I'm not hearing from anybody.* That didn't seem like a very good sign. Somewhere after Baltimore, I spoke to Eric Trump. I'd always felt close to Eric.

"Hey," he said to me, "I want you to know, whatever you're hearing, you're under the most serious consideration. Don't let any of this stuff you're reading discourage you."

"Eric," I told him, "I understand the way this stuff goes, and I'm not worried about it at all."

"Because I really like you, Governor, and I think you would make a great vice president," he said. "And sometime soon, my father's going to make this choice."

Eric was the one person in the Trump family who was saying anything encouraging. I thanked him for calling and said good-bye.

—

On Thursday morning, Nicolle Wallace, the MSNBC anchor and former White House communications director for George W. Bush, came to our house in Mendham for a long-scheduled interview to run during the Republican National Convention. As her crew was setting up and Mary Pat was showing them around, all the news channels were reporting that Newt Gingrich was out of the running for vice president. It was now officially down to Pence and me.

"Is he going to call you today?" Nicolle asked before we began our interview.

"I assume I'm going to hear today," I said.

She seemed excited about that. "Any chance I can be here when that happens? I would love to break this, whatever happens."

I looked down. Just as Nicolle got to "whatever happens," the phone rang. Donald. "Um—" Nicolle said, raising her hand and trying to hold my attention. She wanted to hear the conversation.

I shook my head no and walked out to the patio with Mary Pat to take the call. But Donald wasn't calling with an answer. He had another question for me.

"Are you really sure you want this?" he asked.

I did not take that as an encouraging sign.

So right there, I had to make a fundamental decision. The way he asked the question, it sounded to me like he was asking for an easy way out.

To hell with it, I thought. *I'm pushing for this.*

"Yes, I really want it," I told him.

"You know it's going to be a lot of scrutiny," he said.

"Donald," I said, "you have to choose whoever you think is best. But I am not backing away. I'm ready for the fight. I want to beat Hillary Clinton. I've been in this with you since February. Let's go do it. I'm in."

Mary Pat nodded as I spoke. She was clearly with me on this.

"All right," Donald said. "I'm definitely making the decision today. I just want to make sure that you two are ready for this. These other people, I don't know them. You're my friends. I don't want to see my friends get hurt."

"We're a big boy and girl," I said. "Whatever happens, we're fine."

I did the interview with Nicolle. I kept an eye on the news all afternoon. There was a huge amount of coverage of the impending decision. We also had a huge storm, and the power went out. Early in the evening, I got word from my New Jersey state troopers that Mike Pence was flying into Teterboro, the airport in Bergen County that handles many of the region's private jets.

Now, *that* pissed me off.

Donald had offered it to Pence, and he didn't even call me. So, I called Donald.

"Hey," I said, "the least you could do, when you made a final decision, is to let me know."

"I haven't made any final decision," he said.

"You haven't made any final decision? You haven't offered the vice presidency to anybody?"

"Absolutely not."

"Well, then, explain to me why Mike Pence is landing at Teterboro in half an hour."

"I have no fucking idea," Donald said.

"Well, I'm telling you that I know he's landing at Teterboro within the hour," I said.

"How do you know that?" he said.

"I'm the governor of the state where he's landing!"

"Chris," he said, "I swear to God I haven't offered it to him. This must be Manafort trying to force my hand."

"Well, I don't believe you," I said.

"You really don't believe me?"

"No, I don't. I find that unbelievable."

"What are you doing right now?" Donald asked.

"I'm watching TV."

"Turn on Fox News."

"Why?"

"Just turn it on. I'll call you back."

I turned to Fox News. Greta Van Susteren was on. All of a sudden, Greta interrupted her coverage of a terror attack in Nice, France, to announce she had a special guest, the presumptive Republican nominee for president, Donald Trump. She asked about Nice, then got quickly to the vice-presidential pick.

"You know the rumors out there, I'm sure," Greta said. "I know you've denied you've made a decision. You haven't released it. But Governor Mike Pence, the media is reporting that they think is your vice-presidential nominee."

Donald denied again he'd settled on Pence. "I haven't made my final, final decision," he said. "I've got three people that are fantastic."

"I think Newt is a fantastic person," he said. "I think Chris Christie is a fantastic person. He's been a friend of mine for fifteen years. Just a fantastic person. And there is Mike. And Mike has done a great job as governor of Indiana. . . . But I haven't made a final, final decision."

There were lots of other choices, too, he said. "A lot of people want this position. A lot of people that you don't know about want this position."

As soon as the Greta interview was over, Donald called me back.

"Do you believe me now?" he asked.

Frankly, I wasn't sure what the stunt had proved. "I just don't know what to make of Pence flying in on—what?—a half promise? That makes no sense to me."

"I have not made my decision," Donald insisted.

———

Nothing was announced Thursday night.

Friday morning, I got to the State House early. I did paperwork in my office for a couple of hours, then had a meeting. That's where I was when the phone rang. It was Donald again.

I heard him take a breath, and then he spoke. "Chris," he said, "I'm about to send out a tweet that I'm picking Mike Pence as vice president."

"Okay," I said. "Congratulations, Donald. Good luck. Good luck to you and Mike. Obviously, I'll be there to help you."

"Are you disappointed?" he asked.

"Of course, I'm disappointed," I said, "but these are your choices, not mine."

"You've got to understand, Chris," he said. "He's out of Central Casting."

"Donald," I answered, "whatever reasons you have for picking Mike, Mike's a good man. I introduced you to Mike. These are your choices. You have to make them."

A couple of minutes later, at 10:50 a.m., a tweet popped up from @realDonaldTrump: "I am pleased to announce that I have chosen Governor Mike Pence as my Vice Presidential running mate. News conference tomorrow at 11:00 a.m."

TWENTY-TWO

UNCONVENTIONAL WISDOM

It wasn't until I walked onto the floor of the Quicken Loans Arena in Cleveland that the thought really hit me.

I'm not the one who's about to be nominated for president.

With all the many demands of being governor, transition chairman, peer counselor, and campaign adviser, I had somehow managed to push the pangs of regret into the darkest recesses of my brain. All spring and into the summer, I'd kept my focus on the campaign. But on July 18, 2016, the opening night of the Republican National Convention, I stood with the New Jersey delegation at a prized spot on the floor right in front of the podium and found myself momentarily inundated by a wave of what-might-have-been.

I admit, it felt a lot different from what I had originally envisioned.

Everyone was patting me on the back for the valuable real estate I had snagged for my state's delegation. Paul Manafort, who controlled the seating chart and many other convention details, had actually responded when I leaned on him on New Jersey's behalf: "Don't forget who got here first. Nobody endorsed earlier than I did." Paul had also sounded pleased when I told him I would use my speaking time Tuesday night to make the case against Hillary Clinton. "No one will go after Hillary better than you can," he said.

For the past five months, I felt like I had done everything in my power to ease Donald's path to this nomination. But I'd be lying if I said a voice in my head wasn't still whispering, *Man, I wish things had turned out differently.*

———

Melania Trump spoke Monday night, delivering inspiring words about the importance of solid values and hard work. Unfortunately, some of those words were remarkably similar to the inspiring words Michelle Obama had delivered at the 2008 Democratic Convention in Denver. The media picked up almost immediately on the too-close-to-be-a-coincidence angle, demanding to know who in the Trump campaign had plagiarized the former first lady's speech.

Manafort adamantly insisted that the speech hadn't been lifted at all. "To think that she would be cribbing Michelle Obama's words is crazy," he thundered, finding a way to somehow blame Hillary. "This is once again an example of when a woman threatens Hillary Clinton, she seeks out to demean her and take her down. It's not going to work against Melania Trump."

I can't believe anyone bought a word of that.

I was really angry watching this type of ineptitude. Melania was new at this, had obviously relied on campaign staff, and had been awfully served. She is a bright, tough woman who was made to look less by someone else's mistakes. Also, she was my friend, and I felt protective of her.

Early Tuesday morning, while I was in the gym at the Westin Cleveland Downtown, Jared walked up to my exercise bike. Ivanka was at his side. "What do you think about the stuff with Melania?" he asked me.

Jared was constantly asking my opinion about things and listening carefully to my answers. Whatever he might have been saying or doing behind my back, he was unfailingly polite and respectful when we spoke. He'd been that way since meltdown day and never really changed. It was strangely hypocritical, from everything I would come to learn. But that was definitely his pattern and practice as the campaign wore on.

"It's not good," I said. "It's embarrassing and unfair to her. I don't know who the hell was in charge of writing her speech, but whoever came up—"

Jared cut me off. "It was all Manafort," he said.

"Manafort was involved in that granular detail?"

"Yep. It was Manafort. I told Donald this morning it was Manafort. He's not going to last. Just another reason he's got to go."

I thought the exchange was revealing. Corey was gone. And now Manafort was on his way out, too. It was only the second morning of the convention. The fall campaign hadn't even begun yet. And Jared was already casting around for someone new to put in charge. Whatever else might be said, no one could accuse the Trump campaign of lacking internal intrigue.

As the plagiarism story lingered, it was up to me to give the pundits something new to talk about Tuesday night. I was hoping that would be Hillary Clinton. While I waited backstage, Marla Maples, Donald's second wife, came over to me. She was there with their daughter, Tiffany Trump, who'd just graduated from the University of Pennsylvania and was also set to address the convention that night.

"Governor," Marla said, "Tiffany is really nervous." The giant television audience, the throng of boisterous delegates in the hall, every media outlet imaginable—it wasn't hard to understand why. Convention speeches are high-stakes performances. There's nothing quite like them in American politics. "Do you think you could talk to her?" Marla asked me. "Maybe you can calm her down."

I told her I'd be happy to try.

I went over and sat next to Tiffany. "So, how you feelin'?" I asked her.

"I'm really nervous," she said. "I don't do this."

"Listen to me," I said to her. "Your mother thinks I should talk to you because I do public speaking all the time. But I'm going to talk to you as a father. You could go up there and, as long as you don't throw up on your shoes, your father is going to love whatever you say. He's your father. He loves you. He's not going to care exactly what you say. He's just going to see his daughter standing up there saying great things about him as he gets ready to be nominated for president. What I want you to think about when you're up there is you're not talking to all the people in the hall or all the people on television. You're talking to him."

That seemed to connect with her. She took a deep breath. "That's so great," she said. "Thank you, Governor."

"Just go talk to him," I said. "You'll be fine."

Marla, who'd overheard some of this, lit up, too. "That's amazing," she said. "She'll be great." And Tiffany was, talking straight to her audience of one.

For my turn onstage I had a far more combative message, aimed straight at the presumptive Democratic nominee. I summoned up my experience as a federal prosecutor and addressed the delegates like I was making an argument to a jury, focusing on Hillary Clinton's many failings and abuses as secretary of state. From Libya to Syria from terrorism to trade, I had plenty to work with. With each new particular, I asked the delegates, "Guilty or not guilty?"

"Guilty," they roared backed.

With the whips on the floor stoking the enthusiasm, some of the delegates broke out in chants of "Lock her up! Lock her up!"

I didn't participate in any of that. I thought it was in poor taste, and I thought it was wrong. As soon as I heard it, I stepped back from the microphone and let the chant die down before I started speaking again.

I was no Michael Flynn. Monday night, right after Melania spoke, the retired army general, the campaign's top foreign-policy adviser, had led the convention delegates in rousing chants of "Lock her up!" "That's right, lock her up," Flynn bellowed from the stage. "I'm going to tell you what, it's unbelievable. . . . Lock her up. Lock her up. . . . You guys are good. Damn right. Exactly right. There's nothing wrong with that."

I understand political passion, but I'm a rule-of-law guy. I don't believe political leaders should demand the jailing of their opponents. "Guilty or not guilty" for what Hillary did in office? Fair game. "Lock her up"? I wasn't going to participate in that.

My speech was incredibly well received. I got a huge ovation when I finished and a great call from Trump. "You killed it," he said. "The guilty-or-not-guilty thing—brilliant."

———

Everyone was waiting to hear what Donald was going to say to the convention delegates and the nation on Thursday night. He'd been such an unconventional candidate, anything was possible, right?

But this would be the formal launch of his campaign against Hillary Clinton. The country would be listening. It was crucial that he strike the right, powerful chords.

Stephen Miller had been working on a speech draft with Donald's input. There was a lot of anxiety inside the campaign about what would be in it. Thursday morning, Donald called.

"I think I'm pretty close to done with the speech," he said.

"Good," I said. "You happy with it?"

"Yeah, I'm pretty happy with it. Do you want to see it?"

"No," I told him.

"Why not?"

"I want to hear it tonight," I said. "It's too late for me to be editing anything. You should be locked in by now. Don't let anybody edit it anymore unless it's you. You've got to own this now. It has to be all yours."

Truly, this was a moment like no other, the night this first-time political candidate was accepting the Republican nomination for president of the United States. This wasn't a time he should be smothered by aides and advisers. On this night, he needed to give the speech he wanted to give.

I was truly eager to hear how it sounded in the hall.

"Our convention occurs at a moment of crisis for our nation," Trump told the people packed into the arena and watching on TV at home. "The attacks on our police and the terrorism in our cities threaten our very way of life. Any politician who does not grasp this danger is not fit to lead our country."

Profound change is needed, he declared. "The problems we face now—poverty and violence at home, war and destruction abroad—will last only as long as we continue relying on the same pols who created them in the first place. No one knows the system better than me, which is why I alone can fix it."

He repeated his familiar calls for more conservative judges, tighter border security, and stronger support for law enforcement, though he ended on a more upbeat note. "We will make America strong again. We will make America proud again. We will make America safe again. And we will make America great again. God bless you and good night."

As the crowd sent him off with a long, standing ovation, I thought, *He gave the speech he wanted to give. It was legitimately Donald Trump.*

"It was totally you," I said when he called afterward. "Tomorrow, you'll get a bounce in the polls. Now let's go out and win this thing."

Donald sounded happy to hear my upbeat review before moving on to the next person he was calling. We left Cleveland thinking the campaign was in a relatively good position. The party was fairly united. The race against Hillary would clearly be an uphill run. But against all odds and despite almost every professional prediction, Donald Trump was very much in the game.

———

Donald got the convention bounce I had predicted, though the pollsters couldn't agree on exactly how much of one. Three percent, 5 percent—not a game-changer but definitely real.

When the Democrats gathered in Philadelphia from July 25 to 28, they grabbed their turn in the national spotlight. On their side, there was still some lingering bitterness among the die-hard "Bernie or Bust" crowd, who complained that the Clinton machine was grinding up Sanders as they had anticipated. Hillary's acceptance speech, asking voters to trust in her experience, judgment, and compassion, didn't exactly electrify the Wells Fargo Center. But the party's main message, that Donald Trump would ruin

America, was pounded night after night by nearly everyone who took the stage. That connected with the Democratic faithful in much the same way that Trump supporters liked hearing what a disaster another Clinton presidency would be.

Donald, too, was watching.

In the presidential-campaign calendar, the postconvention period is often a bit of a lull, especially for the party that goes first—the Republicans this time.

Lulls can be dangerous times for Donald Trump.

In the days after the Democratic Convention, the freshly minted Republican nominee was in a decidedly sour mood. Hillary got her own postconvention bump—a few points larger than Donald's, some of the pollsters said. The Republican Never Trumpers, though soundly defeated in Cleveland, had still not entirely thrown in the towel. It was the slow part of the summer. Not much was going on. And day after day, Trump was still seething about Khizr Khan.

A native of Pakistan's Punjab Province, Khan had told his story to the Democrats in Cleveland. He was the father of US Army captain Humayun Khan, who was killed in the Iraq War in 2004. The son, born in Dubai, immigrated to America with his family as a child, graduating from the University of Virginia and hoping to attend law school after his time in the service.

"If it was up to Donald Trump, he never would have been in America," the father said of his son. "Donald Trump, you're asking Americans to trust you with their future. Let me ask you: Have you even read the United States constitution? I will gladly lend you my copy," he said, pulling out a pocket edition and holding it up for everyone to see. "In this document, look for the words 'liberty' and 'equal protection' of law. Have you ever been to Arlington Cemetery? Go look at the graves of brave patriots who died defending the United States of America. You will see all faiths, genders, and ethnicities. You have sacrificed nothing and no one."

I watched the speech on TV. It was an effective piece of political theater. It played to the emotions of Trump's tougher immigration policies. And if Donald hadn't overreacted, the story would have faded in, at most, a day, maybe two. Donald, however, considered the attack totally unfair. Instead of letting the story pass, he proceeded to do everything he possibly could to keep it alive.

"Mr. Khan, who does not know me, viciously attacked me from the stage of the DNC and is now all over TV doing the same—Nice!" he complained in one tweet. "Hillary voted for the Iraq war, not me!" he said in another. In an interview, he questioned why the dead soldier's mother, Ghazala Khan, stood beside her husband at the convention but did not speak, implying that she wasn't allowed to by her husband—a double slam on Muslims and women. Later, the mother explained that she still can't talk about Humayun without breaking down in tears.

Asked by ABC's George Stephanopoulos what sacrifices he'd made for his country, Trump shot back, "I think I've made a lot of sacrifices. I've created thousands and thousands of jobs, tens of thousands of jobs." To Stephanopoulos, that didn't quite measure up to what the Khans had given to the country.

"Those are sacrifices?" the anchor asked.

"Oh sure, I think they're sacrifices," Trump said casually. "I think when I can employ thousands and thousands of people, take care of their education, take care of so many things. Even in military, I mean I was very responsible, along with a group of people, for getting the Vietnam memorial in downtown Manhattan, which to this day people thank me for."

It made no sense to be engaging with Gold Star parents in this way. It was throwing gasoline on a bad story.

Jared and several others on the campaign had urged him to cool it. They weren't getting anywhere. Finally, I got a call from Jared, who said to me, "We're banging our heads against the wall on this Khan stuff. Can you come up and talk to him? Maybe you can get somewhere."

I told Jared I would try, thinking some backhanded humor might be the way to go. I walked into Donald's office like I always did. I just stuck my head in. "Hey, how you doin'?" I asked.

"What do *you* want today?" he grumbled.

"I want to chat with you. Got a couple of minutes?"

"Yeah, yeah," he said.

From his tone, I could tell that Donald wasn't in a very chatty mood as I took one of the chairs across from him. "I'm confused," I said.

"What do you mean you're confused?" he asked.

"I'm confused about what we're doing here. Did the Khans replace Hillary Clinton as the Democratic nominee for president? Are we running against the Khans? Because I've got to tell you the truth. Given the volume of stuff I see coming out of here against the Khans as opposed to the volume of stuff I see coming out against Hillary, I figure we're running against the Khans now. And if that's the case, let me know, because I've got to change my whole approach on TV."

He chuckled. He didn't laugh, but he chuckled. He looked at me and said, "So, you're going to be a wiseass today?"

"No," I answered. "I'm just trying to get you to think about this." I knew at least I had his attention. "There's no margin in attacking a Gold Star family. I know that he was being incredibly partisan. I know that frustrates you when he says things about you that aren't true. But Donald, he's earned it. He gave his son to the country. We're minimizing ourselves by doing this. We've got to stop running against the Khans and get back to focusing on Hillary Clinton."

He looked at me and shook his head. "I know," he said, "but it really, really pisses me off."

"I understand," I told him. "But we've got to let it go. We've got to keep our eye on the ball."

As I was walking out of the office that day, Jared was waiting for me. He wanted to know how the meeting went.

"I think he's in a better place," I said. "We'll see, though, right?"

———

In the depths of the August lull, one other reality became hard to ignore. Inside the Trump campaign, things were lonely at the top. There were hardly any seasoned professionals with actual political experience. What had once been part of the campaign's seat-of-the-pants charm—a swirl of youthful exuberance, an extremely lean crew, a notable absence of Washington insiders—was quickly becoming a genuine liability.

It was one thing to mount discrete races in a few primary states at a time. It was quite another to run for president in all fifty states at once. With Manafort all but officially departed, Donald's three oldest children, Don Jr., Eric, and Ivanka, spoke to their father every day. But none of them had any experience running a national political campaign. Son-in-law Jared, who was pretty much in charge of everything, didn't have much more. Bright as he might have been, Jared still had a whole lot to learn. I suppose that was why he kept phoning me.

One Sunday afternoon, he called me at home to say, "I need your help with Pennsylvania."

"What about it?" I asked.

"How many field people should we have in Pennsylvania?"

Pennsylvania was a crucial swing state, and August was awfully late to be asking questions like that. I explained to him why a ground game is so important in a swing state like Pennsylvania. I gave him my best estimate of how many would be needed in the field. We would need to get our voters to the polls in the rural and collar counties to offset the beating we were sure to take in the wards of Philadelphia and Pittsburgh.

Here they were. They'd beaten everyone to capture the Republican primary. Election Day was less than three months off. And there was no one in the entire campaign hierarchy who knew the very basics. It was slightly unnerving that at this late date Jared was still calling with Campaign 101 questions like these.

He was the de facto campaign manager, and he had never run a political campaign before.

Soon, he was on the phone again, this time with an inquiry I didn't expect. "We want to hire Bill Stepien to run the field operations," he said. "But we won't do it unless you say it's okay."

Stepien, of course, was the person who had managed both my races for governor and served as my deputy chief of staff before being fired in 2014 for showing poor judgment in connection to Bridgegate. He and I hadn't spoken since then.

As I walked into Trump Tower Monday morning to discuss this with Jared, it was one of those instances when I felt like I was being led into a trap. I knew Stepien as an immensely talented political operative. But I told Jared I couldn't predict how the media would react to his joining the Trump campaign. And frankly, I couldn't speak to what Step had been up to in the past two years. There was also the Bridgegate trial of Bridget Kelly and Bill Baroni, which was set to open in September. I certainly had no idea how Bill's name might come up in the testimony.

I wanted to be very cautious here. "I can vouch for his talent, which is unquestionable," I said. "But if you're asking me what the defense and government will say about Step at trial, I just don't know."

Jared pressed me harder. "Come on," he said. "You have to know what his level of involvement was."

"I don't know," I repeated. "I don't believe he had anything to do with Bridgegate. He is one of the most talented operatives in the country. If circumstances had been different, I would have had him manage my presidential campaign. On the merits, I can tell you he's a good hire. But I can't warranty anything else for you."

There were not a lot of top-level political operatives out there who were eager to join the Trump campaign, even then. And Stepien was.

With those caveats, I told Jared that they needed someone like Stepien. Jared seemed pleased with my answer. Stepien was hired. Step and I were finally on a presidential campaign together. Only it was months later than I expected, and it was Donald Trump's campaign, not mine.

TWENTY-THREE

IT'S DEBATABLE

It was August, and everyone knew what that meant: time for a new wave of hires at the top of the Trump campaign.

Corey had been out since June. Manafort was neutered by July, though he wasn't formally given the heave-ho until August 19. Donald hated the way Paul handled himself on television. If Trump doesn't like you on TV, that's a very bad thing. When the *New York Times* started running stories about Manafort's shady dealings in Ukraine, he was quickly history, though his deputy, Rick Gates, was inexplicably allowed to hang around at the Trump inaugural committee.

The day Manafort left, Steve Bannon arrived from the website Breitbart as the campaign's new chief executive officer, and Kellyanne Conway, who'd been a Trump adviser since July, was elevated to campaign manager, soon to be joined by a new deputy campaign manager, David Bossie.

Still keeping all that straight? Hardly anyone around Trump Tower was.

And I was beginning to notice: as all these people were coming and going, I was still very much there, never far from the center of things. I was outlasting almost everyone but the family. You could become a veteran in a hurry on the Trump campaign.

I had never heard of Steve Bannon before he was named CEO. In fact, I called Kellyanne and asked, "Who the hell is this guy"? Breitbart was not a media outlet for a blue-state governor. But once he showed up at Trump Tower, two things were obvious about Bannon right away. He was incredibly bright and incredibly arrogant. Given the arrogance level of most people in politics, that was really saying something.

Steve believed he knew everything about everything. The only thing that seemed to surprise him was that Donald had taken so long to install him in the campaign's "C suite." Personally, I didn't even know campaigns had C suites.

On the surface, Steve was extraordinarily deferential to me. "You're an incredible politician," he said the first day we spoke on the twenty-sixth floor. "You're a phenomenal speaker. You really know the game." I couldn't tell whether he meant any of it. I would describe Steve as a strategic suck-up. Whether he was making nice to me, to Jared Kushner, or directly to the candidate, Steve worked hard to ingratiate himself with people he thought might be useful to him. In my case, the flattery would continue long enough for him to make a judgment about whether I was on his side or not. I wasn't quite sure who was on the other side. Maybe nobody. But Steve was constantly making these calculations as if he expected a civil war to break out at any moment, and he wanted to be sure he had the right allies in place.

Kellyanne could not have been any more different from Steve. She and I actually shared a lot. Like me, she came from New Jersey.

Like me, she had an Irish father and an Italian mother. Like me, she'd graduated from law school then spent most of her adult life in and around Republican politics, in her case as a pollster, consultant, and TV pundit. We had never worked together, but we had plenty of friends in common, and I'd always had a favorable impression of her. Before joining the Trump campaign, she worked for Ted Cruz, even chairing a pro-Cruz political action committee. But with Cruz out of the picture, she seemed all in for Donald now.

Kellyanne was known for her ability to connect with female voters. But I thought her most important talent was that she knew how to speak to Donald Trump. She could get a point across without being caustic but was still frank and direct. She was also seemingly unconcerned about grabbing credit, a rare quality in any campaign, much less this one. Her attitude was that while this could well be a short-term assignment there were countless complexities and a huge amount to be done. She needed to impose some structure. She had to navigate the family and the existing staff. She didn't have time to worry about who was getting credit. Stuff just had to get done. Exactly how you want a campaign manager to think.

When David Bossie arrived in September, the campaign got another pro. David was the longtime president of Citizens United, the conservative-action group behind the US Supreme Court decision that changed campaign-finance law to permit larger donations from wealthy individuals and well-funded interest groups. Politically astute and an excellent evaluator of talent, David could tell who was competent and who was not. This was especially important as people from the Republican National Committee began streaming into the Trump campaign, now that the primary season was fully behind us. But the thing I liked most about David was that he was incredibly honest with Trump.

With David and Kellyanne on the team, I didn't feel I was the only nonfamily person who could speak frankly to him. In this crowd of people with their own agendas, we now had three people other than his family who could have an open conversation with the candidate, even when he didn't want to hear it—Kellyanne, David, and me.

Among Steve, David, and Kellyanne, Kellyanne was clearly the most versatile addition. She had an inside game and an outside game. She gave sound advice to the candidate. She could also represent him in the outside world. You weren't going to put Bannon or Bossie on television, but you could put Kellyanne out there. After twenty years in and out of green rooms, she knew how to handle herself. She was a double threat, while the others had their own lanes—not that they always stuck to them.

How would these three interact with the staffers already in place and with the family? No one could say for certain. How would they get along with each other? That was anybody's guess. This crew might not last forever, I said to myself. What in Trump world does? But at least we had some people in place at Trump Tower who had been around politics and knew what a ground game was. That was progress right there.

Agenda item number one: preparing Donald Trump for Hillary Clinton and their first of three one-on-one debates.

———

I got an unexpected phone call on Labor Day weekend. When I answered, I heard the unmistakable voice of Donald Trump. After we exchanged pleasantries, he said he'd seen a story in the paper saying I was holding a fund-raiser for the transition. He didn't sound too pleased about that. "You know I don't even want a transition—it's bad karma," he said, repeating the phrase he had used with me before. "Now it's costing us money?"

I explained to him that we were not raising much money at all, a fraction of what Hillary was spending on her transition and most of it from people on my donor list, not his. That last point seemed to placate him a bit. "Okay," he said with a sigh in his voice. "But come to the apartment tomorrow morning. I guess I should get an update."

We agreed to meet the next day.

Kellyanne Conway called right after Donald and I hung up. "I explained the fund-raising situation to him," she told me. "He gets it. You know what bad luck he thinks the transition is—that's all this is about."

We met at Trump Tower as planned the next morning, and what actually happened in that meeting bears almost no resemblance to a wildly embellished version that Steve Bannon has been energetically peddling to any reporter who still answers his calls. Through all his many ups and downs, Steve has remained a busy fiction consultant to needy journalists, feeding colorful but patently false anecdotes to Bob Woodward, Michael Lewis, Michael Wolff, and anyone else itching to spice up a dull book chapter or a magazine piece. Steve has spent so much time whispering to reporters "on background," it's anyone's guess how he still finds the time to invent his latest dark conspiracies or claim fresh credit for changing the entire face of modern politics.

In Steve's fanciful version of the Labor Day sit-down, Donald is supposedly yelling and screaming and cursing at me, when he isn't threatening my permanent banishment.

Wrong, false, and completely untrue!

The meeting, which Steve attended part of, was never angry. There was no yelling. No screaming. No cursing. No accusations.

Donald asked me how much money we were raising. I told him not much more than $1 million. He asked if we could shut down the transition. He was still consumed by the bad-karma concerns and the divided focus he thought the transition might mean. I told him we could not shut it down—that closing the transition would be a violation of federal law.

"C'mon, Chris," he said, "just close it down. Chris, you and I are so smart, and we've known each other for so long, we could do the whole transition together if we just leave the victory party two hours early!"

I laughed at that thought and assured him again that closing the transition was not possible. We had to do this right. Steve jumped in to say that doing so would look bad politically, making us look like we believed we couldn't win. And that was it. The discussion was over. Donald said two things to me as I left the apartment: Keep the transition quiet. And go on TV more often to advocate for his candidacy. No acrimony. No drama. Just another day in the Trump campaign.

———

Getting Donald ready for the first general-election debate, to be held September 26 at Hofstra University on Long Island, was a process that began in earnest after Labor Day—and almost immediately turned into a total shit show.

First of all, there were too damn many people in the room, some of whom had absolutely no idea what they were talking about. That was glaringly obvious at the very first prep session, a weekend meeting in the large conference room at Trump National Golf Club in Bedminster, New Jersey. There was the family: Jared Kushner, Ivanka Trump, Donald Jr. There were the Millers: Stephen Miller, who was now the head of Trump's economic policy team, and Jason Miller, who had been with Cruz and was now Trump's senior communications adviser. There was the Fox News and talk radio star Laura Ingraham. There was Republican National Committee chairman Reince Priebus. There was Trump's friend and supporter Rudy Giuliani, the former New York City mayor. There were the generals: Mike Flynn and Keith Kellogg, both now giving advice on all kinds of topics, military and otherwise. And there were us: Steve Bannon, Kellyanne Conway, David Bossie, and me, his closest nonfamily advisers at that point. I'm sure I've forgotten a few. This was like rush hour outside the Lincoln Tunnel on Friday of a holiday weekend.

And nobody seemed to be directing the traffic.

Someone would ask a mock question. Trump would respond with whatever popped into his head. Then he would go around the table and ask, "What did you think?" Someone would gently say, "No, I don't think that quite worked." A couple of others would offer suggestions on how to sharpen the response.

Then, General Flynn—it was usually Flynn—would speak. "That was a brilliant answer, Donald," he would say. "Don't listen to these other people. Stick with it. Don't change a word."

And Trump would say, "Great. Okay, let's move onto the next question."

Flynn was a train wreck from beginning to end. At one point that day, he made a proposal that stunned nearly everyone in the room.

"I have an idea, and I think it's really strong," Flynn said. "Mr. Trump, what you should do is get on that stage and declare that you've changed your mind on abortion, and now you're firmly for a woman's right to choose."

What?

"No, no, no," Bannon declared. "No. He can't do that. He's already changed his position once. He used to be pro-choice. Now, he's pro-life. You don't get to change twice. Not on this issue."

"No, sir," Kellyanne agreed. "That's not a good thing to do."

"It'll totally knock Clinton off guard," Flynn insisted. "It'll take away an issue from her, and you'll be seen as a genius."

"Yeah," Bannon piped in sarcastically. "And for every person he steals from the middle, he loses three from the Right. That's great math. Let's just move on."

What had been clear to me for months—and was becoming clearer by the day—was that Mike Flynn, for all his supposed military and intelligence experience, had no idea what he was talking about when it came to politics. He was a slow-motion car crash.

Laura Ingraham was sitting next to me looking appalled as Flynn barreled on that day, opining boldly on all kinds of subjects he was utterly ignorant about. At one point, Laura leaned over and whispered not too softly, "What the hell is this? Why is he even here?"

I wish I'd had an answer for her.

Afterward, Kellyanne, Bannon, Bossie, and I talked privately. "He plays to the candidate's worst instincts," Bossie complained. "He doesn't know what the hell he's talking about. We've got to figure out a way to get him out of the room." We agreed we wouldn't tell Flynn about the next debate-prep session.

At another prep session for the first Hillary debate, this time at Trump Tower, someone decided to bring into the conference room a podium and a video camera setup. Donald came from his office upstairs, took one look around, and started firing off questions.

"Who's he?" Donald asked, motioning to the man standing beside the camera in the back of the room. "How do we know him? Where's he from? Has he signed an NDA?"

"Um, we're going to get him to," a staffer stuttered.

Donald looked at the cameraman and made himself clear: "Get out. Get out. Take your equipment and get out. I'm not doing this. And get this podium out of here."

The poor camera operator didn't even grab his gear. He just hustled out the door and was gone.

"Make sure that camera is off," Trump demanded before he sat down. "I don't want any videotape of this. How can we have somebody in here we don't even know, who hasn't signed an NDA?"

Needless to say, he didn't do too much prepping that day.

———

Mary Pat came with me to Hofstra on September 27 for the big face-off. From beginning to end, Donald and Hillary's first debate was an awkward encounter. There was a problem with Donald's microphone. Mary Pat and I both noticed it. Sometimes we could hear him clearly. At other times, we could hardly hear him at all. I had no idea if that was just in the theater or also on TV at home. Regardless, Donald seemed to be yelling when his mic was low. I had to assume that made him sound crazy on TV. Hillary's microphone sounded normal. I couldn't say if the problem was intentional or not. But between the microphone and the sloppy debate prep, Donald put on what seemed to me like a substandard performance—not awful, but far from great.

After the debate, as I was waiting to be interviewed on NBC, the Reverend Jesse Jackson came walking by. "Christie," he said, loud enough for everyone around us to hear, "you got the best mouth in the Republican Party, but not even you can put lipstick on this pig tonight."

That wasn't exactly how I would have said it, but it wasn't a winning night for Trump.

Jared called while we were in the car going home. "What did you think?" he said.

"He lost," I said.

"He thinks he won," Jared answered.

"Of course he thinks he won," I said, "but he lost."

"He needs somebody who he respects to tell him he lost. Would you call him?"

It was another of those moments when I wondered if Jared was suggesting I put my head in a noose. Or was this a genuine, necessary request? I decided Jared's motivation didn't really matter. I wasn't sure what Bannon, Kellyanne, or Bossie was saying, or even whether he had asked them. The right thing for me to do was to call Donald and tell him the truth.

When he answered the phone, he was in his car heading back to the city.

"It didn't go well," I told him.

"What do you mean it didn't go well?" he shot back at me. "I got, like, 94 percent of the vote on the *Drudge Report*."

"All the people on the *Drudge Report* are already voting for you," I told him. "I'm surprised you didn't get 100 percent. But it didn't go well. You'll do better next time." He complained about the microphone. I told him he was right. The microphone sucked. "We've got to make sure we have somebody sitting with the audio technicians so no one is playing around. But even if the microphone was fine, you still weren't ready. You've got to get ready."

"I can't believe you think I lost," he said.

"You can believe something else if you want to," I said. "But you lost."

"Fine," he answered. "Thanks." Then he hung up the phone.

Mary Pat shot a look from her side of the car. "That didn't go well," she said.

"He'll call in a couple of days, once he has time to think about it."

And he did. Exactly two days later. "I have to do better," he said. "I wasn't as bad as you said I was, but I have to do better."

That was good enough for me. "I'm glad you know that," I told him, "I'm ready to help out wherever I can."

———

The next night I was back in Washington, working on the transition, when Jared called. Earlier in the day, there had been a leak to *Politico* saying Chris Christie was put in charge of debate prep—floating the idea, I suppose, though no one had bothered to ask me. Now Jared was asking.

"Would you be willing to?"

"If I'm in charge," I told him. "I need to set the parameters for how we do it. Otherwise, no."

Then I laid it out for him. A much smaller room, I said. A few people around a table. Make him as comfortable as possible, then pepper him with questions. His responses will get him used to the rhythm of a one-on-one debate and the length his answers need to be. We'll just keep sharpening as we go along. "That's the most helpful way to do this that he'll be willing to accept," I said.

The next day, I got a call from Donald, asking if I would be in charge of his debate prep. Of course, I said, I would.

This time, the debate-prep team was Bannon, Kellyanne, Bossie, and the Republican National Committee chairman, Reince Priebus. Sometimes Rudy wandered in. So did the occasional family member, but not too many and not too often. And no Michael Flynn. Definitely no Michael Flynn. We met at Bedminster and at Trump Tower. Roger Ailes came once. We did a lot of lightning rounds where no one was allowed to speak to Donald but Priebus and me.

Priebus asked the questions. Donald answered them. I didn't say I was playing Hillary. Donald was not a mock-debate guy. But I delivered the answers as Hillary would deliver them. He needed to get used to a Democratic opponent coming at him hard and coming only at him. That's different from eight Republicans tripping over each other for stage time.

Priebus had a real knack for this. He asked excellent questions. The rest of the people took notes and shared their impressions when we were done. It was a much more efficient, much more effective way to prepare someone who was difficult to prepare. And Donald showed genuine improvement. His answers were crisper. He was sharper and more precise. He still had his trademark bombast. No one could take that from him. But after a few rounds of practice, he was definitely making his points more effectively and in the format of a presidential debate.

Debate number two was set for Sunday night, October 9, at Washington University in Saint Louis. CNN's Anderson Cooper and ABC's Martha Raddatz would lead the candidates in a competitive town hall format. As the big night got closer, I could tell that Donald was going to be ready for most of the curveballs that the moderators would throw at him.

What we didn't realize was that the big curveball would come in the form of a leaked video.

———

Our last prep session was planned for Friday afternoon in the large glass conference room on the twenty-fifth floor at Trump Tower. Most of the usual suspects were there. But one by one, people started leaving the room. First Kellyanne. Then Bannon. Then a couple of others. Priebus, Trump, and I were still at it, going back and forth, with Jared watching us work. But through the glass, I could see the others gathering in the hallway. Finally, Trump spoke up: "What do you think's going on here?"

"In my experience," I said, "when the staff leaves the room and doesn't come back immediately or doesn't tell you why, it's never good news."

Just then, Hope Hicks walked into the conference room, looking positively ghostly. She had some papers in her hand. "Mr. Trump," she said, "we just got this from the *Washington Post*. I think you need to read it."

She handed me a copy. "Governor," she said, "you should probably read this, too."

It was described as the transcript of a videotaped conversation between Billy Bush, a co-anchor of the syndicated TV program *Access Hollywood,* and Donald Trump.

The words were not good. They included "bitch" and "I just kiss. I don't even wait." And maybe the worst part: "When you're a star, they let you do it. You can do anything. . . . Grab them by the pussy. You can do anything."

If you were running for president and those were your words and they were caught on videotape, it would be hard to think of any way to fully capture just how not-good they were. But as with everything else in this crazy 2016 campaign, it crossed my mind that the rules just might be different for Donald Trump.

Priebus, who'd been sitting next to me, began to read over my shoulder and mumbling to himself, "Oh, my God. Oh, my God. Oh, my God."

Trump looked deeply pained. Though he usually shows his upset by yelling and screaming, this time he was stone quiet. "Do you think this is real?" he asked finally.

"Do you have any recollection of this?" someone asked.

"I don't," he said "I don't have any recollection of it at all. But this doesn't sound like me. It doesn't sound like the words I would be using."

Hope said the *Washington Post* was asking for a comment from the campaign. Either way, the reporter warned, the story was going live within the hour.

Someone asked Hope, "Where is the tape? Can't we get a copy?"

She said she had asked but that so far the paper was refusing to provide it.

"That's ridiculous," several of us piped in. "If they want us to comment, they have to give us a copy of the tape." Someone suggested that Don McGahn, the campaign's lawyer, contact the *Washington Post*'s attorney to get a copy of the tape. This provoked more back-and-forth, much of it wishful thinking. *We can't give a comment blindly. We don't know if the transcript is legitimate or not. We don't even know if it's accurate.* The room filled with speculation and suppositions.

At one point, Trump spoke up: "Do you think the tape could have been dubbed or altered?"

Nobody knew. Anything was possible.

Donald turned to Jared: "Remember that guy we had? That expert on examining tape? Get him on the phone and get him ready in case we need him." Jared went off to find the audio guy.

For a while, Donald seemed to have convinced himself that the whole thing was phony. "It can't be true," he said. "No way I said this. There's no way."

Hope walked in with her laptop, saying she had the video.

I looked at Hope. She clearly looked rattled. Hope told us she believed the tape was real. "Come on," she said. "We can all watch it."

She opened the laptop in front of Donald. The rest of us gathered in a semicircle behind him. He turned to me and said, "Chris, it isn't me."

"Great," I said.

Then we pressed Play, and the video began.

The words were the same as the words on the transcript. The voice sounded awfully like Donald. Donald was larger than life, talking in the video.

Five or ten seconds in, he turned around again. "It's me," he said.

TWENTY-FOUR

HOT MIC

The tape was hard to watch. It was harder to listen to.

But we watched and listened to the *Access Hollywood* video all the way to the end. The words sounded crude and vulgar playing through the small speaker on Hope Hicks's laptop, even more so with Donald sitting there with us. We figured we had the tape for an hour or so before the whole world would see it, and that time was already flying by. I noticed something else on the video, and it added another level of complexity to the growing mess. The video was date- and time-stamped.

September 16, 2005.

I knew what that meant immediately.

Donald's wedding to Melania, which Mary Pat and I had attended, was in January 2005. "We don't only have a political problem," I said to the others in the twenty-fifth-floor conference room. "We have a personal problem, too." When Donald was caught on a hot mic making all those comments, he and Melania were still newlyweds.

This was the inner circle of Trump-campaign aides. Truly, there was no one else but us. We all sat around together for a good long while that day, trying to come up with the right response. "Clearly, we need to put out a statement," I said.

People started proposing phrases to quote Trump as saying: "Many years ago." "Bill Clinton has said far worse to me on the golf course." "I apologize if anyone was offended."

It was Donald who offered the best one. "Locker room talk," he said.

There was an intense debate over the "offended" line. I hated it. "If anyone was offended." Rudy, Kellyanne, and I all pushed back. "There's no doubt people were offended," Kellyanne said emphatically. "We can't say, 'If people were offended.'"

"We can't say 'if,'" I agreed. "People were offended. That's the surest bet in the world."

"No, no, no," Jared countered. "It's fine for him to say that. Some people are, some people aren't." He and Bannon liked the distance the phrase conveyed. I knew Donald would agree with them, and they refused to budge.

I made my argument directly to Donald. "If this apology isn't genuine and complete," I said, "we're just going to find ourselves having to do it two or three more times. Let's just do it once and get it over with."

I lost that fight.

The statement the campaign put out had Trump apologizing if anyone was offended. It also took a jab at Hillary's husband. "Bill Clinton has said far worse to me on the golf course—not even close."

Donald went upstairs to talk to Melania. That was a meeting I had no interest in attending.

———

It was Shabbat. Jared and Ivanka had to leave. Priebus left for DC. Kellyanne, Bannon, and I stayed around for a little while longer, discussing the fact that something else was going to have to be done. We weren't quite sure where Reince Priebus stood. But we all agreed the evidence was highly damaging. At that moment, all of us recognized that this was a make-or-break moment for the Trump-for-president campaign.

Later that night in New Jersey, I got a call from David Bossie. "We've done a video we want to put out," he said. "Mr. Trump wants to talk to you about it."

Donald asked if I would listen to the video.

"Why don't you have someone email it to me so I can look at it?" I said.

"We don't have time," he told me. "Just listen to it."

I listened to the audio over the telephone. "I like the first half where you apologize," I told Donald when he came on the line. "But I don't like the second half where you attack the Clintons. Let's save attacking the Clintons for later. Let's just get the apology out there now."

Donald still wasn't buying my argument. "No," he said, "I want to do the whole thing."

It wasn't until after midnight when I actually saw the video on CNN that I realized how bizarre it was. It had a faux nighttime New York skyline behind him. He was talking stiffly to the camera. It was awful. It looked like a hostage video.

As I went to bed that night, this was only getting worse.

When Donald called first thing in the morning, I told him I thought the video was a mistake. He didn't want to hear it.

"How fast can you get over here?" he asked.

"I'll shower and change and come over," I said.

On my way into the city, Reince Priebus called.

"This is a disaster," he said. "My phone is blowing up. Everyone wants him to drop out."

"Well, he's not going to drop out," I said, "so let's move on from there."

"Are you going to this meeting?" he asked. "I'm on the train approaching Philadelphia right now. If you're not going to this meeting, I'm getting off in Philadelphia and going back to Washington."

I told him I was already on my way.

"Don't lie to me," he said.

"I'm in the car on the way to New York," I told him. "I will be there when you get there. You should come to the meeting. You're the national chairman. You have to be there."

"Oh, I hate this," he said. "I hate this. This is awful. It's terrible. I can't believe we're in this position."

——

Outside of a political convention or a Super Bowl, I don't believe I had ever seen more media in one place than when I walked into Trump Tower on the Saturday after the *Access Hollywood* video was released. It was crazy. I was dressed in khakis and a Mets hoodie. The reporters were screaming questions at me. I ignored everyone as I marched into the side entrance and onto the elevator to the sixty-third floor.

The regular crew had already assembled in the Trump family living room just inside the front door. Jared, Kellyanne, Bannon, Bossie, Rudy—they all looked worn out. Mike Pence was on the road, not in New York. I knew he and Donald had been speaking by phone.

Donald was sitting in a chair with his back to a window. When I walked in, the first thing he said was, "Okay, what do you think?"

I knew that was coming. I'd been rehearsing my answer on the ride in.

"The first thing we need to do," I said, "is fix your reputation. The campaign will fix itself if we fix your reputation. We've got to fix your reputation first. And the only way to do that is for you to give a one-on-one prime-time TV interview with somebody tonight. Apologize completely. Get it over with. Be ready for the debate tomorrow night."

As an aside, that is exactly what I said that morning at Trump Tower, not the fictionalized version spewed by Steve Bannon and peddled by Bob Woodward in his book. I never said the campaign was over. I never thought it was over. We were running against Hillary Clinton, after all! More erroneous reporting from Mr. Woodward.

Donald didn't like my suggestion. "I don't want to do an interview," he said.

"I just believe you've got to answer questions face-to-face," I told him.

He didn't want anything to do with that. "I understand what you're saying, Chris, but I don't want to do that."

I sat down while others offered their thoughts, batting around different approaches. "Let's have a till-you-drop press conference," Rudy suggested. Nobody liked that idea.

Then Priebus walked in. Trump asked what he thought.

"There are only two alternatives," Reince said. "Either you drop out—or you will suffer the greatest defeat in American presidential-electoral history, and you'll take the party down with you."

He liked that even less than he liked my idea. "You can forget that," he said. "I'm not dropping out. I don't care whether I get 10 percent. I'm not dropping out under any circumstances."

The party chairman held his ground. "There's no recovering from this," he said emphatically. "You can't recover from it."

As Trump waved off Priebus, he turned to the rest of us and said, "Do you think I need to drop out?" Everyone else said no.

Priebus was eyeballing me, clearly unhappy that I didn't speak up for him. He motioned me into the dining room for a private chat. "Why didn't you back me up on that?" he wanted to know.

"Because I don't believe it," I told him. "I don't agree with it."

"You know he's never going to win," Priebus countered.

"Let me tell you something," I said. "There's two things I know for sure here. One, Donald Trump will never, ever drop out. He'd rather die than drop out. So why give somebody advice that you know they're never going to take? And two, we're running against Hillary Clinton. She's a dreadful candidate. We've still got a shot here. If we do well in the debate tomorrow—this might sound crazy to you—but we've still got a shot here."

"You *are* crazy," he said.

I still didn't understand what Reince thought he could accomplish here. "Why did you give him advice to drop out?" I asked him. "You knew he wouldn't drop out." He looked at me with the most serious face I have ever seen.

Said Reince: "Because when they write the book about this, I want to be on record."

Now I guess he is.

We went back into the living room and kept up the full-court press for Donald to give an interview.

Finally, he relented.

"All right," he said. "I'll do an interview. I'll do an interview, I'll do it tonight. Fine. Who do you want me to do the interview with?"

We started batting around names. I said I thought the interview should be with a woman. I suggested NBC's Kelly O'Donnell.

"No," he said. "I don't want Kelly O'Donnell."

Someone else proposed Diane Sawyer from ABC. He said no to her, as well. Other names were mentioned. For one reason or another, he said no to all of them. One thing was clear to me: he did not want to do this interview.

Ultimately, we settled on a male interviewer, *ABC World News Tonight* anchor David Muir.

Donald said, "Okay, I'll do it."

Hope Hicks went to call Muir and offer up the interview. She didn't have to ask twice. Muir agreed to bring a crew to Donald's Trump Tower apartment. They hammered out some details, deciding the interview would be conducted in the living room with Donald in the same chair that he'd been sitting in when I arrived that morning. Before Muir and his crew arrived, Donald suggested we all go down to the twenty-sixth-floor conference room and order lunch. That would give us time to prepare him for the *Access Hollywood* cleanup interview the same way we'd been preparing him for Sunday night's debate.

Kellyanne got things started, trying out a tough question that Muir would almost certainly ask: "Given what's on that tape, how can you be trusted by women in America?"

He didn't really have an answer. I repeated the question, just phrased it in a different way. "Trust and judgment are important in a president. Would you trust the judgment of the person on this tape?"

And that was it. Trump refused to go on—with the practice session or the interview. "Forget it," he thundered. "I'm not doing this. Cancel it."

At that point, David Muir was already in the apartment setting up. "What are we supposed to tell him?" Kellyanne asked.

"I don't care," Donald fumed.

We went around the table arguing about the wisdom of canceling this interview. Pretty much everyone except for Donald thought canceling was a bad idea. Finally, Bannon said, "If he doesn't want to do it, we're not doing it. That's it. Let's stop arguing about it."

Actually, Bannon was right about that. If he didn't want to do it, it wasn't going to go well. Most of us thought it was a necessary evil, that he had to take his medicine—but Donald just wouldn't do it. He had made up his mind.

It was at that point that Bannon brought up a lingering question about Sunday night's debate: whether the campaign should bring Bill Clinton's alleged sex-assault victims into the hall.

Under the circumstances, I thought it was too much. Several others agreed. Donald initially wasn't sold on the idea, but someone had obviously been working it behind the scenes. The women had already been contacted and were ready to come. There was some more back-and-forth around the table, but the issue wasn't resolved. For the moment, the idea was dropped.

"Okay," Trump said, "who's going to do the Sunday shows tomorrow? Chris, why don't you do Tapper and Stephanopoulos?"

I looked at him and said, "No.

"I'm not going to answer questions that you haven't answered yet," I explained. "How do I know what your answer is going to be? How do I know whether I'm giving the answer that's your answer? It's a personal thing. It's just not appropriate for me to do these interviews."

Donald glared at me.

Then, he turned to Kellyanne. "Well, you do those."

She echoed what I said. "I think the governor is right. Sir, you're the one who has to answer these questions. It's not right for us."

Then Rudy spoke up. "I'll do all of them," he said. "I'll do every Sunday show."

That didn't surprise me, coming from Rudy. He was up for anything, including a round of Sunday shows that were certain to be the network-television equivalent of walking into a lion's den.

Rudy and I had first gotten to know each other while I was US Attorney. We had mutual professional friends. I was rooting for him in 2007–08 when he was running for president. After that, when Obama won and I resigned to run for governor, Rudy was my first big endorsement. He announced the endorsement on the front lawn of Jon Corzine's apartment in Hoboken—a great event. He was a regular on the trail for me in 2009 and was a very big help. We have remained friends ever since.

When Rudy spoke up, Kellyanne and I looked at each other, both thinking exactly the same thing: *Why did he just say that?*

I think it came from a good place, Rudy wanting to be helpful. But it was the wrong thing to do. Still, Trump grabbed the offer like a life preserver at open sea. "Okay," he said, "Rudy's going to do the shows."

With that settled, we went back to discussing the idea Bannon was pushing, that we bring the Clinton women to Sunday night's debate.

I said I thought it was unnecessary. It might be a mistake, I said. I wasn't sure it was a mistake, but I was certain it was unnecessary. "Why do this?" I asked. But I was outnumbered. Bannon was totally in favor, and most of the others went along. Finally, we dispatched Kellyanne up to send David Muir home. Donald wasn't doing the interview.

It was then that Donald, Steve Bannon, and a few others decided to meet with a group of supporters who had gathered downstairs. I decided not to join them. Feeding more tall tales on background to Bob Woodward, Steve would later claim that he and I had a confrontation at the twenty-fifth-floor elevator bank, where I supposedly yelled and cursed at him. The truth? We never had a confrontation that night of any kind. In fact, until that point, Steve and I had never had a cross word between us. There are a few folks who stayed in the conference room that night with me who will back up these facts.

Why did Steve invent this lie? I suspect it was to make himself sound tough at a time when chaos was everywhere. As for a deeper explanation, I'm afraid I would need years of psychological training to unwind all the post-campaign utterances of campaign CEO Steve Bannon.

I left Trump Tower Saturday night feeling terribly down. Donald needed to answer the questions raised by that videotape. He needed to answer them publicly. I didn't know what those answers were going to be. No one did. And now we were bringing the Clinton sexual-assault victims to Saint Louis for the debate? There was no way I was going to be there.

I'm the only elected official on this team of advisers, I thought, *the only person here who currently holds public office.* If I showed up at the debate, I'd be pummeled with questions. It was his life, his issue, his public reputation, his marriage. I was firm with Donald about all that. He had to go first. He had to answer the questions before I could. Now none of that was going to happen before the debate.

I called David Bossie on Sunday morning. "I'm not flying out to Saint Louis," I told Dave. "I can't answer these questions until he does."

"I totally understand," Dave said, "and I'll convey that to the candidate. You're an elected official. You're in a different position than the rest of us." The New Jersey media certainly thought so.

———

The next morning, news cameras were parked at the bottom of my driveway when I looked out the window, waiting to see if I would leave the house. It was just Bridget and me at home. Mary Pat and the other kids were away somewhere. "The trucks are still out there," Bridget, who was thirteen, would report back to me.

I avoided the media the rest of the day. That night, I watched the debate at home on TV. Donald did really well. The work we'd done actually paid off for him.

The *Access Hollywood* tape, as everyone expected, consumed the first part of the questioning. Moderator Anderson Cooper did not hold back.

In his very first question directed at Trump, the CNN anchor said, "We received a lot of questions online, Mr. Trump, about the tape that was released on Friday, as you can imagine. You called what you said locker room banter. You described kissing women without consent, grabbing their genitals. That is sexual assault. You bragged that you have sexually assaulted women. Do you understand that?"

It had taken him a while to get here, but Donald stepped up.

"I'm not proud of it," he said. "I apologize to my family. I apologize to the American people. Certainly, I'm not proud of it. But this is locker room talk." Then, as we'd discussed, he quickly pivoted to other issues of the day, "a world where you have ISIS chopping off heads, where you have—and, frankly, drowning people in steel cages, where you have wars and horrible, horrible sights all over, where you have so many bad things happening, this is like medieval times. We haven't seen anything like this, the carnage all over the world."

Anderson didn't back down quickly, asking Trump if he did "actually kiss women without consent or grope women without consent."

"I have great respect for women," Donald answered. "Nobody has more respect for women than I do." Then again, he shifted the conversation elsewhere, this time to immigration and borders and jobs. The vulgar video was obviously a challenging subject, not something he wanted to feature in a national debate. But as a piece of political performance, which any debate is, he didn't allow it to throw him completely off his game. He was there to debate Hillary Clinton, and, even under the relentless pressure, he won the debate.

Ten minutes after the debate was over, my phone rang. It was Donald. "What did you think?" he asked.

"You won it," I said. "You knocked it out of the park. Clear win. Great job."

Donald sounded thrilled. "You are the greatest debate coach in the history of debate coaches," he said. "When you get out of office, you should open up a debate school and teach people on how to do debates. You killed Marco. You helped get me ready. I could not have done this without you."

He wasn't done. "You know what I was thinking when I was onstage tonight and she would give answers? I was thinking, 'This was so much harder with Chris than it is with her. This is easy. She's not nearly as good as he is. That's how well you got me ready. I can't thank you enough. And you're going to do it for the next debate, right?"

I said, "Of course I will."

"Great. Great. Thanks."

And then half an hour later, on the way to Trump Force One, he called me again and said, "The reviews are incredible. Everyone is saying I won. You did a great job for me. I can't thank you enough. You're in charge again for number three."

"Okay, great," I said.

Then I got a call from Rudy Giuliani. He said just one thing. "We couldn't have done this without you. We're back in the game. You're the best."

As I hung up that night, it seemed to me that Donald understood why I hadn't gone to Saint Louis. Even why I'd chosen not to appear on the Sunday shows. He definitely didn't like it. But our relationship was still our relationship. He knew I brought value to him and this effort. He had just lived it on the debate stage. If he was really mad at me, he wouldn't be calling to thank me ten minutes after the debate was finished, then calling me after that to thank me again. It was another affirmation that this was a peer relationship. It's more proof that Steve Bannon's self-aggrandizing accounts on *60 Minutes* and in Bob Woodward's one-sided version of these tales in his book *Fear* are patently false. If I was "off the team," as Bannon claimed, then why was Trump calling me, effusively thanking me after the Saint Louis debate? Why did he ask me to lead debate prep for the third debate? Why was I in the room for all the preparations before the third debate, playing the role of Hillary Clinton? Here's the real truth: Steve Bannon is a fraud, a nobody, and a liar. After getting fired by the president for being the biggest leaker in the West Wing—and that is quite a distinction, given the leaky crew that was there for the first seven months—Bannon launched a never-ending mission to diminish others and rehabilitate himself. It was a shame and a surprise that Bob Woodward allowed himself to be used on such a fool's errand.

In September 2017, Bannon would go on CBS's *60 Minutes* with Charlie Rose and deliver a version of "Billy Bush Weekend," as he liked to call it, that was totally made up. An utter and complete lie. Bannon claimed he warned me that if I didn't get on the plane to the debate in Saint Louis, I would be thrown off the campaign.

"The plane leaves at eleven in the morning," he quoted himself as telling me. "If you're on the plane, you're on the team. He didn't make the plane."

Total bullshit.

He never said that to me. He never said anything like it. The entire incident was a fabrication. Bannon and I never spoke about whether or not I would travel to the debate in Saint Louis. The only campaign official I discussed that with was Dave Bossie, who fully understood my reasoning and shared it with Trump.

Despite my supposed banishment, I remained deeply involved with the team and the candidate. We never missed a beat. Donald had gotten through the fire of a huge crisis—and so had our relationship.

Now there were thirty days left to elect him president. And the only thing standing in our way was a very flawed Hillary Clinton.

PART FIVE

PRESIDENT TRUMP

TWENTY-FIVE

BELIEVE IT

Busy as I was with the transition, it made no sense for me to stay out on the road with Donald. He called and left voice-mails, urging me to join him in Ohio, Texas, Tennessee, or wherever Trump Force One was landing next: "Hey, Chris, it's Donald. We had a great day in New Hampshire and Maine and just had a big, big celebration with Hindus—it was amazing—in New Jersey, actually. It had to be close to ten thousand people. It was amazing. So anyway, I'm here. If you need me, call me and let me know what's happening. I'll see you soon. Bye."

I stayed in my lane, Amtrak's Northeast Corridor between New York, New Jersey, and Washington. We couldn't afford to lose our focus. If we somehow managed to pull this off and Donald was victorious on November 8, he would have just seventy-three days until the inauguration. I knew better than anyone in the inner circle how daunting a task that would be, because hardly anyone else had spent five minutes setting up a government.

The *Access Hollywood* weekend made things harder for everyone, including the people who'd been toiling diligently at the transition office. When they heard the tape, they were as dispirited as anyone. I got down to DC right away to deliver an in-person pep talk to the vetters, lawyers, and other staffers and volunteers.

"We can't forget what we're doing here," I reminded the troops. "This has never been about whether we won or lost. Our job has never been certain. We can do all this work and, if Donald loses, none of it will be put to use." They all got that, I think.

"Either way," I said, "we want the most professional, well-prepared transition plan that we can have in our hands on Election Day, when the people are going to decide. If you can't bring the same intensity to your job today as you did last week, I completely understand, and you can leave. We can't have anybody here who's not one hundred percent in."

I was pleased though not surprised that no one stood to leave. I think they appreciated that I'd come down immediately and addressed the situation directly.

Donald still had one more debate with Hillary Clinton, scheduled for October 19 at the University of Nevada, Las Vegas. By now, we all knew the drill. He wasn't fighting debate prep anymore. After our final session, at the golf club in Bedminster, Donald walked me to my car in the parking lot. Just before saying goodbye, he asked a question that, in all this time, he had never asked before.

"Do you think I still have a chance to win?"

It was as though, at this late date, he was still trying to get his head around the possibility. I gave it to him as straight as I could. "Before the *Access Hollywood* video," I said, "this was your race to lose. Now you've got to win it. We're going to need a break. I don't know where that break is going to come from—or if it's going to come at all. But we need a break to change the narrative here."

That break came on Friday, October 28, three weeks after the *Access Hollywood* tape and nine days after the debate. On that morning, FBI director James Comey sent a letter to Capitol Hill saying that he wanted to "supplement" testimony he'd given in July about the bureau's long-running investigation into Hillary Clinton's private email server. During that testimony, Comey had defended his decision not to bring charges, though Clinton and her staff had been "extremely careless in their handling of very sensitive, highly classified information."

In his follow-up letter, Comey wrote: "In connection with an unrelated case, the FBI has learned of the existence of emails that appear to be pertinent to the investigation. I am writing to inform you that the investigative team briefed me on this yesterday, and I agreed that the FBI should take appropriate investigative steps designed to allow investigators to review these emails to determine whether they contain classified information, as well as to assess their importance to our investigation."

Comey cautioned "this material may be significant or not," and he couldn't say "how long it will take [the FBI] to complete this additional work." But as a political matter, that hardly mattered. What mattered was that Jason Chaffetz, the chairman of the House Oversight Committee, quickly made Comey's letter public, tweeting, "FBI Dir just informed me, 'The FBI has learned of the existence of emails that appear to be pertinent to the investigation.' Case reopened."

The day the Comey letter came out, Donald called me from the plane. "Is that the break you were talking about?" he asked.

"Yes, it is," I said.

A couple of days later, I was in New York for a meeting of the transition executive committee. Ivanka walked into the room.

The first thing she said to me was, "What do you think of the Comey letter?"

"I think it's a game-changer," I said. "I think it really puts us back on even footing with them, and this can go either way."

"You think he's going to win?" she asked.

I wasn't going quite that far. "I think after this letter, he's got a chance, a real chance now to win."

She seemed surprised by that.

———

By this point, the transition plan was almost finished. A couple dozen binders. Everything backed up on thumb drives. A day-by-day, week-by-week compendium for how the Trump administration should get right to work, all drawn from the candidate's positions and promises on the campaign trail. This would be the new president's own personal checklist for delivering on the promises he'd made.

We had a concrete rollout schedule for tax cuts, infrastructure overhaul, and the repeal and replacement of Obamacare. Sessions and Mnuchin had signed off on a highly impressive short list of candidates, all pre-vetted, for cabinet and senior staff posts— four for each position, to be passed on to the president-elect for interview, consideration, and final choice. These were people of unquestionable talent, experience, and integrity, men and women who really knew what they were doing and could hit the ground running in key top jobs.

For secretary of defense, our pre-vetted candidates included FedEx CEO Fred Smith, a retired marine.

For national security adviser—the job that would ultimately go to the disastrous Michael Flynn—we had retired general Peter Pace, former chairman of the Joint Chiefs of Staff, and retired admiral William McRaven, who'd led the assault on Osama bin Laden. These were military men of the highest caliber, not whackazoids whose hubris and greed would quickly embarrass the president.

For secretary of education, former Indiana governor Mitch Daniels

For secretary of labor, Wisconsin governor Scott Walker.

Imagine the launch the new president would have gotten if he'd been surrounded by talent like this.

For secretary of health and human services, which would ultimately go to the luxury-loving Tom Price, we cleared former WellPoint CEO Angela Braly and the man who would ultimately replace Price, former Eli Lilly executive Alex Azar.

To head the Environmental Protection Agency, we had former Home Depot CEO Frank Blake and former California secretary of environmental protection James Strock. You can't even compare them to the swamp creature who would ultimately get the job, the perk-grabbing former attorney general of Oklahoma Scott Pruitt. Our guys were in a totally different league.

Then there was attorney general, the position Sessions and I both eyed. Despite that, he and I also put forward the names of former US attorney general Michael Mukasey and former Oklahoma governor Frank Keating, two impressive and strong contenders.

Just a first-class lineup all around.

I was signing off on the calendar for our first executive orders. The team had done a splendid job. We'd already gotten full buy-in from the transition executive committee. Everyone had been included in the process. Everyone seemed to be on board with the results.

US attorney Paul Fishman had dragged the Bridgegate saga out as long as he possibly could. The trial had finally opened on September 19, three full years after the temporary lane realignment, sixteen months after the indictments, and six weeks before Election Day. There'd been one last effort to drag my name into the trial, this time by the attorneys for Bill Baroni and Bridget Kelly. They tried to subpoena my "missing" cell phone, which was never missing at all. Right from the start, I'd handed it over to Randy Mastro, who had a forensic evidence firm analyze every byte of data on it, performing a complete review of all of the phone's contents and any remnants of deleted information.

When I retained my own lawyer, Christopher Wray, Mastro turned the phone over to him, and he turned over all information in response to requests by the government. My personal lawyers still have the cell phone today. All along, everyone knew where the phone was—except for the media. Even to this day, some members of the media write that the phone was "missing" or that the government never got to see the contents of the phone. Both were wrong then and are still wrong today.

US District Judge Susan Wigenton quashed the defense lawyers' Hail Mary motion, calling their subpoena "so sweeping and so broad" that the court "could not justify such a request."

On November 4, 2016, four days before the election, the jurors finally returned a verdict with the exact same conclusion Mastro had laid out in his media-maligned March 2014 report. Kelly and Baroni were convicted on all counts, she ultimately receiving eighteen months in prison, he twenty-four. Wildstein, the truth-challenged mastermind of this idiotic plot, would get the lenient treatment he was promised by Fishman—three years' probation and five hundred hours of community service.

The endless saga finally ended—with a whimper.

How disappointed Paul Fishman must have felt.

One last note about Bill Baroni: Of the three people at the center of the Bridgegate scandal—Baroni, Wildstein, and Kelly—Bill was the only one I considered a friend. He is a good lawyer, and I believe he is a good person. In the end, I am convinced that the only part of Bill I misevaluated was his strength. I don't believe he came up with this plot. He is too smart for that. I think he was not strong enough to say "no" to his best friend, lying felon David Wildstein. It was Bill's inability to do that one, simple thing—to say no to David Wildstein—that may ultimately cost him his freedom. And it was my failure to see that in him that may have cost me the presidency of the United States.

———

I voted early on Election Day, arriving with Andrew at Mendham's Brookside Engine Company right at six a.m. We came back to the house and I immediately began flipping among the morning shows. It was clear that everyone in the media thought Hillary Clinton was going to win. So did most of the people I knew in politics, the so-called political professionals. Frank Luntz, the pollster, invited me to join his five p.m. conference call with clients. "The exit polling says that Hillary Clinton is going to get approximately 350 electoral votes," 80 more than needed, Frank said. "It's going to be a blowout. According to the exit polls, Republicans will lose the Senate and take heavy losses in the House."

As I dressed for the evening, Mary Pat asked what I was hearing. Mentioning Frank's call, I said, "If the exit polls are right, Donald is going to lose and lose substantially." I said I should probably get over to Trump Tower soon. "He probably knows by now," I said. "He's going to need someone to talk to."

I told Andrew I would drop him at his apartment in the city or, if he'd rather, he could come with me and watch the returns trickle in. "If the night is over early, we'll go out to dinner. If it's not, we'll hang around the campaign." He agreed to come with me.

When we got up to the fourteenth-floor campaign headquarters, David Bossie was the first person I saw. "The exit polls are really bad," he said, then added, "but I'm not sure they're completely accurate. The sample may be skewed a little."

I didn't know whether the polls were skewed or not. But Steve Bannon sure looked depressed. He was pacing and moping, then moping and pacing. I didn't hear him doing his usual bragging. Of the people I spoke to, Kellyanne Conway was the most upbeat. "I don't believe these exit polls," she said. "They were wrong with Bush Forty-Three both times. I'm not going to even get myself bothered about exit polls. I still think we had the momentum going into Election Day."

It was Jared who suggested we head to the campaign war room, which was outfitted with banks of computers and experienced number crunchers from Washington and New York. "Let's go see what they know," Jared said to Andrew and me.

When we walked into the bustling room, Vermont had been called for Clinton while Trump took Kentucky and Pence's home state of Indiana. No big surprises there. Standing in front of a giant wall map was Bill Stepien. It was the first time we'd laid eyes on each other since January 8, 2014, the day I'd fired him for poor judgment in connection with Bridgegate. Bill looked up when we walked in but said nothing. I went over and put my hand out.

"Mr. Stepien, good evening," I said.

"Good evening, Governor."

There was a lot of history packed into those seven routine words.

We shook hands and spoke briefly but only about the campaign. He was focused on Florida. The state hadn't been called yet, but the Trump numbers looked stronger to me than what I remembered Mitt Romney getting in 2012. "Step," I said, "I think we're going to win Florida."

"I think so," he agreed.

That was my first indication of just how historic this night might turn out to be. If we grabbed Florida's twenty-nine electoral votes, the "blowout" exit polls were definitely wrong. We could still lose, but from what I was seeing, this was no blowout. Before the Florida results were final, Ohio was called for Trump, his first swing state of the night and a state whose voters had correctly picked every US president since 1964.

Florida came in soon after and, twenty minutes after that, Trump grabbed North Carolina, a state that was declared a dead heat just a day earlier. At that point, Clinton had to pin her hopes on pulling a pile of electoral votes out of Pennsylvania, Michigan, or Wisconsin. It was still early, but we were ahead in Pennsylvania. We were neck and neck in New Hampshire. We were ahead in Michigan. We were ahead in Wisconsin.

By then, whatever emotional resistance I had—or self-protective low expectations—had pretty much melted away. *Holy crap*, I was realizing, *if we've won Florida and Ohio and we're roaring across the industrial Midwest, we* are *going to win this thing.* There was no high-fiving yet, but for me at least the conclusion was sinking in.

At that point, Andrew and I followed Jared into a larger room full of people. I didn't see Donald at first. But a few minutes later, I looked over and noticed that he was sitting in a random chair in front of a couple of TVs. He patted the chair to his left and motioned for me to sit. Mike Pence was in the chair to his right.

He didn't say much. Mike and I just sat there with him and watched the states roll in. We won Utah. We won Iowa.

He was very quiet, highly unusual for him. Every once in a while, I took a phone call. Terry Branstad called from Iowa with congratulations. The mood was brightening around Donald, but he stayed quiet, intently staring at the screens. He gave off the clear impression that he didn't want to be spoken to.

One of the networks, I don't remember which, said that unless things changed radically, Donald Trump was going to win the Commonwealth of Pennsylvania. He turned and looked at me and said, "I think we should go upstairs."

It was at that moment, I believe, that the thought was first setting into Donald's head—apart from all the boasting, apart from all the competitive juice—that he was really going to be the next president of the United States. But he wasn't ready to talk about it. He just wanted to get out of the busy room as fast as he could.

A small group of us, a couple of family members and the very senior campaign staff—Bannon, Priebus, Conway, Bossie, Stephen Miller, Mike Pence, and me, plus Andrew—rode with him to the apartment on the sixty-third floor. He didn't say anything on the ride up, and nobody else did, either.

We'd been there just a few minutes when a tense-looking Stephen Miller came over to me with his laptop. "We have a little issue," he said. "I have an exquisitely crafted concession speech, but only bullet points for a victory speech. It isn't fleshed out."

"All right," I said. "Let's go to work."

Stephen opened up the laptop. He and I sat at the dining room table, soon to be joined by Pence, Jared, and Ivanka. With Stephen typing and the rest of us offering lines, we crafted the speech as quickly as we could, as Donald sat in the kitchen watching TV and growing increasingly impatient.

"Where's the draft of the speech?" he called out into the dining room.

"We're polishing it," Ivanka answered. "We're polishing it. You'll have it in a minute."

As the speech drafting continued, the victory was growing increasingly secure. Pennsylvania was called for Trump at 1:35, a key piece of Clinton's supposedly impenetrable firewall. That got us to 264 delegates and counting—of the 270 required for victory. Still no final word from Wisconsin, Michigan, or Arizona. But any one of those three would put us over the top.

So where was Hillary?

The folks at Clinton headquarters seemed to be having a difficult time wrapping their heads around what was unfolding in front of all our eyes. At 2:02 a.m., her campaign manager, John Podesta, came out onstage at the Javits Center, where Hillary's massive victory party was supposed to take place, and tried to put a good face on things. Sounding like mere formality was all that stood between his candidate and victory, Podesta told the crowd, "It's been a long night, and it's been a long campaign, but I can say we can wait a little longer." He had to know the hard truth. Yet he was telling the Hillary supporters that "everybody should head home. You should get some sleep. We'll have more to say tomorrow." Hillary wouldn't be addressing her supporters immediately, Podesta made clear. "Let's get these votes counted, and let's bring this home," he said.

Even across the TV feed, I could hear that his words were met with only scattered applause.

Trump was clearly aggravated hearing Podesta's bedtime story and then seeing his own enthusiastic supporters on TV. He was itching to ride the three blocks from Trump Tower to the Hilton and address his supporters. He was exasperated when I and a couple of others told him, "Not yet." It wasn't time. Hillary had to concede first. But after a few more minutes of grumbling, Donald said it like he meant it, "We're going to our hotel and talking to our people."

"You can't go out there until she concedes," Priebus told him. "You just can't." But he insisted we at least *go* to the hotel, and people started getting ready to leave. Jared stopped me in the foyer. He said to Andrew, "Can you do me a favor?"

"Sure," Andrew said.

He handed Andrew a phone and said, "Would you take a picture of me and your dad at this moment? No one would ever believe that we would be standing next to each other having, together, just helped elect a president of the United States."

Then we headed down and climbed into the motorcade.

We were all backstage at the Hilton when Wisconsin was called at 2:30, its 10 electoral votes putting Donald Trump over the 270 victory threshold. Since no one had heard a word from Hillary, Donald finally agreed to let Reince Priebus, as national party chairman, go out and speak. With Donald standing over his shoulder, Priebus began to jot down a few bullet points.

My son Andrew and I were standing on three little steps with a clear view of the podium. Kellyanne was right in front of us, chatting with us excitedly. She knew she'd be addressing the media in a matter of minutes. Her cell phone was resting beside her on the railing, as Reince prepared to take the stage.

"Kellyanne," Andrew said, as she kept writing.

"Excuse me, Andrew," she said. "I just have to finish—"

"Kellyanne."

"What, Andrew?" she said, sounding like a mom who is used to being interrupted by her kids.

"Huma Abedin is calling you."

"What?"

Kellyanne had her phone on vibrate. But the way the phone was positioned on the railing, Andrew had a straight-on view. He could hardly miss the glowing name of Hillary Clinton's top campaign aide.

"Oh, my God," Kellyanne said as she reached for the phone.

"Hi, Huma. It's Kellyanne. How are you?"

I heard a slight pause.

"Oh, I guess that's not a great question."

Another pause.

"Yes, Mr. Trump is here. Is this *the* call, Huma, because I don't want to put him on the phone unless it's *the* call."

Kellyanne walked her cell phone over to Donald, who was standing perhaps ten paces away. "Mr. Trump," she said. "it's Secretary Clinton, and she wants to concede." We all gathered around as Donald took the call.

All I could hear was his side of the conversation, but he was at his gracious best. "You were a tough, tough competitor. . . . You and your husband have contributed so much to this country. . . . You really made me fight for it."

We were gathered around the most unlikely president-elect in modern American history, and, by God, Hillary Clinton was conceding to Donald Trump. He hung up the phone. He looked at Reince and said, "You're not giving that speech anymore."

Reince nodded, and Donald asked Pence to go out and introduce him. As Pence made his first public appearance as vice president–elect, Donald said to those of us gathered around him, "I want you all out there with me. This is the team that made this happen. I want all of you out onstage."

Kellyanne had tears in her eyes. She was screaming and hugging me. Jared could not stop smiling. The sons, Eric and Don Jr., were high-fiving each other. The evening had started with such low expectations. And now, look.

Pence was just shaking his head. He looked stunned and overwhelmed. He went over to Andrew and said, "I hope you don't think it's presumptuous if I give you a little bit of advice tonight."

"Absolutely not, Governor. What's your advice?"

"In politics," the vice president–elect said, "don't ever, ever bet against your father. He was right."

Pence looked at me and said, "You understood this before anyone else."

"Not before anyone else," I corrected him. "I didn't understand it before him."

The crowd was insane. It was just past 2:45 a.m. as Trump finally took the stage. "Sorry to keep you waiting, complicated business," he said. "Thank you very much." He congratulated Hillary Clinton on a hard-fought campaign and pledged to be "a president for all Americans."

I really don't remember what else he said, even though I helped draft it. As I stood up there in the middle of all this mayhem, I couldn't hold it all in my head at once. All I could think was, from the Trump Tower escalator in June of 2015 to this almost unimaginable night, I couldn't believe that Donald Trump had actually won this race. But it was much, too early for reflection. My mind was already full speed ahead.

———

For the past six months, my job had been to prepare Donald for what would come after this very moment. Hardly anyone thought it would ever arrive. Well, here it was now, and a whole lot of business would need to get done. No more bad karma.

My mind was racing.

Okay, when do I want to have the first transition meeting?

When is my first conversation with him?

He's not going to want to hear it right now. I'll have to do it tomorrow. I hope he understands we have no time to waste.

As soon as Donald left the stage at his victory party, I grabbed Andrew and we got out of there.

I dropped Andrew at his apartment and headed home to New Jersey. It was after four by the time I pulled into the driveway in Mendham. When I walked into the bedroom, Mary Pat, who can sleep through anything, was sitting straight up in bed.

"Hey," I said.

"Hey," she said back. "Are we going to Washington?"

"I don't know," I told her.

"I really don't want to go to Washington," she said.

"I know," I told her before climbing into bed at the end of a very long day. "We'll just have to see what happens next."

TWENTY-SIX

NO THANKS

I didn't want to go to Bedminster. There was nothing there I was looking for. As far as I was concerned, this was no way to staff up a new administration. I was still angry about the lousy stories that were being leaked about me. They hadn't stopped. I hated how the hard work and clear path of the transition had been thoughtlessly cast aside. I was very worried about what that might mean for Donald Trump's new presidency. It all just felt foreboding to me.

Instead of executing the meticulous plan he'd assigned me to craft for him, the president-elect had decided to summon a parade of job seekers to the Trump National Golf Club in Bedminster, New Jersey. The only thing I liked about that was the fact that the club was in New Jersey. Everything else seemed haphazard to me. The scene resembled nothing so much as a casting call, right down to the bank of TV cameras planted just outside the golf club's heavy front door.

All sorts of individuals were turning up with their résumés— the good, the bad, and the who the hell knows. Each of them marched in from the parking lot, past the TV cameras, across the club's white-columned portico, through the front door, and into a spacious conference room, where the president-elect was waiting with a few close aides, usually Reince Priebus, Steve Bannon, and Jared Kushner. That was the drill. When the interview was over, each candidate would take the reverse course out, only this time joined part of the way by the president-elect, who would stop in front of the cameras and make a few flattering remarks. Then the applicant would promptly depart, perhaps to turn up later in a cabinet, subcabinet, or White House staff role, or perhaps never to be heard from again.

The whole thing concerned me for the president-elect. It was motion without progress. It looked good but could not possibly lead to the best results for him. I had been through government transitions. This was everything we had worked so hard for five months to avoid.

The smear stories about me had started right after Election Day. They hadn't stopped. They were still popping up in the media, attributed to unnamed people close to the president-elect and dumping all over me. As usual, I couldn't prove who was behind them, but they sure seemed to carry Jared's and Bannon's fingerprints. Donald had assured me, several times, that he hadn't ordered up the hit pieces and insisted that he didn't approve of them. In fact, he would call me, outraged about the "leaks" and assuring me they would stop. But the anonymous insults kept showing up.

The other reason I wasn't rushing to Bedminster was that I already had a job. A great job. I still had more than a year on my second term as governor. I wasn't at all sure I wanted to go to Washington. Jeff Sessions had already gotten attorney general, the one position other than vice president that was enticing to me. So, at this point, I really couldn't think of any reason that I should take part in the Bedminster parade.

Between the smears and my displaying no interest, I was surprised the second week of November when I received a message from a staff scheduler asking when I'd be available for a meeting in Bedminster.

"No thank you," I said when I returned the call. "I don't think so. Not for me."

But that wasn't the end of it. David Bossie followed up. Bossie, who'd been deputy campaign manager since September, was part of the transition now. "I hear you said you're not coming to Bedminster," Bossie said when he called. "You really need to come. Don't make this your argument with the president-elect. Your problems are with other people, not with the president-elect. Please come."

David was one of the people around the president-elect who knew what he was doing. In my experience, he'd always been a straight shooter with a keen grasp of the politics around him. Most important, he was strong and confident enough to tell the president-elect the truth. Maybe he had a point.

"All right," I told David. "I'll come."

So, on Sunday afternoon, November 20, I threw on a blue blazer and rode over to Bedminster, fifteen minutes from my house in Mendham.

I managed to slip inside the clubhouse without the reporters noticing and was escorted into a hold room, where I met with Mike Pence, Rudy Giuliani, and David Bossie. They all made a point of saying they hoped I would be joining the new administration. When Donald was ready for me, I was brought out of the back of the clubhouse to stage an arrival for the reporters and

photographers who were camped out front. This was all a part
of the show that they were creating up at Bedminster. I was not
offended by the show. I was very concerned that, with the transition thrown out and all the players participating in the show, who
was doing the actual work of putting together a government? Priebus, Bannon, and Kushner always wanted to be in the room with
Donald. Who was putting together the intricacies of running the
largest government in the world now that our six months of work
was in the trash?

I walked up to the front entrance where the president-elect
was waiting to greet me. We stood outside together and shook
hands while the journalists shouted questions and the photographers got their shots. Donald said nice things about me: "Very talented man. . . . a great guy. . . . Many qualities, including smart
and tough." Then we headed inside to the conference room, where
Reince, Steve, and Jared were already waiting for us. I nodded
hello to everyone. Donald was the first to speak.

"I hate these stories that are out there about you," he said to
me. "But all that stuff about Jared being the guy who's doing it to
you, that's totally false. Isn't it, Jared?"

"Absolutely," Jared told his father-in-law—he had nothing
to do with any of it. Then Jared turned to me. "I never speak to
the press. I told you all the way back last spring, Governor, that
any animus I had was now behind me," he said. "That the most
important thing was electing Donald president and, now that
we've done that, making him a great president. I would never do
anything to harm you in any way."

"See?" Trump said. "He wouldn't do anything like that."

Right there, I had to decide how I wanted to handle this.

Steve Bannon had told me it was Jared who'd ordered my firing. Top folks in the campaign had told me Jared was criticizing

me and the transition effort to Donald on a daily basis. Friendly members of the media had assured me that "Team Jared" was planting stories on me. The eleventh-hour assurances to the contrary were tough for a former prosecutor to swallow. But I didn't see much benefit in pressing the point in that room. These people had an administration to assemble and not much time to do it. Now was not the moment to rehash ancient bitternesses. So I decided to let the subject pass.

"Well, Mr. President-Elect," I said, "if that's what you tell me, I have no reason to disbelieve you."

"Okay," Donald answered, sounding relieved to move on. "I want you to be special assistant to the president in the White House."

I already knew my answer to that.

"No thank you, sir."

Donald looked surprised. "What do you mean 'No thank you?'" he asked. "I haven't even described the job yet."

"Mr. President-Elect," I said, "I didn't come here with a résumé. I already have a job. I'm not looking for a job. I'm not looking to come and work in the White House. So why don't we just sit here and have a pleasant conversation about how I can help from the outside, because I'm not looking for anything."

Donald shot me an expression that said maybe, he hadn't heard me right. "You really don't want to even consider this position?" he asked.

"No, sir, I don't," I answered. "But thank you."

And that seemed to settle it. For the moment.

We talked about how Donald was feeling—"Just great!"—and a couple of the people they'd already interviewed. Then Reince said to me something that struck me as almost surreal.

"That transition work you did," he said, "who else do you think we should be considering? What other people should we be talking to?"

Could Reince be serious? Was he joking? I couldn't believe he was asking me that. I felt like saying, *Go look in the garbage where Bannon and Dearborn threw the shit out. Look for it yourself.*

I didn't say that. I just thought it as I sat there—how these three people were so ill serving the president-elect in the way they were handling the transition. And I gave a rote response to Reince: "There are plenty of talented people out there." I just wanted to leave.

After less than half an hour in the conference room, I could tell we were done. I got up and Donald got up, and we shifted into the standard Bedminster exit drill. He walked me out to the lobby and I stepped outside for another round of shouted questions.

"How'd the meeting go?"

"Great," I said, before heading back to my car.

——

Apparently, our preinaugural job dance still had a few steps left.

In early December, I got a call from Steve Bannon, who said that he'd been speaking with Rebekah Mercer. The Mercers are among the party's largest donors, giving many millions of dollars a year to Republican causes and candidates. Steve went on to say that Rebekah and other family members had decided they wanted me to consider being chairman of the Republican National Committee.

Well, that certainly came out of the blue!

As soon as a Republican is elected president, that person designates someone to chair the Republican National Committee, the official body that runs the party. At its next meeting, the committee's voting members rubber-stamp the choice of the president-elect. The position opened in mid-November when the previous chairman, Reince Priebus, was announced as the White House chief of staff. The names of several possible replacements were already floating around. One was David Bossie. That sounded promising. Another was Ronna Romney McDaniel, chair of the Michigan Republican Party and a niece of 2012 presidential nominee, Mitt Romney. She'd earned good will among Trump supporters—"my Romney," Donald was heard to call her—by bucking her uncle's anti-Trump attitudes, even publishing a preelection op-ed in Utah's *Deseret News* in which she stated, "Donald Trump is the president we need." Corey Lewandowski was mentioned in media reports. So was Nick Ayers, who had run Mike Pence's vice-presidential campaign.

But on high-level leadership decisions like this one, I knew, the Mercers carried real weight. Party chairman wasn't anything I'd given any thought to. But when Steve asked if I'd be willing to meet with Rebekah Mercer, I said, "Of course."

"Good morning," I texted her. "Steve Bannon suggested I give you a call and set up a time to meet this week or early next week. Tried to call you, but your voice mailbox is full. This is my cell. Feel free to call when you get a moment."

She got right back to me, and we set up a time to meet.

Before we got together, I poked around a little. I wanted to see how far the idea had gone. Was it just Steve and Rebekah talking about my being chairman? Was the president-elect on board? How about the others in the inner circle? I'd been around long enough to know that, in the end, an incoming president always has the call on who runs the party. That's one of the spoils of winning on Election Day. This would make sense only if he and those around him wanted me. The early signals I was hearing were all quite upbeat.

When Rebekah and I sat down together, she had lots of questions and lots of compliments about how I had run the Republican Governors Association in the pivotal 2014 midterms. She sounded as encouraging as Steve had predicted. We really hit it off. After the meeting, I called Roberto Mignone, a Wall street hedge fund titan and big supporter of my presidential campaign. He and his wife, Allison, were also friendly with Rebekah. I asked if he could get feedback. It was all very positive.

I also got a totally unexpected call—from Jared Kushner. He asked if I was truly willing to consider the party chairman idea. I said I was if the president-elect wanted me. Jared said he thought it was a great idea. He said they wanted the benefit of my advice, as they had during the campaign. He assured me he was supportive.

I texted Steve after the Jared phone call: "I had a very good meeting with Rebekah on Friday."

"She raved about it," he texted back

"Well, that's good to hear," I answered. "Also had good convos with JK as well as others."

"Yes," Steve answered, "we were with each other all day. He is very enthusiastic."

After the weekend, I got another text from Steve. "Are you free Wednesday afternoon to meet with Rebekah Mercer again re: the RNC?"

"Okay," I answered. "Any intel?"

"Yes. The Mercers are very interested in you running the RNC."

I met with Rebekah again, this time in the offices of the Mercer Family Foundation on Manhattan's West Seventy-Second

Street. We had another great talk. I was beginning to think I really might like to do this—and I could be good at it. With a new, outsider president, the Republicans needed someone party officials could relate to—who also had a long and close relationship with the new president. There weren't that many people who had both. There still aren't.

I got a call from the president-elect the following weekend.

"Are you willing to be chairman of the RNC?" he asked me straight out.

"Sir, I'm willing to do it, if you can change the rules that allow me to accept outside income. I've got to be able to accept my gubernatorial salary. I'm happy to be chair of the RNC if that's what you want me to do. It will allow me to help run your political operation, and that will be fine."

"I love the idea," he said. "Let me talk to the guys around here, and then I'll get back to you."

We scheduled a meeting at Trump Tower for 3:45 p.m. the following Wednesday, December 7, to seal the deal.

I got a call that afternoon before I left New Jersey. The president-elect was running late. Could we push our meeting back to 4:30? Sure, I said. When I arrived at 4:30, I got word that Trump was still tied up, and I should go see Reince Priebus first.

"You can't be chairman of the RNC," Reince said as soon as I sat down in front of his desk. "He's already decided to give it to someone else."

"That's not what he told me," I said.

"Well," Reince continued, "I'm telling you. But he wants you to consider some other things."

That's when I blew up.

"This is bullshit," I erupted, "and I don't want to consider other things." The truth was I wasn't the one who had been pushing for Republican chairman. That was Steve Bannon, Rebekah Mercer, Jared Kushner, and the president-elect. I was willing to consider the position because it was outside of government and would allow me to stay as governor. Reince obviously wanted *his* person.

"Enough of Bannon calling me and the president-elect calling me," I said. "I don't know what's going on here, but I've had enough."

This clearly wasn't what Reince was hoping to hear.

"He wants you to consider being secretary of labor," Priebus said.

"No," I shot back. "No interest."

Reince still wasn't done. "Well, how about secretary of homeland security?" he said.

"No. No interest."

"No interest?" Priebus repeated, sounding just a little incredulous.

"No interest," I said.

Reince pressed valiantly on. "Well, he also told me, if you were more interested in being an ambassador, he was willing to make you ambassador to Italy or ambassador to the Vatican."

I couldn't believe what I was hearing. This was truly off the rails. Nice as Rome might be to live in, it also made no sense in my life.

"I'm not rich, and my children are still in high school," I said. "So I'm not moving to Italy. The answer is no."

Reince looked truly frustrated. He told me he had been sent down by the president-elect with an explicit instruction: "Make Chris happy."

"Then, tell the president-elect to make me RNC chair," I replied. "You're going to have enough to do as chief of staff without worrying about the RNC. With me there, you won't have to worry about it."

"Not possible," Reince said.

Reince was running out of options now. He certainly wasn't getting any of the responses he expected from me. "I just want to be clear on this, so I can tell the president-elect," he said. "You've refused secretary of labor, secretary of homeland security, ambassador to the Vatican, and ambassador to Italy."

"Yes," I said. "I've refused them all. You guys raised the RNC thing with me. If you don't want me to do that—"

"You need to be a member of the RNC to do it," Reince said.

I knew that wasn't correct.

"No, you don't," I shot back. "Don't BS me about this. I know what the rules are. Whoever the president wants, the RNC will elect."

He didn't press the point.

"I'm supposed to go meet with the president-elect," I told Reince. "I should probably get going."

"I have to go talk to him first," Reince told me.

Whatever, I shrugged as Reince practically sprinted to Donald's office.

———

I didn't wait to be called upstairs. A few minutes after Reince left, I rode the elevator up to Trump's office on the twenty-sixth floor. As usual, the Secret Service didn't say anything. Nobody stopped me. As I reached the door, Reince was sitting with Steve Bannon, Jared Kushner, and the president-elect. I could tell they were talking about Reince's meeting with me.

"Oh, Chris," Trump said as I walked in.

"Hey, how are you guys?" I said, completely matter-of-fact. "What's going on?"

"Ah, can you give us a minute?" Trump asked me.

"Yeah, sure," I said.

I waited outside until Jared, Steve, and Reince left the office. But just as I was standing to walk in, Trump came out with his jacket over his arm like he was heading up to his apartment.

He spotted me immediately. "Chris," he said, "I can't meet with you tonight. I'm too tired."

"Mr. President-Elect," I said, "I don't need a meeting."

"You don't?" he asked.

"No, no, I don't need a meeting," I said. "I think Reince already handled everything. I don't need a meeting. I'll walk you to the elevator."

"If you don't need a meeting, what are you doing up here?" he asked.

"I'll explain it to you," I said. "Let's walk."

I looked at him as we made our way toward the elevator bank. "I just came to say goodbye," I said.

He seemed surprised at that. "Goodbye?"

"Yeah," I said. "You know, Mr. President-Elect, it's pretty obvious that there are people around here who don't want me around. And that's fine. I don't want that ever to affect our friendship. So, I wanted to come here and say to you, 'I'm proud of you.' You won an amazing race. I wish you all the best to be a great president. I want you to do that because you're my friend, and I want you to do it because I'm an American, and I want you to be successful. If you are, the whole country will be. But I don't want you to worry about me or think about me anymore. I'm the governor of New Jersey. I'm fine with being the governor and then moving on to private

life after that. But I do not want to come back here again and discuss any other jobs, because I'm done."

"No, no. Chris," he protested. "You come back here tomorrow.
What did they do to you? You and I can fix this together."

I put my hand on his arm, and I said, "No, Mr. President-Elect.
I'm done. I'm not angry with you. Believe me, I don't blame you
for this. It's other people, and I get it. I know how this game is
played. So I'm going to go home, and you go home, too. We'll continue to be friends. I wish you all the best. If you ever need my
advice or my help or you just want to talk, I'll always take your
call, sir."

And I left.

The president-elect and I didn't speak again for another ten
days. After that, it was on a totally different basis. As far as I was
concerned, the transition saga had finally ended that day. Those
who thought they would increase their own influence by ditching
the carefully planned transition process and excluding people
from the government who might actually persuade the president-
elect—those selfish people had won. They put themselves ahead of
the president-elect and the country they were supposed to loyally
serve.

And we all know what happened next.

TWENTY-SEVEN

MR. PRESIDENT

There was a mix-up with the tickets to the inauguration. Of course there was.

When Donald Trump was sworn in as the forty-fifth president of the United States on January 20, 2017, Mary Pat and I sat with my fellow Republican governors, not on the platform with the inner circle of the Trump campaign. Our tickets never showed up at the Willard hotel, one of many balls that got dropped by the inept leadership of the longtime Paul Manafort aide and future federal felon Rick Gates at the Presidential Inaugural Committee.

We had fine seats—no complaint there—six rows behind the platform with a clear view of everything. Tennessee's Bill Haslam was on one side of us. Maine's Paul LePage was on the other. But when Rudy Giuliani noticed the two empty chairs in his row on the platform, he yelled up to Mary Pat and me, "You're supposed to be down here!"

"I don't have any tickets for down there," I called back.

Suddenly, Rudy was waving two cardboard placards that he'd just ripped off the backs of our reserved seats: GOV CHRIS CHRISTIE and MARY PAT CHRISTIE. The whole thing had Haslam and LePage shaking their heads and cracking up.

"Perfect," Haslam said.

"Just perfect," LePage agreed.

That is why, if you look at video of the Trump inauguration, you will see two empty seats near the center of the platform. We'd gotten a stack of invitations to parties, balls, receptions, concerts, church services, and other inaugural events, but Mary Pat and I had decided to skip all that. We just wanted to be there when Donald raised his right hand and became the president.

At precisely noon, Donald placed his left hand on two Bibles—one his mother had given him and the historic Lincoln Bible—and took the oath of office with Chief Justice John Roberts. The Marine Band played "Hail to the Chief" and Trump was honored with a twenty-one-gun salute. His sixteen-minute inaugural address struck a tone that was surely familiar to anyone who had attended any of his campaign rallies or watched him on TV. He described the United States as a "land of abandoned factories, economic angst, rising crime," pledged to end the "American carnage" and promised "a new era in American politics" in which, "from this day forward, it's going to be only America first."

It was, almost everyone agreed, an unconventional curtain-raiser on what was destined to be an unconventional presidency.

When the ceremony was over and the crowd began to disperse, Kellyanne Conway made her way over to us. "Why didn't you sit in your seats on the platform?" she asked me. "Are you upset about something?"

"Not at all," I told her. "The only thing I'm upset about is nobody told me we had seats on the platform."

Apparently we'd also been invited to the congressional luncheon in the Capitol Statuary Hall, but we needed our platform tickets to get through security. We just walked over to Union Station, where we got a train home to New Jersey.

It was the next week when Donald called. "I heard they screwed up your seats at the inauguration, and that stinks," he said, even before *hello*. "I was looking for you two."

"Mr. President," I started. It was the first time I had addressed him that way. It felt a little strange. But he'd certainly earned it, and the words tumbled comfortably off my lips. "Mr. President," I said, "don't worry about it. We had a great view. We saw you get sworn in. We heard the speech."

"No, no, no," he countered, sounding just like he always sounded, despite the big change in his life. "I need to make it up to you and Mary Pat right away. Bring her down in the next couple of weeks. Let's have lunch."

I said we'd love to.

I did bring up one other topic before we got off the phone: "About the travel ban. . . ."

As one of his first official acts, Donald had signed Executive Order 13769, which temporarily blocked travel to the United States by citizens of the majority-Muslim nations of Iran, Iraq, Libya, Somalia, Sudan, Syria, and Yemen and suspended the admission of refugees from around the world. Green card holders were also affected. The media said the order was inspired by Steve Bannon and drafted by Stephen Miller, both of whom now had senior positions on the White House staff.

That order sparked immediate protests at airports across the country—including Newark and Kennedy—and almost fifty legal challenges in federal court. The courts issued orders, including a national temporary restraining order that barred enforcement of major parts of the travel ban.

The whole thing had turned into a giant mess.

"I think your staff might have screwed up the EO," I said to Donald, using the initials for executive order. "It doesn't sound like what we had in mind in the transition plan." I didn't have to remind him that the transition plan, the one that Bannon and Dearborn so famously trashed, included detailed drafts of key executive orders that were prepared by experienced government attorneys to withstand court scrutiny, not hurriedly thrown together by inexperienced White House aides.

To me, the order Trump signed looked more like a campaign brochure than a legal document. It was so broadly drafted there was no way it was going to be upheld in court. Clearly it hadn't been approved by White House counsel Don McGahn, who had plenty of experience at this sort of thing.

"No, no," Donald said, dismissing my concerns. "They all told me it was fine."

"Well," I said, "I know what they told you. But I think this is going to be a problem."

I didn't want to get into a lot of detail with him on the phone. All I said was, "It's not good. Have the lawyers check it out. You may want to amend it."

But I could tell he was only half-listening. "I'll talk to somebody," he said noncommittally.

He had no idea how bad this would get.

This was exactly what I had been concerned about when those transition binders were tossed into the trash. With half a year of careful planning out the window, it was a free-for-all in there. The reality was no one was in charge. People were pushing their own agendas. Nothing was coordinated at all. Important responsibilities were being grabbed by people who had never done anything like this before.

These were precisely the kinds of problems our transition process was designed to avoid, amateurish moves by inexperienced staffers operating with no master plan. And the travel ban fiasco was just the start of it.

This wasn't effective government. It was back-of-the-envelope winging it from Bannon and the others. I had feared this would happen, and it did—over and over again.

▬

A parade of screwups followed on issues large and small, with the White House staff dividing quickly into feuding factions with no transition plan to refer to. Bannon had his human hand grenades. Priebus had his Washington insiders. And Donald seemed content to let them all fight it out.

Clearly that was no way to launch a new administration, especially one purportedly dedicated to businesslike efficiency and draining the Washington swamp. Nothing was rolling out like it was supposed to, at a time when there was so much that needed to be done. Top-level staff appointments. Cabinet and subcabinet nominations. Diplomatic postings around the world. The order of major-issue rollouts. This was the gritty business of forming and operating a government. Too much of it wasn't getting done—or wasn't getting done nearly as well as it should have been.

I was back in New Jersey, being governor. Donald and I kept talking. But I had no position in the administration. Maybe that gave me a clearer perspective. Who knows? But I'll say this much: a lot of it was painful to watch, nothing so much as the fiasco of Michael Flynn.

———

Against my strong and repeated advice, Donald had appointed that walking car crash to be his national security adviser, one of the most important positions in the White House. As the president's chief in-house adviser on national security issues, Flynn was responsible for coordinating all the incoming from the Defense Department, the State Department, the intelligence agencies, and anything else related to our national defense, providing the president with the best possible information and guidance. This takes a keen mind, a calm disposition, vast experience, and unquestioned integrity. Flynn was lacking three, possibly four of those categories. He had never been one of the four pre-vetted officials identified in the transition plan for such a sensitive role.

The retired general certainly didn't waste any time making himself a real liability to the president who'd shown such trust in him. Even before Flynn went to work, questions were being raised about his close ties to Russian military and intelligence officials—and his own verifiable lies about the relationships. Congressional Democrats were pounding him about a December 2015 gala in Moscow where he sat next to Russian president Vladimir Putin, while taking a $45,000 speaking fee from RT, the Russian propaganda TV network. Others asked about work Flynn had done for the government of Turkey and a meeting he'd held at Trump Tower with Heinz-Christian Strache, the leader of Austria's far right Freedom Party.

Twice in January, the acting attorney general, Sally Yates, an Obama holdover, met with White House counsel Don McGahn to warn that Flynn was "compromised" and possibly open to blackmail by the Russians. Yates also reported that Flynn had misled

Vice President Pence about his communications with Sergey Kislyak, Russia's ambassador to the United States.

He couldn't last, and he didn't. Flynn submitted his resignation as national security adviser on February 13, his twenty-
four-day tenure the shortest in the history of the job. Again, all of
this could have been avoided if someone had bothered to pull our
transition plan out of the trash.

The morning after Flynn was fired, Mary Pat and I were on
the train to Washington for a Valentine's Day lunch with Donald when I got a call from Hope Hicks. Hope was calling to let
me know that Steve Bannon, Reince Priebus, and Jared Kushner
would be joining us for lunch with the president.

The three senior aides were clearly at each other's throats on
some matters, but they were fully united in not wanting me alone
with the president. Who knew what I might say about *them*? I'd
said some things on TV about the botched travel ban and a few
other issues that made clear I didn't believe the president was
being well served.

"Hope," I said, "you tell whoever told you that, that if all three
of them are coming to this lunch, I'm not going. I'll get off at
Union Station and take the first train north. And they can explain
to the president why Mary Pat and I are not there."

Hope didn't sound entirely surprised to hear me say that. "I
know you're serious," she said.

"Dead serious," I answered. "So you need to go find out what's
going to happen here, because I don't need this."

She called back a few minutes later and said, "Bannon and
Priebus will not be at lunch. Only Jared."

"Fine," I said. At least I would not have to contend with the president being distracted by all three of them.

Donald welcomed us warmly into the Oval Office. He was excited to show us how he'd set everything up, the prized piece of real estate that it was. "You know what?" he said. "This might have been you guys here if it hadn't been for Bridgegate."

I thought Mary Pat's head might explode at that, even though (I think) Donald was just trying to be nice. We took some pictures with us standing behind Donald, who was sitting at the desk, then moved directly into the private dining room.

He told Mary Pat to order whatever she felt like. "The food is amazing here," he said. "The chef is great. You can have whatever you want, whether it's on the menu or not. He'll make you whatever you like." She ordered the salmon. I was about to order when Donald spoke up. "You and I are going to have the meatloaf."

Immediately, my mind flashed back fifteen years to our very first dinner together at Jean-Georges. At least now he wasn't ordering something I hated.

Jared walked in and sat with us. He ordered his typical salad. Priebus, despite skipping lunch, appeared several times and whispered to Trump, lingering each time until the president shooed him off. "Okay, Reince," he said. "I'll see you later."

At one point during the lunch, Donald said to me, "This Russia thing is all over now, because I fired Flynn."

I started to laugh.

"What are you laughing about?" he asked.

"Sir," I said, "this Russia thing is far from over."

"What do you mean?" he said. "Flynn met with the Russians. That was the problem. I fired Flynn. It's over."

"That's right," Jared piped in, "firing Flynn ends the whole Russia thing."

I couldn't believe how naive all this sounded. "Guys," I said, "my guess is that we're going to be sitting here at Valentine's Day of 2018, maybe longer, and we're still going to be talking about this."

"You're crazy," Jared said.

"Well, you may think I'm crazy," I told him. "But I've been through this kind of stuff both as a prosecutor and as someone who was being investigated. And it's never what you think it's going to be. Firing Mike Flynn is not going to end this conversation. Mr. President, I'll give you one bit of advice as someone who's been through it. There is no way that you can make this process shorter, but there's lots of ways you can make it longer. And the biggest way for you to make it longer is by talking about it. Don't talk about it. That's the biggest, most important bit of advice I can give you. Don't talk about it."

He looked at me like I was talking another language.

"You think I had to fire Flynn, though? I mean, you think I had to get rid of him, right?"

I said, "Sir—"

He cut me off before I could answer. "How did you feel about Flynn?"

"No, no, no, no," I said. "Let's not play this game. You know how I felt about Flynn. You know I didn't want you to hire Flynn in the first place. So let's not play around thinking you're not sure how I felt about Flynn. You know how I felt about Flynn."

"Yeah," he said, "you didn't like him."

"That's right," I said. "I didn't like him, and I didn't think he should be hired in the first place, and I'm glad he's gone. You're doing the right thing by getting a new person."

In the midst of our back-and-forth, we could see Sean Spicer on the TV in the dining room. The president's press secretary was speaking from the White House briefing room, addressing the controversy around General Michael Flynn. Just then, Jared's phone rang. It was Flynn complaining about whatever it was that Spicer was saying.

I turned to the president and said to him, "You see? When you have a crazy person in your life, you can never get rid of him. Crazy people don't act like sane people. They're crazy. You're never going to be able to get rid of this guy. He is going to be like gum on the bottom of your shoe for years to come."

Before Mary Pat and I got out of there, Donald pulled me aside and asked me, "Of the big priorities that we have in front of us, what order would you do them in?"

I was momentarily taken aback that he was now seeking my advice on that. Hadn't he already ignored my advice? "Well," I said, "that was all laid out in the transition plan. But I would do tax cut first, infrastructure second, and then Obamacare. Obamacare will be the hardest of the three, but you will gain a lot of credit with members of Congress by cutting taxes and by creating an infrastructure plan. There will be something for everybody then. The Democrats will love the infrastructure plan and the spending and the redevelopment of the nation's roads and bridges and mass transit and airports. The Republicans will love the tax cuts. The public will love both. Then, when you've strengthened yourself politically, you can take on Obamacare."

I don't think that was the answer he was expecting or the answer that he wanted.

"I hear you," he said. "But Paul Ryan and Reince are telling me that I have to do Obamacare first or I won't have the money for the tax cut."

"That's complete bullshit," I said. "Ronald Reagan didn't care about those arguments when he did the tax cut in 1981. He just went ahead and did it and figured it out later on. You can't allow the propeller-heads to tell you what you're supposed to do here. It's a political judgment, not a math equation. Do the tax cuts first."

That's where things were when Mary Pat and I left.

The president called me a couple of days later and said, "I can't do what you told me to do. Gotta do Obamacare first. Everyone around here is telling me I have to do Obamacare first. Reince is telling me. Bannon is telling me. Everyone says I have to do Obamacare first."

"Okay," I said.

Everyone knows what happened next.

The Wisconsin axis, Priebus and Speaker Ryan, kept assuring Donald Trump they had the votes in the House and the Senate to repeal Obamacare. It was going to be a grand slam home run for the party and the president, and everything else would fall in line after that. All spring and into the early part of the summer, I kept having my own conversations with the president, saying as firmly as I could, "The votes aren't there. . . ." "You will regret this. . . ." "It'll make everything else that much more difficult." And the truth of the matter was that the votes weren't there. The staff didn't have a plan. They had wishful thinking. They had red meat rhetoric. But they didn't have a plan. And that ill served the president.

I'm not claiming I had a crystal ball on any of these early mistakes—the shoddy travel ban, Flynn's toxic instability, the unvetted personnel moves, or the extraordinary difficulty of replacing Obamacare. But I had an advantage over the crew of people who became the new inner circle and White House senior staff. I had spent six months thinking about all this stuff, consulting with the nation's top experts, drafting vital documents, identifying potential allies, drawing up lists, and making plans.

I'm not saying any of that made me a genius. But it put me light-years ahead of the rest of them. And one last thing: I had the president's agenda as priority one. I was not playing *Game of Thrones* in the West Wing.

▬

On his way to his new job as Donald Trump's labor secretary, Andy Puzder was getting it from all sides. And Donald was reaching back to me.

The former chief executive of the Hardee's and Carl's Jr. fast-food chains, Puzder was being accused by Democrats of mistreating his workers, opposing the minimum wage, and promoting heartless workplace automation. At the same time, some conservatives were knocking him for employing an undocumented immigrant as a housekeeper. Even worse, a videotape had surfaced of his ex-wife on *The Oprah Winfrey Show* in 1990 saying he'd threatened her—"I will see you in the gutter. . . . You will pay for this"—after she publicly accused him of spousal abuse.

With all that swirling around, Puzder's confirmation hearing kept being delayed by the Senate Health, Education, Labor, and Pensions Committee. Unable to extract himself from this particular version of Washington hell, he finally faced the inevitable and withdrew his name.

I was in the kitchen at home eating dinner with Mary Pat, Patrick, and Bridget when Donald called. "Have you been reading this Puzder stuff?" he asked.

I told him I had.

"It's a shame, because he's a nice guy," Donald said. "Who would have known? I'm calling because I want you to take labor secretary. Get down here. Get around the table. I know you want one of the big jobs, and you're entitled to that. You're smart enough for it. People have those jobs right now, but they won't have them forever. You gotta come down here and get at the table so that when one of those big jobs comes open, you're sitting there and you're ready to go."

"No thank you," I said.

Hadn't we been down this road before?

"Why not?" he pressed.

"Three reasons," I told him. "Reason number one is I have no interest in being labor secretary. I'd be bored to death. Reason number two is that I'd have to leave home. Mary Pat is not coming with me—the kids, either. They're not leaving high school to move to Washington. So I'd have to become a weekend father, and the job would have to be more interesting to me than labor secretary for me to do that. And number three is because of all of the arguments I had with the public-sector unions in New Jersey. This would be a really hellacious confirmation hearing. How do you expect me to trust your staff to have my back during that when they're the very same people who fired me as transition chairman?"

Up until that moment, Donald Trump and I had never spoken once about my being fired from the transition. He never talked to me about it. I never brought it up to him. I never said how unfair I believed it was, how I thought the decision poorly served him. I knew where it came from, and I wasn't going to bother him with complaints about a decision that had already been made.

But I bristled at what he said to me next on the phone: "Chris, you didn't get fired. You got made part of a larger team."

That wasn't what happened.

"Mr. President," I said, "I've never, ever brought up my leaving the transition chairmanship, because you were the president-elect of the United States and you had much bigger fish to fry. And I'm a big boy who understands the way this business works. But please, sir, don't ever, ever, tell me again that I wasn't fired."

From the immediate change in his tone, I could tell he wasn't about to argue the point. "Okay," he said, trying one, last time. "How about labor secretary?"

"I'm not going to do it, sir. I really appreciate the offer. I'm honored. But it's not for me."

"I figured I'd give it a try," he said. "You're my first choice."

It was very flattering. I felt like I could say exactly what I was thinking. The same as I did in television interviews. The same as I did when I spoke with people on the White House staff. Donald didn't always enjoy my answers. I am certain of that. But I do believe he liked that I gave them.

TWENTY-EIGHT

OPIOID BEACH

hated the whole idea of being a lame duck.

I'd seen what happens far too often: A successful two-term governor reaches the final stretch of that second term, totally exhausted. Grumpy and insular. Distracted and irrelevant. Unable to summon the spark for anything new. I knew what the law said, and I could read a calendar. Someone new would be sitting at my desk on January 16, 2018.

So I decided to up my efforts on one of the toughest causes around: treatment for substance abusers. I had been interested in the issue ever since my time as a Morris County freeholder, when I'd gotten to know a miracle worker named Father Joe Hennen. Executive director of the Daytop Village drug-treatment program, Father Hennen helped me see how addiction touches nearly every family and treatment saves lives. Neither of my parents had drug or alcohol problems, though we knew several people who did. Even as a child, I understood the grip of addiction. All I had to do was watch my mother smoke.

As governor, I'd already had some success expanding New Jersey's drug court, where nonviolent offenders were funneled into treatment, not prison. Now, with a deadly epidemic of opioid abuse sweeping the state and the nation, often fueled by the overprescription of legal pain pills, I knew we needed to do more.

The answer was obvious: we had to reduce the stigma of addiction and get more people into treatment. So we expanded the state's drug-treatment hotline. We launched a $25 million advertising campaign featuring the real-life stories of people in recovery. We reduced first prescriptions for opioids to five days, the shortest in the nation at the time. We established America's first drug-treatment state prison to give addicted inmates a chance to get clean before release. We held candlelight vigils outside the State House, where family members commemorated the lost lives of their loved ones. Anything to focus attention on the cause.

With my encouragement, Donald Trump stepped up, too. On March 29, 2017, he asked me to chair his President's Commission on Combating Drug Addiction and the Opioid Crisis. This was an issue the president also took personally. His older brother, Fred, had died an alcoholic in 1981 at age forty-three, further proof that addiction touches every family. With that recognition, Donald and I agreed the commission should be utterly bipartisan. I was pleased that former congressman Patrick Kennedy, who is in recovery, agreed to participate, as did Republican Massachusetts governor Charlie Baker, Democratic North Carolina governor Roy Cooper, Republican Florida attorney general Pam Bondi, and professor Bertha Madras of the Harvard Medical School, who knows more about the evolution of the opioid crisis than any other clinician in the world.

We got right down to business. Holding hearings. Taking testimony from active addicts, people in recovery, pharma companies, family members, and the nation's top experts. Crafting an action plan of practical steps the government could take or encourage that would help people find the tools to change their lives.

———

That summer, while our national opioid commission was searching for answers, I ran into a wall of drug-treatment resistance from our own state legislature. As a key part of my eighth and final state budget, I had an inspired idea. I proposed that Horizon Blue Cross Blue Shield, a state-owned entity that had billions of dollars in surplus, contribute $300 million to make drug treatment more accessible to pregnant women, addicted newborns, and others who desperately needed help. Senate president Steve Sweeney backed the concept and got a bill through his chamber. But Horizon's management balked, and so did Vinnie Prieto, the Speaker of the assembly. With the June 30 deadline approaching, Vinnie vowed he would never pass a state budget that included the Horizon contribution to drug treatment. If we couldn't make a budget deal by then, the state would have to shut down.

I was proud to have signed seven state budgets without a single government shutdown, including some killer negotiations in the early years. I pushed the assembly with every ounce of strength I had. People were dying, I pointed out. They needed access to treatment. The money was there. But Vinnie refused to budge. There was no doubt in my mind he had some kind of secret arrangement with Horizon's executives. That suspicion would be heightened later when the health insurance giant quickly settled major litigation with hospitals in Vinnie's district and his chief of staff joined the Horizon board of directors.

There could be no budget without the assembly, and Vinnie stood in the way. This was the kind of dirty deal that Hudson

County politicians had been famous for since the days of the corrupt Jersey City mayor Frank Hague. Vinnie Prieto now joined that Hall of Shame by putting politics ahead of helping addicted pregnant women.

All week I had been telling everyone in Trenton that I didn't know if the government would close. "But if it does," I said, "I am going to the governor's beach house at Island Beach State Park for the Fourth of July weekend, just like I promised my family I would." Months earlier, I had told all four kids they could invite friends to the beach for our final Fourth of July weekend. A dozen friends were flying in from all over the country and, in one case, from London. l wasn't going to hold my family hostage to Vinnie Prieto's sleazy maneuvering and the resulting dysfunction in Trenton.

The dysfunction won. The legislature failed to send me a budget, so there was nothing for me to sign. At midnight June 30, all nonessential state services shut down, including New Jersey's state parks. Regardless, I headed to the governor's beach house with my wife, our kids, and their friends. The beach house was on the property of Island Beach State Park, a state-owned beachfront. When the park was open, people paid by the carload to swim and sunbathe at a portion of the beach three and a half miles from the entrance gate. The beach house was one mile from the gate and had been there for decades for governors and their families to use.

I kept working on the budget, traveling back and forth each day between the State House and Island Beach, trying to facilitate an agreement. On Sunday, July 2, before I headed to Trenton, Mary Pat said to me, "You know, we have all these people out there on the beach, all these friends of our children. Just come out and sit for an hour so they can at least spend some time with you."

I didn't really feel like it, but I said okay. My wife was asking, and she had a point. I pulled on shorts, a T-shirt, and a baseball cap and walked out to the sand. I settled into a beach chair and spent an hour sitting with my kids and their friends. I was being a husband and a dad, just as I had promised. It turned out to be a bad decision.

Unbeknownst to me, the *Star-Ledger* had hired a plane to fly over the beach and take pictures of us. It just so happened that they chose the one hour I was sitting out there. Talk about bad luck! After an hour, I left the beach, took a shower, got dressed, and went back to work in Trenton.

Those photos exploded in the media. Within a few hours, they were all over the internet and leading cable news. It was a slow news holiday weekend, and they were everywhere. The message the photos were meant to convey—entitled governor lounges with his family while New Jersey beaches are closed to regular folks—was factually wrong in several respects. First of all, it wasn't true the beaches of New Jersey were closed. Quite the opposite. Every single beach in the state was open to the public, except for the one beach I was sitting on. That's because, up and down the coast, all the beaches are municipally run. The only state beach is Island Beach State Park. Every other beach was completely unaffected by the state-government shutdown. There were literally hundreds of thousands of people on those beaches that July Fourth weekend, even as the media commentators kept insisting otherwise.

The aerial photos showing an empty beach except for the Christie family advanced another false impression. This was no flash of special treatment. That's the way this beach always looked. The state troopers maintain a one-mile security buffer, north and south of the governor's beach house. No one is ever allowed to sun themselves there. It's not like anybody who wants to could open a beach umbrella next to mine and announce on Facebook, "Hey, I'm hanging with the governor's family today." That's not allowed for security reasons, whether the rest of Island Beach State Park is open or not. Those inconvenient facts were never featured in the coverage, of course. If the newspaper had taken those pictures on June 30 or August 15 or any other day that summer, they would have looked exactly the same.

I understand the power of images. But now I was at the end of my term, and I had taken a beating in the polls. Both those facts played into this. Do I wish I hadn't gone on the beach for that one hour? Of course. I certainly didn't need the aggravation. But my family still would have been there, and the fly-over stalkers still would have gotten pictures of my family on the beach. Would the images have been less compelling if I hadn't been there? Sure, and they would have been more representative of our time at the beach house.

But you know what? My family has always come first. There was no shortage of open beaches that weekend. I always care how I'm characterized publicly, as anyone would be. But I had eight years as governor. I had wonderful moments and difficult ones, far more of the first category. This was just another event during my eight-year run. When I went to bed that night, I asked myself the same question I always asked: Was I true to what I believed in? The answer was yes. Everything I did that day was true to myself, true to my family, and true to the people of New Jersey.

In the early hours of July 4, I was finally presented with a budget. It didn't have the Horizon money I was hoping for, but I signed it at 2:39 a.m., reopening the government. I vowed to find other ways to keep expanding drug treatment. The scourge of addiction was still taking thousands of lives.

—

On November 1, the President's Commission issued our 128-page report, proposing sixty-five specific steps to combat the opioid crisis. The report was incredibly well done. Bertha Madras's academic research gave the report historical heft. The most credit belongs to my chief of staff, Amy Cradic, and my policy chief, David Reiner. They spent countless hours turning my vision, the contributions of the other commissioners, and the input from our numerous public hearings into a report that could form the basis of the national response to this crisis. President Trump accepted our recommendations immediately. Kellyanne Conway took on the duties of White House drug czar, making sure these things got done. They included opening drug courts in ninety-three federal jurisdictions, easing access to the anti-overdose medication Naloxone, mandating tougher sentences for fentanyl traffickers, ensuring better training for physicians, and waiving Medicaid rules to open treatment beds for people who couldn't otherwise afford them. A lack of money should not prevent anyone from getting clean. To get things rolling, the president declared a national opioid emergency under the Public Health Service Act, and Congress got busy turning many of our proposals into legislation.

The president held a signing ceremony in the East Room of the White House, declaring "a national public health emergency" and directing all executive agencies to use their emergency powers to fight the opioid crisis. It was a powerful event. Melania introduced Donald and shared her touching stories of meeting families that had struggled with addiction. Various family members and survivors were invited to stand behind the podium. I sat in the audience with the cabinet, members of congress, and senior staff.

Then the president called an audible.

He waved me up to his signing desk and, smiling widely, handed me the pen he used to make the declaration official. He'd asked me to chair his commission. He made sure to recognize my service. It was a great moment for me and all the members of the commission who had put in so much hard work

I kept beating the treatment drum wherever I went. "One hundred and seventy people are dying every day," I said, making the case for crucial funding in the House and the Senate. "Imagine if that many people were dying at the hands of a terrorist organization." We need that kind of response to the drug crisis.

———

Since the state constitution prohibited a run for a third term, Lieutenant Governor Kim Guadagno campaigned with my support to replace me. It is never pleasant to be the incumbent who is term-limited out. You are sure to be attacked, and you really can't defend yourself. I would have enjoyed highlighting our eight-year record. I would have loved to run against Kim's opponent, Phil Murphy, a Democratic Party fund-raiser who'd had a twenty-three-year career at Goldman Sachs, served as Democratic National Committee finance chair for Howard Dean, and had been rewarded with an ambassadorship to Germany. Believe me, I could have found some points to make on the campaign trail. But I wasn't the candidate. Kim Guadagno was. And Murphy beat her.

I was disappointed for Kim, who had been a loyal lieutenant governor. I was sad for the state, which was about to experience an increase in taxes and a vast expansion of the state government by a true Massachusetts liberal. Right after the election, Governor-Elect Murphy and I had lunch in the governor's office, and I walked him through the important pending issues and answered the questions he had. Thanksgiving weekend, he and his wife, Tammy Snyder Murphy, and their four children wanted to see the governor's mansion. The staff had the weekend off. So I gave them the tour myself. I did everything I could to be open and welcoming. I had no hard feelings.

I felt strange, waiting for someone else to be sworn into the job I had held for eight years. I knew my new life would take some getting used to, not being the constant center of political attention and not being able to affect the day-to-day lives of the people I served. Mary Pat and I attended the inauguration on January 16 and wished the new governor well. When the ceremony was over, we walked out of the State House with our heads held high. The State House beat reporters followed us to the parking lot, shouting questions as we walked, including "Governor, what did you think of the speech?"

As I reached the SUV, I looked back at the reporters, who were in a tight semicircle around us, and I said, "You know what? I don't have to talk to you people anymore."

I climbed into the car. I shut the door, and we drove off.

With the State House receding out the back window, I reached into my shirt pocket and pulled out my phone.

I tapped my right index finger on the Twitter app. I called up the names of those local reporters and unfollowed every one of them.

In the car. Riding away from the capital. Unfollow. Unfollow. Unfollow.

Barely a minute after I had left the building, I had unfollowed all of them on Twitter.

I didn't need to know what they were writing about. I didn't need to know what they were talking about. It wasn't my responsibility. It was time to go now. I had proudly, energetically, honestly, and unapologetically served my state for eight years. And I had loved it.

That chapter was over. Time for the next challenge.

TWENTY-NINE

PRICE PAID

I was waiting in the West Wing lobby for a meeting with Kelly-anne Conway about the opioid commission, when Reince Priebus came stomping in.

"I want to see you in the Roosevelt Room," the White House chief of staff demanded, very loudly. It was now three months into the Trump presidency. The day before, April 24, I had been on CNN with Jake Tapper saying that President Trump was being failed by his staff. Reince must have caught the interview.

"Why do you keep saying he's being failed by the staff? You know when you say that, people think it's me."

"I didn't say *you*," I told him. "I said *the staff*."

"Well, I'm the chief of staff," he said.

"I'm aware of your title," I told him, "but I didn't say you specifically. You're just one part of the problem."

He let out a long sigh, like I was just the latest of the many burdens he was forced to bear. "Do you know how impossible it is to operate in this job?" he asked me. "Do you know how difficult it is to work here?"

"I think I do," I said.

"And the family, they're all here," he continued. "They walk into the Oval Office whenever they feel like it. They're in his ear all the time. This is an impossible job for me to do, and people are blaming me for it."

Part of me did feel for Reince.

"I know what I would do if I were you," I said.

"What?"

"I would stop yelling at me. I would walk to the other end of the Roosevelt Room, go into the Oval Office, and say, 'Mr. President, I need ten minutes alone with you. Can I have ten minutes alone, please?' And when he said yes, I would close all the doors and tell the Secret Service to keep everybody else out. And then I would say to him, 'Mr. President, the way this is structured is bound for failure. You need to give me, as chief of staff, the authority I need to succeed. Everybody on the staff has to report to me, and I report to you. And sir, if you're unwilling to do that, I'm resigning.'"

Reince looked skeptical. "You'd really threaten to resign?"

"Absolutely," I said. "Because if you don't do that, no one around here is going to treat you with any respect. And if they're not going to treat you with any respect, why would you want to be here anyway?"

Reince let that sink in.

He was hoping to remain chief of staff for a year. I'm not sure where he got that benchmark, but I know he had it firmly in his mind. He barely got halfway. He never did what I suggested. And so the decision to leave was made for him before he could make it for himself.

On July 28, six months and eight days into his tenure as White House chief of staff, Reince was ousted by President Trump and replaced with John Kelly, the retired army general who'd been serving as homeland security secretary. Reince's departure came as a surprise to almost no one, including Reince, I suspect. He was getting dissed from all directions. He never walked into the Oval Office and drew the line. He had just been the target of a furious, foul-mouthed attack by the new White House communications director, Anthony Scaramucci.

In those first months, Donald Trump lost a national security adviser (Michael Flynn, after twenty-five days), a deputy chief of staff (Katie Walsh, seventy days), a deputy national security adviser (K. T. McFarland, eighty days), a communications director (Mike Dubke, 119 days), a press secretary (Sean Spicer, 183 days), and a chief of staff (Priebus, 190 days). He was about to lose another communications director (Scaramucci, eleven days), and that doesn't count the revolving door of people leaving from various *acting* and lesser roles.

For all his trouble, the outgoing White House chief of staff and former chairman of the Republican National Committee got an *attaboy* tweet on his way to the sidewalk. "I would like to thank Reince Priebus for his service and dedication to his country," Trump said. "We accomplished a lot together and I am proud of him!"

———

Just as Reince Priebus was handing off to John Kelly as White House chief of staff, Obamacare repeal was going down in flames. Donald wasn't happy at all.

The last gasp for Obamacare repeal came in the Senate on a 49–51 vote when Arizona's senior senator, John McCain, battling brain cancer, gave a silent thumbs-down to signal that he was joining Susan Collins, Lisa Murkowski, and all the Democrats in saying no. The symbolism was terrible. Despite controlling both houses of Congress and the White House, Republicans had been unable to deliver on one of Donald Trump's top campaign promises to overturn one of Barack Obama's signature domestic achievements.

But tax cuts were a far more promising terrain for a Republican president in need of a win. For one thing, Donald understood the issue. Economics, unlike health care policy, was a subject he knew a lot about. He didn't need to subcontract this fight to Paul Ryan and Mitch McConnell, as he had with Obamacare repeal. And General Kelly was turning out to be a far more assertive figure than Reince Priebus ever was. Kelly didn't try to micromanage Trump. As the new chief of staff, he was starting to bring some discipline to the many independent fiefdoms of the West Wing. Not everyone loved the new structure. Some people felt hemmed in. But for the first time since Trump was president, everyone and his mother wasn't able to wander into the Oval Office any time they felt like it.

On the transition team, it was one of three positions we called the spine-of-steel jobs, along with secretary of defense and attorney general. These three jobs were where crises, domestic and international, were most likely to come to roost. To fill those three positions, a president needed someone who could deliver bad news and could take the particularly ugly issues off the president's plate. That took a special breed.

Kelly still had to prove himself, just like anyone at the White House. But he's a strong person so, even with no real nonmilitary political experience, he was a needed step in the right direction. So was Defense Secretary Jim Mattis, a former Marine Corps general who'd seen action in Iraq and Afghanistan and had run US Central Command. Again, just the kind of guy Trump needed in one of those spine-of-steel spots. Unfortunately, the same could not be said for Attorney General Jeff Sessions.

I recognized why the US senator from Alabama was considered for a top job in the administration. Sessions was early to the party in 2016, endorsing Trump for president two days after I did, the first and for a long time the only US senator on the Trump train. But once he was nominated by the president and confirmed by his fellow senators, Sessions showed himself not ready to stand up.

Despite testifying during his confirmation hearing that he had never met with any Russians, he later had to admit to a serious "misrecollection" on that topic. Back in September, he had in fact met in his office with Sergey Kislyak, the Russian ambassador to the United States, at the height of what US intelligence officials called a Russian cyber campaign to influence the 2016 presidential election. That wasn't all. The two men also had a phone call in July. Under pressure over that falsehood, Sessions hastily decided to recuse himself from any Justice Department investigation of alleged Russian interference in the election, citing his prominent role in the Trump campaign.

To me, that decision to recuse was a perfect indication of why Jeff Sessions was the wrong choice to be attorney general. If he did it because of his involvement in the campaign—well, he knew about that on November 18, when he was nominated by the president-elect to be attorney general. If he did it because of his contacts with the Russian ambassador—well, that went back to July and September of the previous year. Why wait until March to recuse himself? And why not discuss all of it with Donald Trump *before* agreeing to take on the important responsibilities of attorney general?

It's always been my belief—and it remains my belief today—that Sessions recused himself because he couldn't take the heat that came from his incorrect testimony. Being a conservative

Republican in Alabama, I suppose, means never having to stand alone. Suddenly, Sessions was being harshly questioned in the media and on Capitol Hill, and he folded rather than fight. That decision incredibly ill served the president. The ramifications have been felt every day since March 2, 2017.

It put the Russian hacking probe into the hands of deputy attorney general Rod Rosenstein. It sparked the firing of FBI director Jim Comey and the political fallout that flowed from that. It led to Robert Mueller's appointment as special counsel and his nearly limitless investigative portfolio. It launched a wide-ranging and long-running probe of alleged collusion, obstruction of justice, and whatever strikes Mueller's fancy, potentially roping in anyone from the president down. Who knows where this will ultimately lead? Indictments, guilty pleas, felony trials, ruined reputations, paralyzed government, deepening political divisions, and a damaging whack at America's respect and power around the world.

All that from one hasty decision by a single presidential appointee.

If Jeff Sessions felt such a burning need to recuse himself because he had somehow been compromised by his role in the campaign, he certainly had an obligation to tell the president-elect *before* being nominated as attorney general. He never mentioned it to me when we discussed putting him on the short list for attorney general. Trump could have chosen someone else who was in a position to do the full job.

Or if the issue from Sessions's perspective was his interaction with Russian officials, then why didn't he say, "By the way, if this Russia thing turns into anything, I'm going to have to recuse myself, because I met with the Russians and had conversations with them"? That would have saved everyone a whole lot of trouble.

Like too many in the administration, Sessions put his own ambitions ahead of the best interests of the president. He was gone the day after the 2018 midterm elections, but the damage had long since been done. The president and the country are still paying the price for Jeff Sessions's early silence on recusal.

———

Donald Trump had been thinking for many months about firing Jim Comey. I know because back in November, immediately after the election, he had asked what I thought about the idea. I gave him the best advice I had.

"If you're inclined to do that," I told him, "do it now. Start fresh with a new FBI director. Nobody will really give you a hard time about it if you do it now. I'm not telling you to fire him or not to fire him. What I am telling you is that if you think there's a chance you're going to want to do that, you need to do it right away. You'll get a lot more grief if you do it later."

This had nothing to do with hackers or Russians or WikiLeaks or collusion or witch hunts or any of that. No one had any idea in November 2016 how all that would blow up. Our conversation was sparked by Comey's antics over Hillary Clinton, the way he'd been zigzagging around Hillary's missing emails, not charging her, then blasting her for being sloppy with government secrets, then announcing he was reopening his investigation a week before Election Day. Comey's performance had left people in both parties shaking their heads. He had violated Justice Department guidelines and traditions. He had a real impact on the 2016 election. That is not what FBI directors are supposed to do. His conduct certainly merited termination, if that was the president-elect's wish.

I hardly gave it another thought until the following May 9. I was in meetings at Drumthwacket. When I came downstairs to leave, my body guy, Dan Robles, said to me, "You will not believe what just happened. They just fired Jim Comey."

"What?"

"Yeah," Dan said, "they fired Comey. In fact, they fired him while he was in Los Angeles. They fired him long-distance."

"Let's get out of here," I said.

We'd been in the car ten minutes when Jared called, saying, "I want to get your read on what we did."

"I can't speak to the substance of why you fired him, because I wasn't read in on the reasons for the firing. I will guarantee you one thing, though. It's going to cause an enormous shit storm."

"Respectfully," Jared said. "I believe you're wrong about that. The Democrats have said nothing but awful things about Comey. They hate him. So they're going to be vapor-locked from criticizing the president for firing him. It would be inconsistent with what they've said before."

I had to remind myself, again, that even after the campaign and a few months in Washington, Jared was still new to the ways of the capital. "That would be true," I told him, "if you were operating in a place where intellectual integrity is treasured. You, however, are working in Washington, DC. And I'm willing to bet you that within fifteen minutes Chuck Schumer is going to have a statement saying the president fired Comey because Comey was getting close to him on the Russia investigation."

"That's crazy," Jared said, a position he was able to hold for the next fourteen minutes.

"Well, it's going to happen," I said.

"Governor, we just disagree on that."

Again, the president was ill served by poor advice, in this case on the timing and method of firing Jim Comey.

In the end, there were lots of reasons to fire Jim Comey as FBI director, some of them laid out in the detailed memo written by deputy attorney general Rod Rosenstein. But *when* it was done and *how* it was done was abysmal and caused unnecessary grief for the president. Case in point: no one at the White House apparently knew that Comey was in Los Angeles when they sent Keith Schiller, the chief of Oval Office operations, to hand-deliver the dismissal letter to FBI headquarters in Washington.

Unacceptable.

Just because the decision was executed poorly doesn't make it a bad decision. But it sure helped make it a more politically damaging one for the president.

It made Trump look as if he were trying to interfere with an investigation that might be inching closer to him.

It was all so avoidable. The whole thing made me want to scream. The failure to follow the transition plan on policy and personnel rearing its head again. Steve Bannon later called it the worst mistake in modern political history. Witnessing the profound impact of Bob Mueller's investigation, I think on that point Steve and I agree.

———

Personally, I never saw any signs that the Russians and the Trump campaign colluded or that any such efforts tipped the results. Looking back, I don't think the Trump campaign was organized enough to collude. The existence of such a meeting, whatever precisely was discussed, is just another example of how chaotic the campaign was. In any normal political campaign, no one would have the son of the candidate, the son-in-law of the candidate, and the campaign chairman take a meeting like that without clearing it first with the campaign's lawyers. I know for certain that no one discussed it in advance with Don McGahn. That's come out publicly. I also know it because I know Don. He never would have allowed that meeting to occur. I know what Don would have said: "Are you kidding? No way."

Normal processes that are part of almost every major presidential campaign—the close involvement of lawyers, the vetting of questionable information that arrives over the transom, the protection of high-level staffers from outside influence—none of that existed in the Trump campaign. That fly-by-the-seat-of-your-pants approach is part of what gave the campaign its grounding and its energy. But it also left the staff and the candidate vulnerable in many different ways.

The cost of all that has turned out to be extraordinarily high.

Donald's taunting sense of humor didn't help, nor did his insistence on being flip about serious subjects. Even before the Republican Convention in July, he was mock-urging Moscow to hack the Clinton computers: "Russia, if you're listening, I hope you're able to find the thirty thousand emails that are missing. I think you will probably be rewarded mightily by our press." By fall, WikiLeaks was a running rally punch line. "WikiLeaks, I love WikiLeaks," he declared at a rally in Wilkes-Barre, Pennsylvania, on October 10. Two days later, he was at it again in Ocala, Florida: "This WikiLeaks stuff is unbelievable. It tells you the inner heart, you gotta read it." And also the day after that in Cincinnati, Ohio: "It's been amazing what's coming out on WikiLeaks."

By November 4, WikiLeaks had almost turned into a comedy routine. "Getting off the plane," he told the crowd in Wilmington, Ohio, "they were just announcing new WikiLeaks, and I wanted to stay there, but I didn't want to keep you waiting." He turned and pretended he was leaving the rally platform before turning back to announce "Boy, I love reading those WikiLeaks."

Crowd-pleasing material? You bet it was. A genuine criminal conspiracy? Not even close. He was just riffing on media reports and getting a reaction. Of course he wanted bad stuff to come out about his opponent. Most people in politics hope bad stuff will come out about their opponents. But the idea that, via a stump speech, Donald Trump was directing Russian hackers to invade Democratic Party email—I'm sorry, I call that aluminum-foil-hat craziness.

The US intelligence agencies tell us that the Russians have been targeting the American electoral system for many years. The Russians didn't need Donald Trump's instructions to launch something like that. And seriously: If he were really colluding with the Russians to subvert American democracy, wouldn't he communicate with backdoor secrecy? Would he really do it on live national television with millions of viewers at home?

The Donald I know is smarter than that.

Did Donald Jr. and Jared and Paul Manafort do some things that were dumb or, in the young peoples' case, signs of profound inexperience? I'm afraid so, meeting the Russian attorney most prominently. But was Donald giving instructions to Moscow—or taking them? I just don't believe that, and I haven't seen any evidence to the contrary.

As Mueller's investigation pressed on and Donald expressed his growing impatience and frustration to me, I kept telling him to stop talking about it and quit tweeting. He would never listen, of course. He kept calling the probe a witch hunt and insulting Bob Mueller and professing his innocence and ridiculing the evidence and giving everyone new rabbit holes to chase down. When you're facing a special counsel who has an unlimited budget, a limitless agenda, and no deadline, you don't want to dangle fresh facts in front of him. Anything but silence lengthens the probe.

Bill Clinton's experience is instructive here. He didn't meet Monica Lewinsky until nineteen months after the special prosecutor was appointed, ostensibly to look into the Clintons' tainted Whitewater real estate venture. I feared that history would repeat itself. Once a special prosecutor is in place, it's nearly impossible to control the scope of an inquiry.

"Why do you need to put new stuff out there?" I asked Donald repeatedly as the months wore on. "You're making the prosecutors' job that much more interesting. There is nothing you can do to make this investigation shorter. There are many things you can do to make it longer."

The abandoned transition process that I had headed was an extraordinary effort performed by more than 140 exceptional folks. It would have served the president, the vice-president, and the country so much better than the slipshod work of Rick Dearborn, Steve Bannon, and the others who parachuted into this process after Election Day.

Is it any surprise that, except for family members, all the people who gave the president such catastrophic advice are now gone from the administration? Priebus, Bannon, Dearborn, Porter, and Walsh—not one of them remains.

The result of their thrown-together approach? Bad personnel decisions over and over again. What competent, professional process would have yielded Omarosa Manigault Newman anywhere in the White House? Empty desks throughout cabinet departments? Or, worse yet, Obama holdovers not pushing the president's agenda? Bannon's phone call to former congressman Mike Rogers, head of the transition's national security efforts, revealed just how selfish these decisions were. When Rogers asked why he was being fired, Bannon said, "You didn't do anything wrong. You're a Christie guy. We're firing all of the Christie guys."

Professionals like Chief of Staff Kelly and Johnny DeStefano, overseeing the White House Office of Personnel, were left trying to play catch-up after childish maneuvers like Bannon's. In this environment, it's almost impossible to catch up. Those crucial months, once thrown away, can never be recovered. The ability to govern is inevitably diminished as a result.

The special counsel's actions have not only chipped away at trust. They have been an enormous distraction that has slowed the president's progress in implementing his agenda. The criminal convictions of George Papadopoulos, Michael Flynn, Rick Gates, Paul Manafort, and Michael Cohen have caused distractions and disillusionment. A competent and prepared transition wouldn't have allowed folks like those anywhere near the White House.

The president-elect had the plan he needed. The plan was ready to go into effect. Self-interested folks around him decided to throw it into the trash.

We are all still paying the price.

EPILOGUE

This book's subtitle touts "the power of in-your-face-politics."

I'm one version of that. Donald Trump is a very different version.

There's no doubt about it: my aggressive personality, my outspoken nature, and my no-holds-barred political style have all contributed to my successes as well as to my failures along the way. Nothing, however, has matched my disappointment as I watched truly selfish people trash a remarkable governing blueprint for the president-elect. That trashing was done for petty and personal reasons. It served no grand purpose. Yet many of the frustrations of Trump's first two years in office can be traced directly to that one reckless act. Fortunately, the vast majority of my twenty-five years of public service has felt far more purposeful.

The joys and challenges of my public life are obvious, and I've had more than my share of both. Serving as a local officeholder, as United States attorney, as governor of my home state, as a candidate for president, and as the chairman of the transition for a winning presidential campaign, I've had some truly extraordinary opportunities to lead. Rebuilding my state after Superstorm Sandy. Establishing a more robust educational system. Bringing prison and sentencing reforms that made New Jersey a more just place to live and work. I've had my share of disappointments, too. Losing elections for myself and others. Being betrayed by aides I handed power to. Failing to make government as fully accountable as it ought to be, especially in education and public pensions.

Today, I am enjoying private life for the first time in sixteen years, as a private-practice lawyer, as a member of corporate boards, and as a contributor to philanthropic causes that I have cared about my whole life. Yes, some things have taken getting used to. People in New Jersey keep expressing surprise the first time they see me drive. Day and night for two terms as governor, I had New Jersey state troopers drive me everywhere. I tell people that driving is like riding a bike. Once you learn, you never forget how to do it. But parallel parking? That's a totally different story. After eight years without a steering wheel in my hands, I am a total disaster. The excellent news is that I am able to support my family and still do work of consequence. It is different from public life. But I am finding it rewarding and relaxing in its own unique ways.

No one spends as much time and energy as I have fighting for causes like these, only to suddenly disappear. Thankfully, my TV commentary has kept my voice in the public arena, as has writing this book and chairing the President's Commission on Combatting Drug Addiction and the Opioid Crisis. I have cared about that work since 1995. It will continue to be a public focus of mine. Every life is an individual gift from God and deserves to be protected, including the lives of those suffering from the disease of drug addiction.

As I have said throughout this book, none of this would have been possible without a great family and extraordinary friends. A pair of strong women, my mom and my Nani, made me believe that if I worked hard enough, I could achieve anything. They taught me toughness, integrity, courage, and loyalty. These are all traits that prepared me for the rough-and-tumble of political life.

My dad is now eighty-five years old. He and his wife, Fran, live a great life at the Jersey Shore. He has always served as an example to me of hard work, love, and the value of education. He gave me the second great passion of my life after public service—a love of baseball. His team is the Saint Louis Cardinals. Mine is the New York Mets. But baseball still brings us together today.

My brother, Todd, is still an everyday presence in my life. He is the father of five great children. He is a youth football, basketball, and baseball coach. He has a successful career on Wall Street. He and his wife, Andrea, have been unfailingly supportive of me in public and in private.

My sister, Dawn, continues to be a gift in my life. While Todd has been deeply involved in my public life, my sister has preferred to keep her support in the background. A mother of five with a wonderful husband, Russ, she asks little of me but provides unconditional love and support. I am a lucky big brother.

Mary Pat is now home full time with our children, enjoying a well-earned break after a thirty-year career on Wall Street as the true breadwinner of the family. We are now enjoying a much more relaxed and private life together at our homes in Mendham and Bay Head, New Jersey.

Our four children have always been the joy and inspiration in our lives.

Andrew is twenty-five years old now, a graduate of Delbarton School and Princeton University, pursuing his lifelong baseball dream in the front office of the team he rooted for at the urging of his dad, the New York Mets. Even in the crib, he was one great son. Today he is a great example as the oldest brother to his three siblings.

Sarah, twenty-two, is a 2018 graduate of the University of Notre Dame. She works in sports marketing at Genesco Sports Enterprises in New York and lives in New York City. The girl who declared that I was "ruining her life" when I decided to run for governor has been an enthusiastic participant in all aspects of our public life. I couldn't be prouder of her.

Patrick is eighteen and has always been the straw that stirred the drink in our family. He is now a senior at Delbarton School and will be heading off to college next fall.

Bridget is fifteen and a sophomore at Villa Walsh in Morristown. She is an avid basketball and lacrosse player and is the go-to person for Mary Pat and me when any of our technology is not working. She is one smart young lady.

———

In American politics, as soon as one presidential race is over, the next one begins. The 2020 campaign is already revving up. I presume that the president will be seeking reelection. People across the country are still genuinely angry about the failures of government to get things done. This still exists in spite of record-low unemployment, excellent wage growth, and lower taxes. In the past, all of those things would act as pressure valves to lower the nation's political temperature. That's not happening as we approach the next presidential election. Part of this is because Americans have a sinking feeling about our future as the preeminent world power of the twenty-first century. Part is because both parties keep choosing gridlock and further frustration over reasonable compromise. As America's forty-fifth president, Donald Trump stands at the center of this political firestorm. While some polls may cause some people to feel pessimistic about his chances, I am not. I caution all the Democrats thinking of running what a formidable opponent he will be. He will have the incumbency, his fifty-four million Twitter followers, and more money than he'll be able to spend. He'll also have a unique ability to campaign on the issues he wants to discuss.

As someone who ran against him, I know this much: underestimate him at your own peril. Just ask Hillary.

I hope we begin to focus more over the next few years on getting the big issues fixed. While I agree with what the president has done on taxes and regulation, there is so much more to do. We need to invest in our infrastructure. We need to reform Medicare, Medicaid, and Social Security. We need to deal with the divisive issue of immigration in a way that honors our national heritage. We must secure our future by strengthening our alliances around the world to protect against aggressive dictators in Russia, China, and North Korea. We must work to stop the scourge of the opioid crisis by investing in treatment and by securing our borders against the importation of fentanyl and heroin.

Now, with Democrats controlling the House of Representatives and Republicans controlling the Senate, there is no reason that common-sense compromises can't be reached on many of these issues. President Donald Trump will now have his deal-making prowess put to the test. This could be the time to pass a major infrastructure bill. This could be the time to finally deal with comprehensive immigration reform *and* border security. Maybe the second half of the first Trump term will prove that compromise is not a dirty word. Maybe we can stick to our principles and also reach beyond our tribes. Election division can lead to progress, not gridlock.

I hope I will have a role to play in making positive things happen for our country. That may be as a commentator from the outside, an agitator from the private sector, or, perhaps, in another public role in law enforcement or political life. Whatever that role turns out to be, I am not ready to give up on achieving the big things that got me into public life in the first place.

Let Me Finish is not just the title of this book. It is my fervent hope for the tasks that lie ahead—for me and for us as a nation.

ACKNOWLEDGMENTS

Writing this book has been a joyous and cathartic experience. There are many people to thank in its creation and in the stories it tells.

First and foremost is Mary Pat, my wife of thirty-two years. She has believed in me, supported my dreams, celebrated our triumphs, and been at my side for life's disappointments. She has been a true partner in every way. This extraordinary life would not be mine without her love and confidence.

Our four children are the part of my life that has brought me the most joy. Andrew, Sarah, Patrick, and Bridget have lived exemplary lives while being thrust unavoidably into the spotlight of their dad's career. I could not be prouder of my wonderful children.

My own father, Bill Christie, has been my role model for making hard work a way of life and always putting the family first. From the many hours pitching to me at Little League batting practice to the door-to-door in the New Hampshire snow, Dad has always sacrificed for me, and I love him for it.

My brother, Todd, and my sister, Dawn, have been lifelong gifts. They have supported my dreams and ambitions, Todd loudly and publicly, Dawn quietly and privately.

My mother-in-law, Pat Foster, now ninety years old, has been a source of strength and wisdom for our family and a regular supporter of my public life, as was my late father-in-law, Jack. I am so glad she is here to read this book and even happier she lived it with us every day. I only wish we'd experienced the same with Jack.

This book would not have been possible without my collaborator, Ellis Henican. I first met him in the office of my agent, Mel Berger, and there was an instant connection between us. I love his style and his sensibilities. A native of New Orleans, he is hardworking, smart, funny, and, most of all, a fabulous writer. He never ceases to amaze me in the way he can take my thoughts, experiences, and feelings and turn them into wonderful prose. I have enjoyed every minute of our work together.

My agents at WME are wonderful folks. Jordan Bazant and Kate Urquhart believed in me when I left office and have helped guide me in the months since to make some very good decisions in this next phase of my career. I am also very fortunate to have the incredible Mel Berger as my book agent at WME. Mel is honest and experienced, and he has been in my corner for every step of this process. He also made real contributions to the manuscript, for which I will always be grateful.

Paul Whitlatch, my editor at Hachette Books, provided extraordinary freedom and valuable guidance. He has shown great enthusiasm for this project from our very first conversation and challenged me to make this book all it had the potential to be. His thematic ideas and his careful editing have produced a better read for everyone.

I cannot thank Roberta Teer enough for her meticulous research to help verify (or debunk) my recollections of key events over the fifty-six years of my life. The task of transcribing the dozens of hours of conversations between Ellis and me fell to Janis

Spidle. She did an extraordinary job in keeping up with our pace and allowing us to do so with the utmost confidence in the accuracy of her work. She now knows more about my life than anyone other than my family and Ellis. I will always be grateful for her hard work and admirable discretion. Amanda Kain, Timothy Shaner, Chris Measom, Melanie Gold, and Lauren Hummel, key players on Hachette's editing and design team, brought extraordinary talent and finesse to the manuscript, instinctively capturing the spirit of my public service and the satisfaction that's come from working hard at the many great jobs that I have had in my life.

Thanks to the late Jack O'Keeffe, my first political running mate, who taught me the need for consistent honesty in public life and the lesson that holding grudges is a waste of valuable energy. Jack set the example many years ago, and I hope my service has made him proud.

I owe a great deal to my former law partner and constant political adviser Bill Palatucci. In the business of politics, it is very rare to find a friend whose loyalty is beyond question every day. Through the ups and downs of my career, Bill has always been there to give me forthright advice and friendship. He is a true wartime consigliere.

My friendship with Jeff Chiesa over the last twenty-seven years has been an incredible journey for both of us. Jeff is a man of unquestionable talent as a lawyer and integrity as a person. He came to me at the law firm of Dughi & Hewit as a partially formed lawyer but a fully formed man. He joined me on this journey as an associate and partner, as an assistant United States attorney, as chief counsel to the governor, New Jersey attorney general, and United States senator. At every stop, he made me and the people he served both proud and happy. Even with all those fancy titles, his most important title to me is still friend.

Thanks to two of my colleagues and friends from my days as US Attorney—Ralph Marra and Michele Brown. Ralph served as my first assistant and Michele as my counsel. They both followed me to state service in Trenton. They both reviewed the chapters of this book on our years together at one of the great law-enforcement offices in America and made sure I recounted those years with complete accuracy.

Besides Mary Pat, I shared this manuscript with only one other person, my alter ego and message warrior during my time as governor and on the presidential campaign trail, Maria Comella. From the 2009 campaign to the years in Trenton to the cold and snow of Iowa and New Hampshire, Maria was there twenty-four hours a day, seven days a week, helping me turn my ideas into something we could use to elevate my state and our nation. She was way ahead of her time in understanding the social media phenomenon and the role it would play in our politics. She made me a better candidate and a better governor. Her selfless review of this complete manuscript has undoubtedly made it not only a better book but also one that is truer to the mission we both tried to accomplish together.

I owe much to the fellow governors I have had the honor of serving with over my career.

Haley Barbour, who as chairman of the Republican Governors Association in 2009–10, believed I could beat Jon Corzine when almost no other national figure did. I would not have been elected governor without his support.

Larry Hogan, the 2014 Maryland underdog who won my political heart and showed me that courage and loyalty are indeed alive and well in elected politicians. His fight to be elected in a deep-blue state and his subsequent fight against cancer still inspire me.

Charlie Baker, the man who came back from a discouraging 2010 defeat to be a better and winning candidate in 2014, is a living example of intelligence and class in leading a blue state. His friendship is a real gift to me and Mary Pat.

Paul LePage, the combative governor of Maine, is the genuine article. Rising from an abusive childhood to a successful business career and an against-all-odds, two-term governorship in blue Maine, Paul is a man who sees his word as his bond. I've never had more fun than I did on the campaign trail with Paul in 2010, 2014, and 2016.

Each of those men also stood with me when I sought the presidency while so many others stayed comfortably on the sidelines. They did not let history shape them. They tried to shape history. I will be eternally grateful for their support.

I always saw my leadership as the captain of a team of extraordinarily talented people, men and women I cajoled to stay in public life despite its challenges. My core team from those sixteen years of service are all doing well: Bill Palatucci, Mike DuHaime, Maria Comella, Rich Bagger, Jeff Chiesa, Kevin O'Dowd, Charlie McKenna, Michele Brown, Chris Porrino, Wayne Hasenbalg, Deb Gramiccioni, Richard Constable, Hal Wirths, Tom Scrivo, Amy Cradic, Cam Henderson, Bob Martin, Lou Goetting, Dan Robles, Russ Schriefer, Regina Agea, Paul Matey, Matt Mowers, John Hoffman, Ed Dickson, Rick Fuentes, Marc Larkins, Phil Kwon, Rick Mroz, Marc Ferzan, Lauren Fritts, Dave Reiner, Rosemary Iannacone, Lee Solomon, Adam Geller, Amanda DePalma, Ken McKay, Phil Cox, and all the others are gainfully employed in the private and public sectors now and still a part of our extended family. I miss seeing them on a daily basis. They were the foundation of my success in public life.

Finally, I want to thank the people of the State of New Jersey. They gave me the honor of sixteen consecutive years in what I consider the two best jobs in public life: United States attorney and governor. No one before me had ever been given the honor of holding both those jobs consecutively in the 240-plus-year history of our state. I cannot describe how wonderful and rewarding the ride has been—and I owe it all to you.

INDEX

Note: Abbreviation CJC stands for Christopher ("Chris") J. Christie.